ROYAL
BRITISH
SOCIETY OF **SCULPTORS**

Sculpture Shock

Site-specific interventions in Subterranean, Ambulatory and Historic contexts

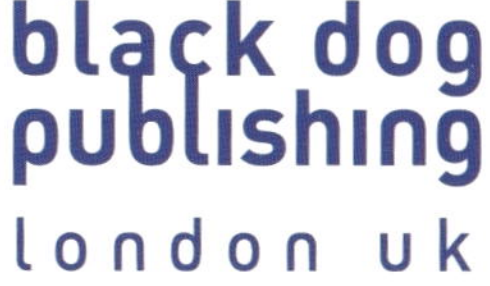

black dog publishing
london uk

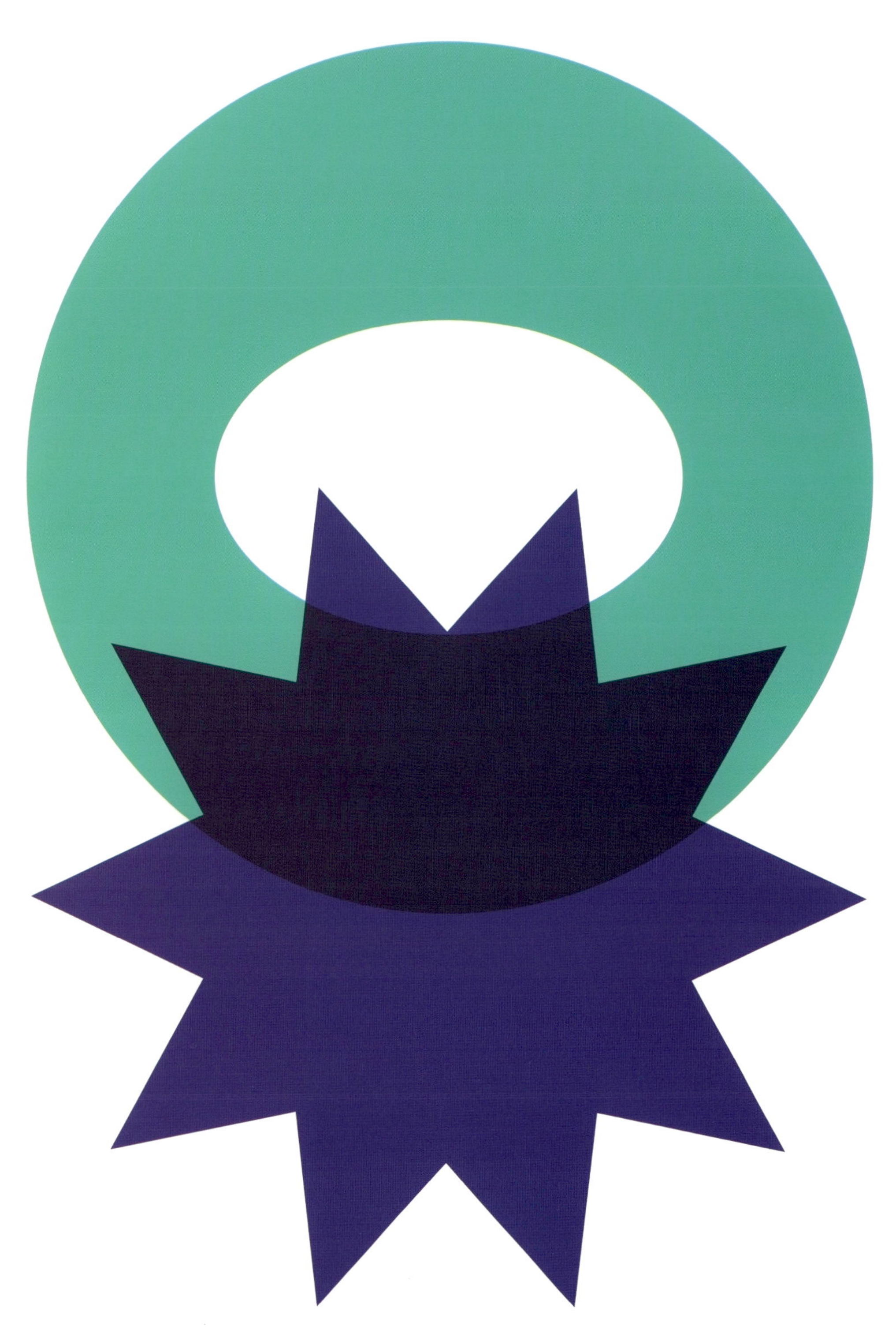

Curator's Notes

Art is far too important to be confined within galleries alone,
and our environment desperately lacks the humanising force
of the artist's imagination.

Richard Cork[1]

The best site-specific interventions possess a vitality, an urgency born from
their short-lived and often ephemeral existence in the fleeting present, with an
intellectual impact that outlives their physical manifestation. Sculpture Shock
was born from the premise that there are few places were art could not or
should not be.[2] This publication provides a contemporaneous account of this
experimental project with a view to demystifying the process and encouraging
further manifestations of site-specific work.

To illustrate the vitality of site-specific interventions, it is worth considering
Susan Philipsz's *Study for Strings*, 2012, at dOCUMENTA 13, a 24-channel
sound installation sited along the disused train tracks leading from the Kassel
Hauptbahnhof where, from 1941 to 1942, deportations to concentration and
extermination camps departed. One of the deportees was a composer who,
washed and suited, took applause after a performance for the purposes of
a Nazi propaganda film of the piece of music used by Philipsz.[3] A few days
later he, and most of the orchestra, were sent to Auschwitz where they were
exterminated. In this desolate industrial setting, the melancholic, haunting and
yet defiant sound of the strings have an unparalleled and unforgettable impact.

Nothing could be further from the reverential stand-offish experience of
viewing contemporary art in the gallery. At times it feels as if these clinical
interiors are holding the art hostage with their deafening neutrality. Making
one's way apprehensively past burly bouncers into commercial gallery spaces
or hurriedly glimpsing a favourite work past the hoards of art lovers snapping
selfies, cannot aspire to the impact of seeing or experiencing a work made for
a specific place and time. Increasingly, the overbearing clinical logic of the
white cube has infiltrated contemporary art, with artists seemingly producing
work of a scale and a saleability with this enclosure in mind. It is similar to the
many artists that draw who feel confined by the universal standardisation of
paper sizes and their dry nomenclatures of A1, A2, A3, A4.

The title of the project, Sculpture Shock, was inspired by Dave Beech's article
"Shock v Awe" in which he argues that, "Instead of learning to love artworks
in the avant-garde tradition, we need to learn to be shocked by them again so
as not to steal from them their *raison d'être*."[4] Shock is a human and humane
reaction and we become insensitive to it at our peril. The existence and pursuit
of shock signals the survival of the avant-garde beyond the demise of its
movements. Sculpture Shock encouraged this transgressive tendency in order
to rattle us out of our preconceptions of what may or may not be understood as
sculpture and where it can or cannot exist, rather than to provoke moral outrage.

The mission of Sculpture Shock, launched in 2013 by the Royal British Society
of Sculptors (RBS), was to move away from the anonymous, undistinguished and
predictable and to embrace risk, freedom of expression and trust. It operated
annually from 2013 to 2015 as an open call to artists working in three dimensions
to create a work in response to a nontraditional space. Three winners each year
received £3,000 and a three-month residency in a London studio culminating in
a surprising spatial intervention in one of three spaces: subterranean, ambulatory
or historic. Each artist's work was installed in the location for which they were
selected and remained there for at least four days.

The groundwork to establish the project was immense. RBS spent two years
locating and negotiating the use of places that would provide stimulating and

unusual sites and would draw in not only an art audience but also the curious public. It was not an easy case to make. The artists had not been selected at the time and the winners of the award were far from being household names. The work they were going to produce was not formulated, the process not prescribed and the form it took was intended to be far from a traditional understanding of sculpture. As with so much of the work of RBS,[5] the opportunity was for those who would benefit from the exposure, the challenge and the opportunity to develop their work, rather than through a high-profile commission of an already successful artist.[6] The sites, especially those that offered themselves without any payment, were asked to embrace this element of risk. Sculpture Shock aimed to instil in those who care for historic buildings such as Chiswick House and Gardens or Holy Trinity Sloane Square, or have responsibility for public highways, a renewed confidence in the professionalism of sculptors and an appreciation of their sensitivity to space, the physical world around them and their audience. As Claire Doherty points out in her analysis of Situations, a scattered-site art project in Bristol, the process of engagement and intervention needs an interlocutor and the role of the curator as mediator becomes vital. The RBS as curator and commissioner needed to manage "the complex processes of initiation, development and mediation of this work".[7]

The categories of sites were broad and enticing. The subterranean, the world underneath our feet, with its connotations of concealment, secrecy, wrongdoing and mystical darkness is far beneath our everyday experience. The 6,000 square feet of space in the tunnels under Waterloo station was reached through a graffiti adorned passageway full of the acrid smell of urine mixed with the heady chemical charge of spray paint. Its waterlogged, dripping interior with trains rumbling overhead was revealed in all its immensity by David Ogle's massive but delicate light installations. The Horse Hospital, built to stable sick cabbies' horses and the immense feat of engineering that is Marc Isambard Brunel and his son Isambard Kingdom Brunel's Thames shaft were venues for the intrepid artist and viewer, willing to open themselves to new challenges and new ways of considering space and artistic possibilities they hold. Sarah Kent explores the history of the use of such spaces by artists and examines the particular approaches of the Sculpture Shock artists in the "Subterranean" chapter of this book.

The ambulatory brought to the fore the contingent and transitory spaces of the city. It naturally embraced performance, live art and socially engaged practice. Sculpture has evolved to occupy "the expanded field" and incorporated aspects such as time and the body operating in space, manipulating their three-dimensional qualities.[8] Sculpture Shock embraced these practices. Artist Amy Sharrocks made use of the public pavements and hidden walkways of Kensington, hosting groups of bodies allowing themselves to fall, be caught and to fall again in a collaborative casting off of the shame of falling. Bringing together the marginalised, the young and the old, Sharrocks fell from trees, plunged into the Serpentine lake and coerced the lame and the fit alike to fall publicly and proudly, surrounded by the housing estates and grand buildings of Chelsea.[9] A converted river barge made its way through the canal system of North London with the white-suited Alexander Costello attached as figurehead to its bow in the name of *Making Progress* while William Mackrell ambushed passengers on central London bus routes with voices responding to the *Gaps, glitches and speed bumps* of the journey, arousing a new awareness of space and the movement of our bodies in response to the urban environment. In the "Ambulatory" chapter Dave Beech explores the relationship of performance's mobility and conceptual breadth to its site through the differing approaches of the Sculpture Shock artists.

Historic sites are imbued with the often overwhelming narrative of the past, expressed in careful architectural language. The Sculpture Shock artists negotiated this overbearing wealth of material through rigorous selection and rejection of potential influences. Nika Neelova conscientiously explored not the rich architectural detail of Holy Trinity, Sloane Square, but its underlying rational and geometric forms to create an uncompromisingly quiet interpretation of the polyhedral Platonic solids. *North Taurids: Following the Meteor Shower* saw her first abstract forms sit amidst the noise and colour of the church, as if excavated or fallen from above. Joanna Sands' work was originally conceived for a dilapidated former Huguenot house on Princelet Street off Brick Lane. The insuppressible construction of Crossrail underneath the fragile site made its realisation impossible, and the site was changed late in the day to the decaying chapel at the Asylum, a nineteenth-century almshouse complex in Peckham. In the short time remaining before its exhibition, the work could not be commenced anew. However, as the artist's interests and aesthetics are founded in the language and concerns of Minimalism, and the resulting work was an essay in proportion, form and the precise manipulation of material and how its dimensions related to its physical surroundings, its resiting did not destroy the artwork.[10] By adjusting its dimensions it successfully responded to the new site and acted as a catalyst for heated debates about the meaning and parameters of site-specificity. Hanna Haaslahti researched her site of the Ionic Temple, which stands proudly if diminutively by the Mirror Lake in the gardens of Chiswick House. She worked closely with English Heritage's expert curator and decided to invert the lavish gilding of the interior of Lord Burlington's Chiswick House by lining the Temple in the ultra-modern, ultra-cheap clarity of PVC and to reclaim the lost limbs of the antique statuary in the grounds, casting them on the blackened lake. Richard Cork shares his impressions of the work in his essay for the "Historic" chapter.

Sculpture Shock showed the broad range of site-specific "practices that evade the easy recuperability of 'public art' and the congealing of significance to which it is prone".[11] Public art ignites debates over the desirability of permanence and the ownership of public space and is thus often burdened by the weight of compromise. The site-specific works of this project demonstrate the freedom that site-specific interventions boast.

Today's world is characterised by its duality: the bewildering mobility of people, information and images flowing at ever greater speeds, but also the homogenisation and standardisation of our surroundings. This impacts on our sense of self and our sense of belonging and, ultimately, our sense of place. Alienation, fragmentation and the "drive toward a rationalised universal civilisation" requires a cultural counterbalance. Sculpture Shock provided a platform for exploring what this counterbalance or cultural expression is or could be. As Miwon Kwon advises, there are "no other options than to confront an ongoing predicament as a predicament. It bears the burden of necessity and impossibility of modelling new forms of being in-place, new forms of belonging. This precarious and risky position might not be the right place to be, but it is the only place from which to face the challenges of the new orders of space and time."[12]

The site-specific interventions created by the Sculpture Shock artists faced this challenge. The project asserted the cultural need and the cultural appetite for the subversive and the unpredictable and in a small way allowed us to reconsider space, belonging and our own sense of place.

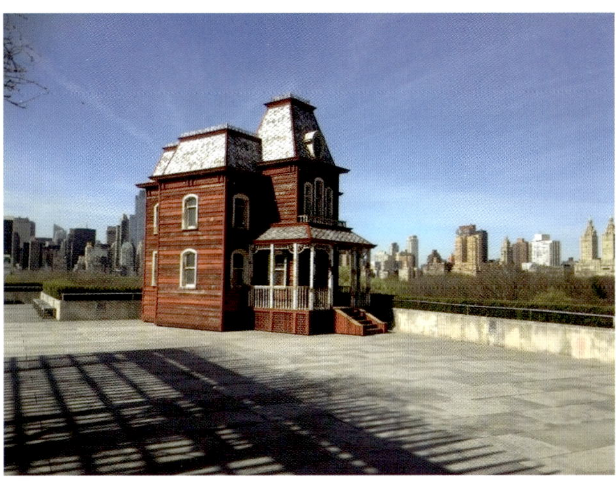

Cornelia Parker, *Transitional Object (PsychoBarn)*, 2016, The Metropolitan Museum of Art. Image courtesy the artist.

1. Cork, Richard, "Shaping the World", *First@108*, exh cat, London: Royal British Society of Sculptors, 2011.

2   Please see sculptureshock.rbs.org.uk.

3. For Philipsz's work *Study for Strings*, 2012, see https:// www.youtube.com/watch?v=s_yMZJkzbcw, last accessed 14 July 2016.

4. Beech, Dave, "Shock v Awe: We Need to Learn to be Shocked by Avant-Garde Art Again", *Art Monthly*, no 300, October 2006.

5. RBS is an independent artist-led organisation that promotes the practice and appreciation of contemporary sculpture. Established in 1905, it is a membership society of over 600 professional sculptors practising across all forms of sculpture. See www.rbs.org.uk.

6. There are many excellent high-profile commissions of site-specific works including Francis Alÿs, *The Guards*, London, 2005 and *When Faith Moves Mountains*, Lima, 2002; Elmgreen & Dragset, *Tomorrow*, Victoria & Albert Museum, London, 2013; Cornelia Parker, *Transitional Object (PsychoBarn)*, 2016, The Metropolitan Museum of Art, New York; Gabriel Orozco, *Empty Club*, 1996; Theaster Gates, *12 Ballads for Hugenot House* and Tino Seghal, *This Transition*, both 2012, dOCUMENTA 13, Kassel; Richard Wilson, *Turning the Place Over*, 2008, Liverpool; Alex Chinneck, *A Pound of Flesh for 50p*, 2014; Ragnar Kjartansson, *The Visitors*, 2015 and Michael Johansson, *Facelift*, 2015, on the facade of the RBS.

7. Doherty, Claire, *Contemporary Art: From Studio to Situation*, London: Black Dog Publishing, 2004, p 12.

8. See Krauss, Rosalind, "Sculpture in the Expanded Field", *The Originality of the Avant-Garde and Other Modernist Myths*, Boston: MIT Press, 1985.

9. Which we are told are located in the ninth most deprived borough in the United Kingdom.

10. Richard Serra, in the famous public debate and legal action over the removal of *Tilted Arc*, 1981, from Federal Plaza in New York in 1989, stated that "To move the work is to destroy the work". See Serra, Richard, *Writings, Interviews*, Chicago: Chicago University Press, 1994.

11. Rugg, Judith, *Exploring Site-Specific Art: Issues of Space and Internationalism*, New York: I B Tauris & Co Ltd, 2010, p xiii.

12. Kwon, Miwon, "The Wrong Place" prepared for the International Lecture Series as part of the 1999 exhibition In all the Wrong Places at the Ottowa Art Gallery, curated by Sylvie Fortin and modified for *One Place After Another: Site-Specific Art and Locational Identity*, Cambridge, MA: MIT Press, 2004.

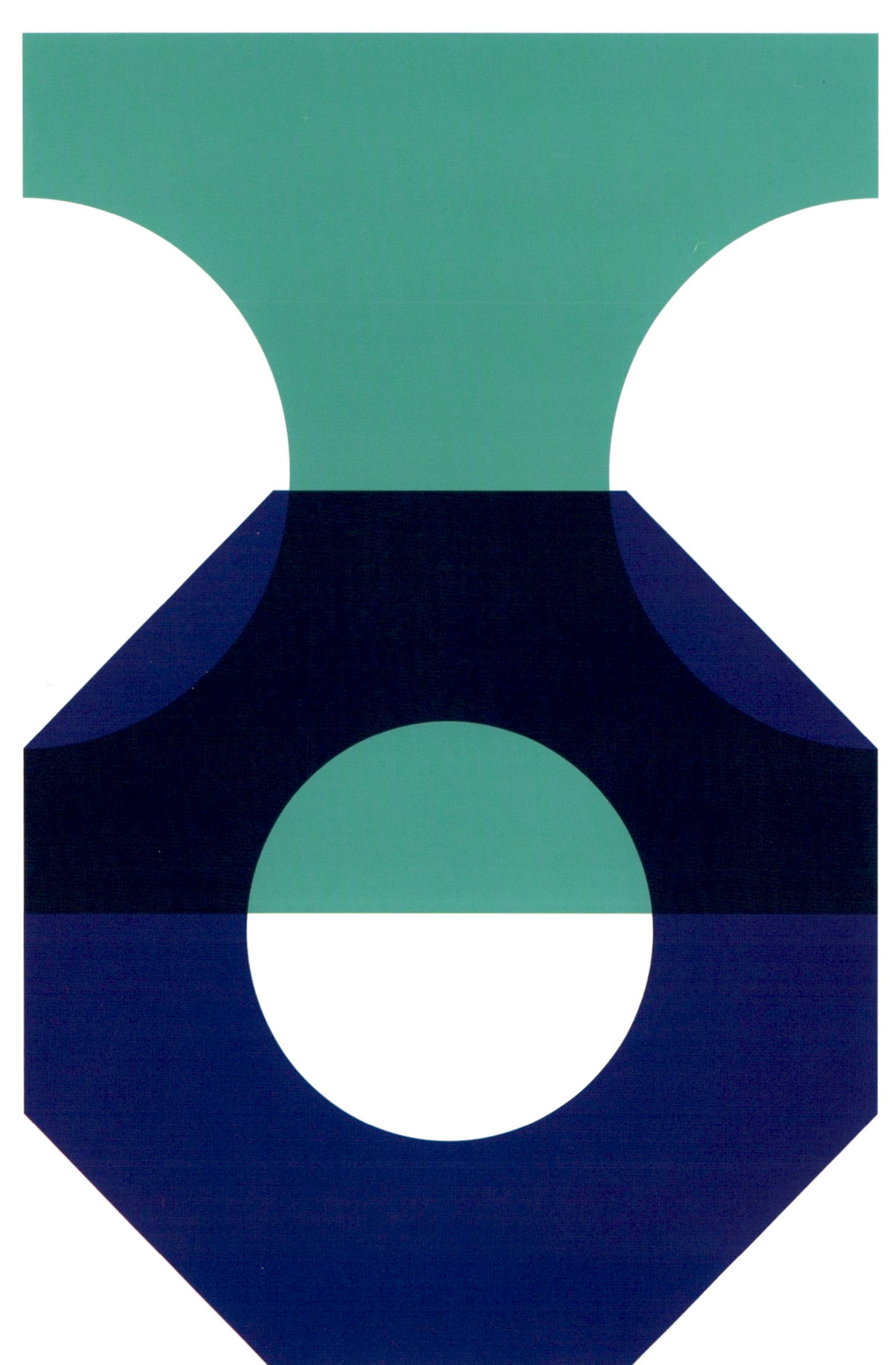

Subterranean

David Ogle
Tunnels under Waterloo Station, London

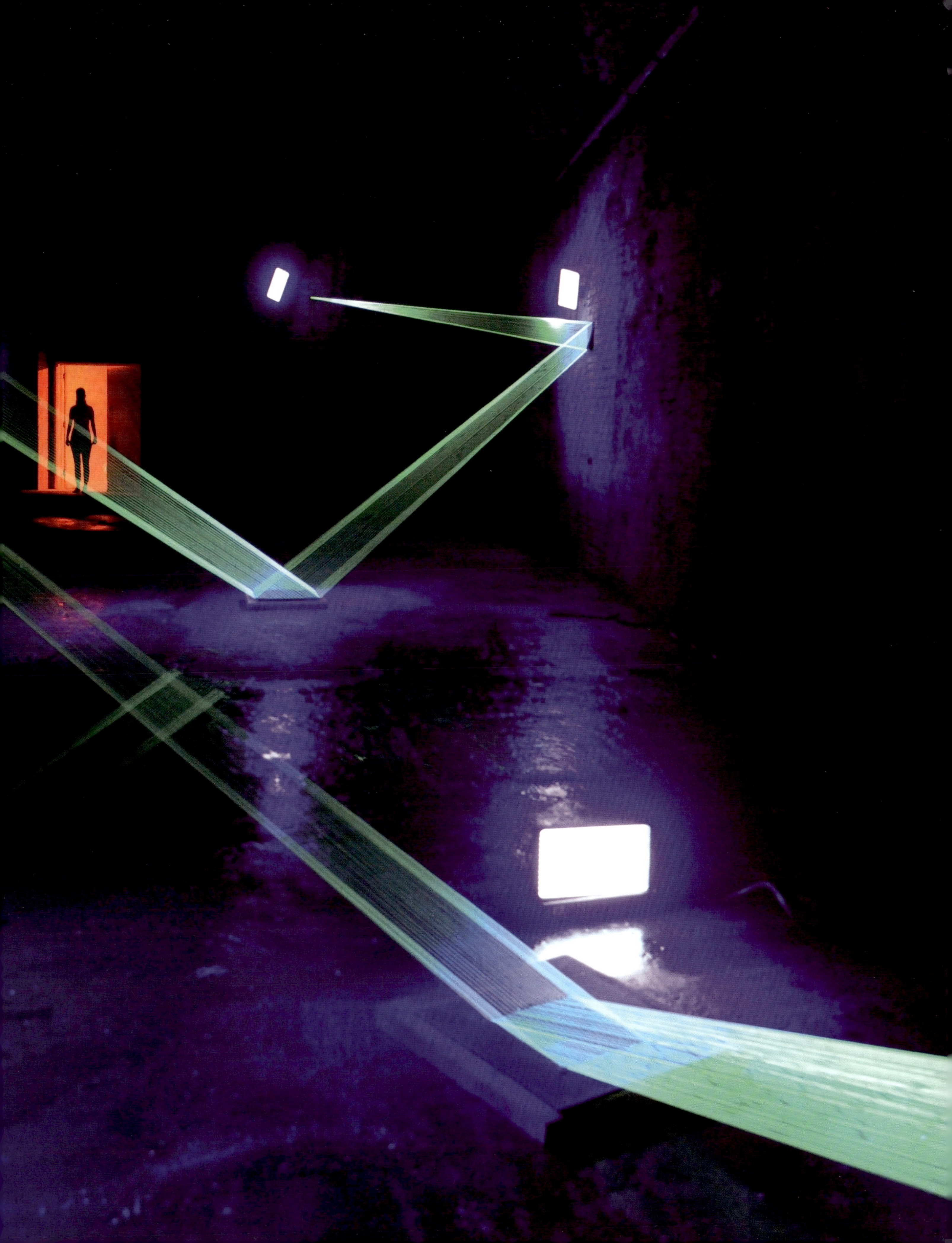

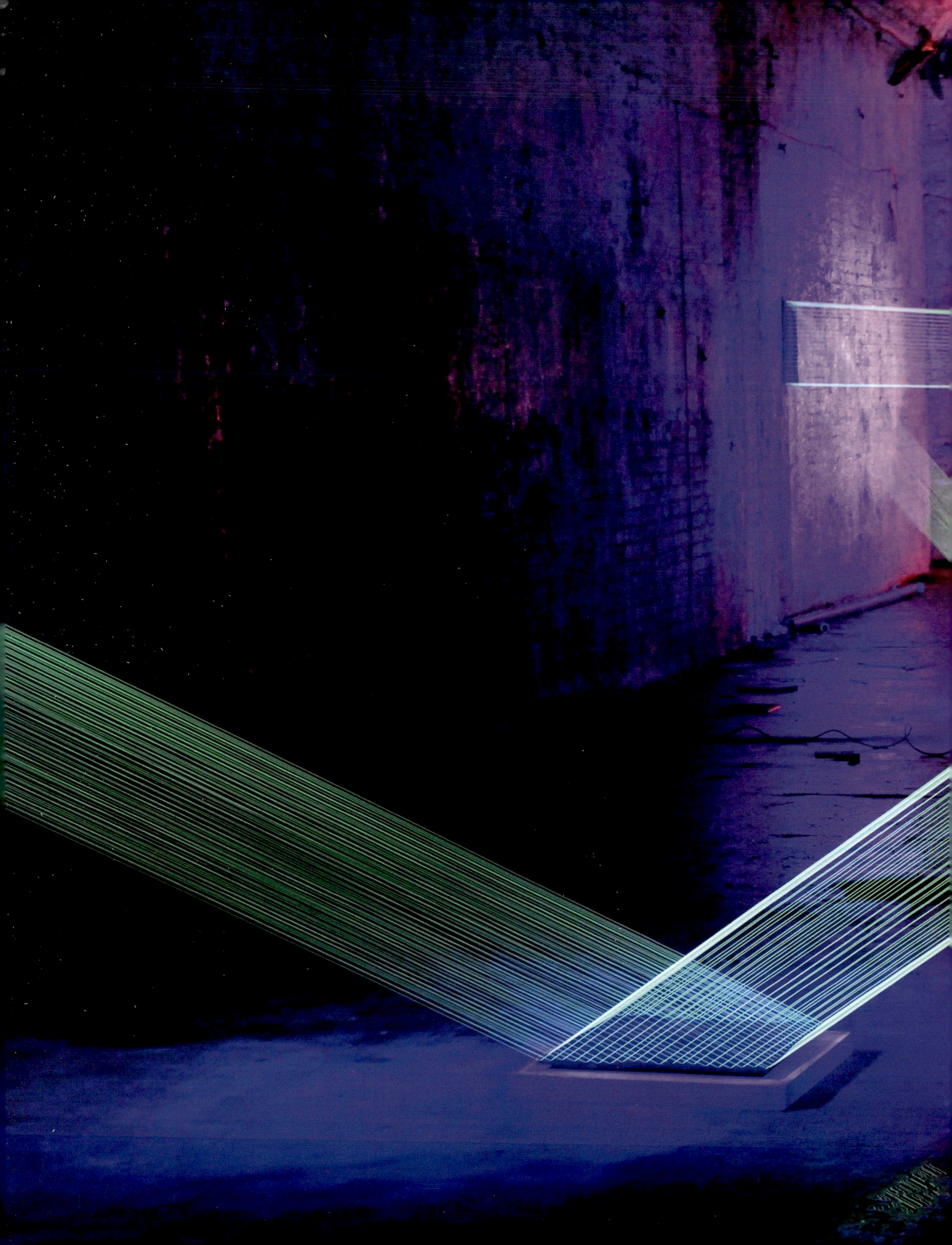

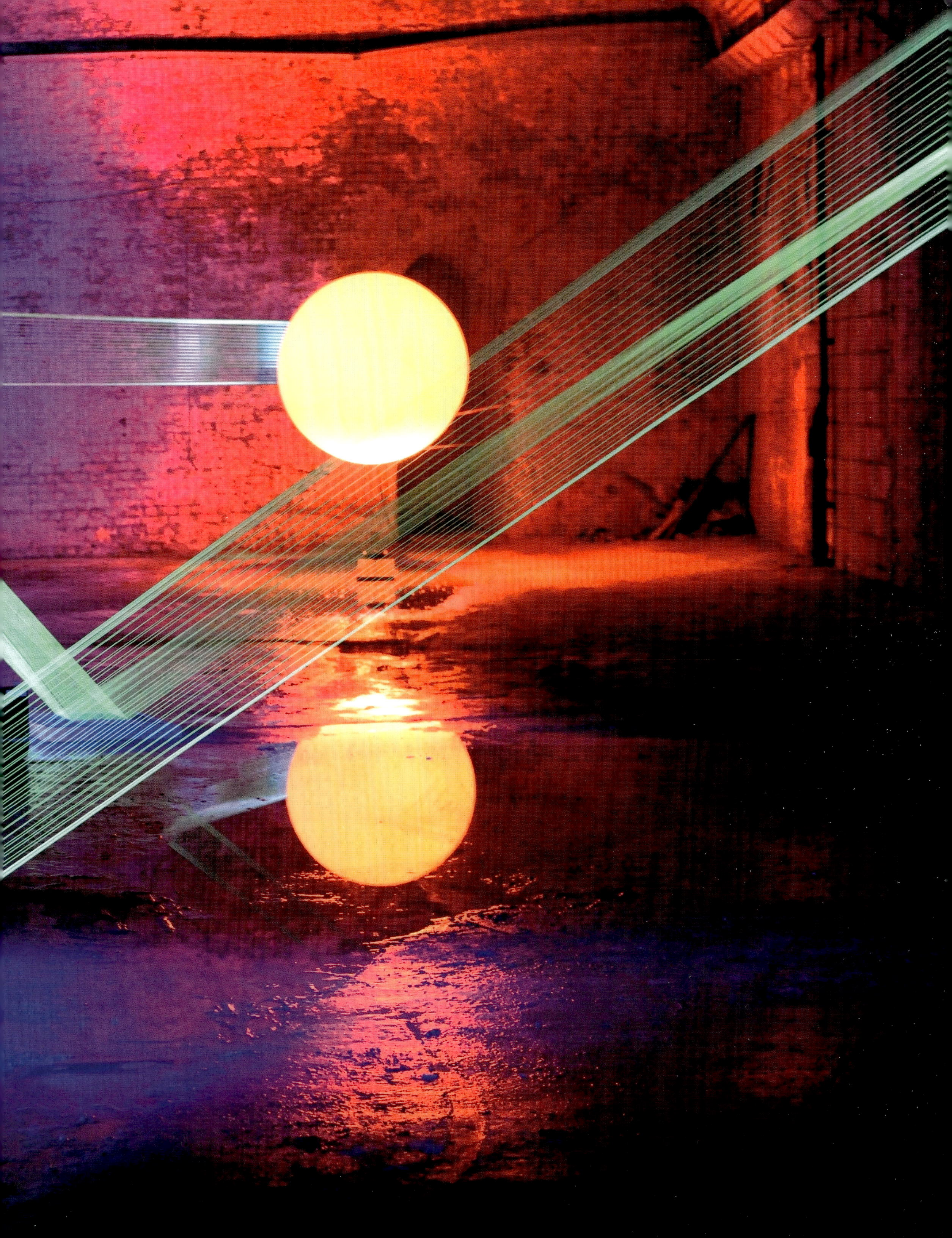

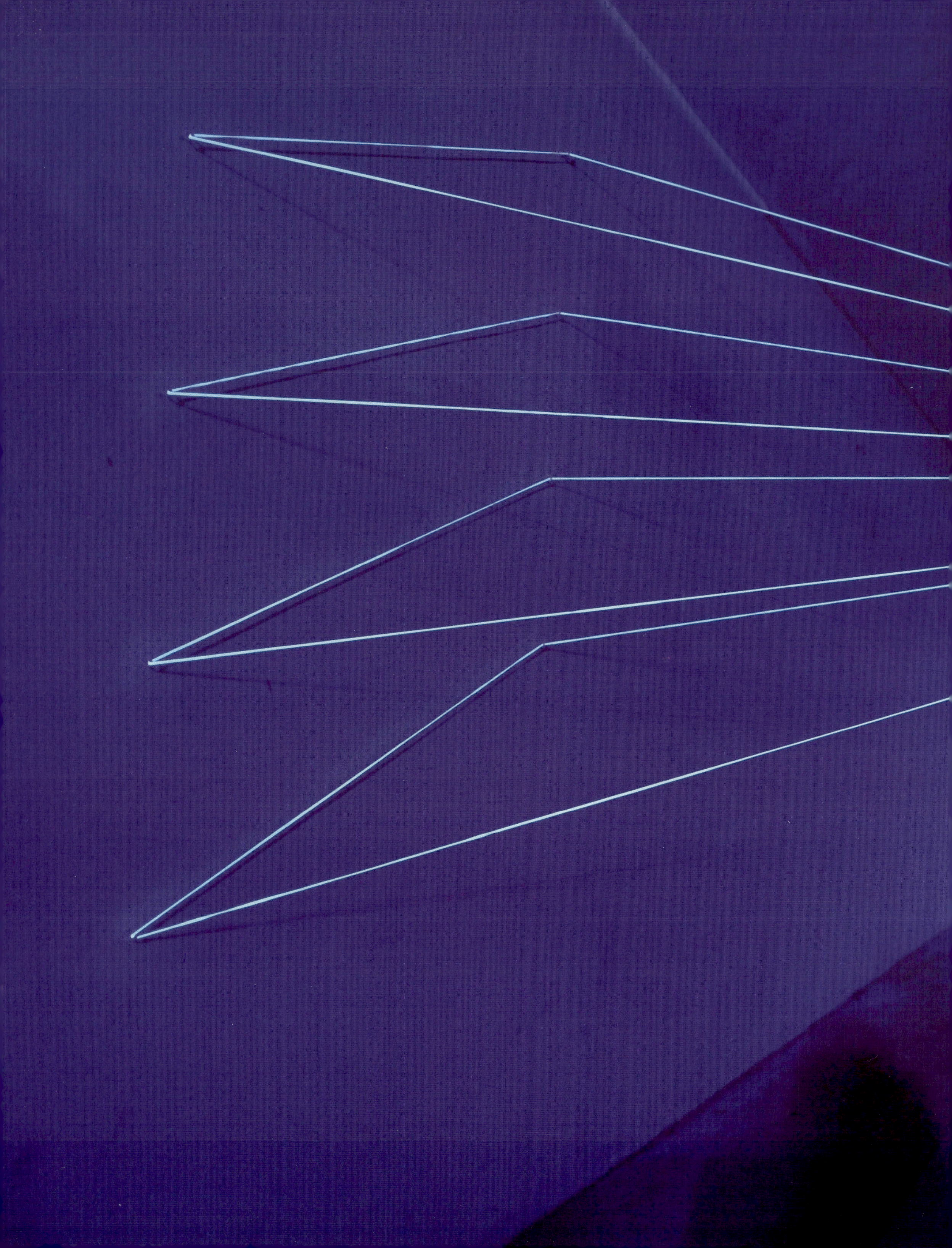

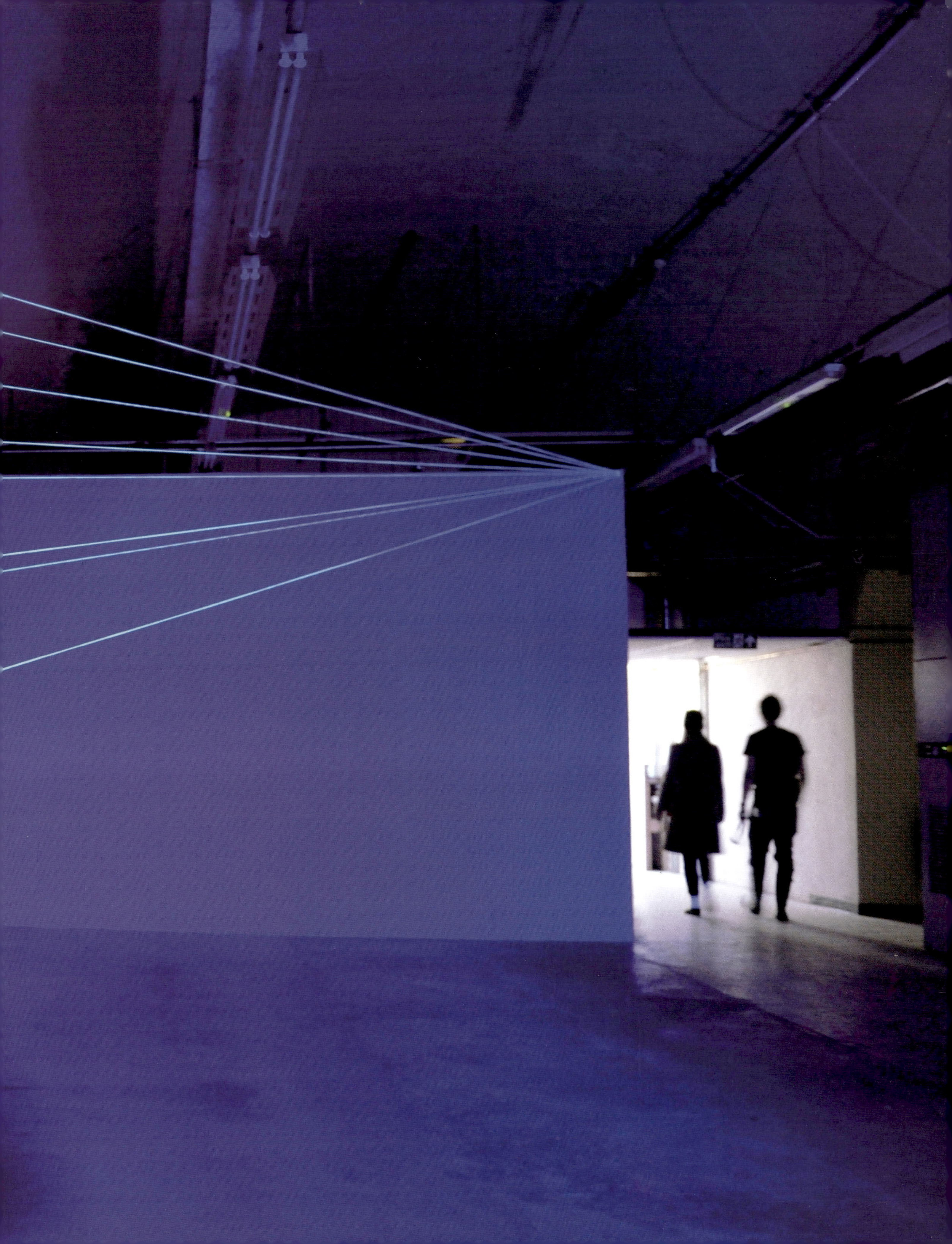

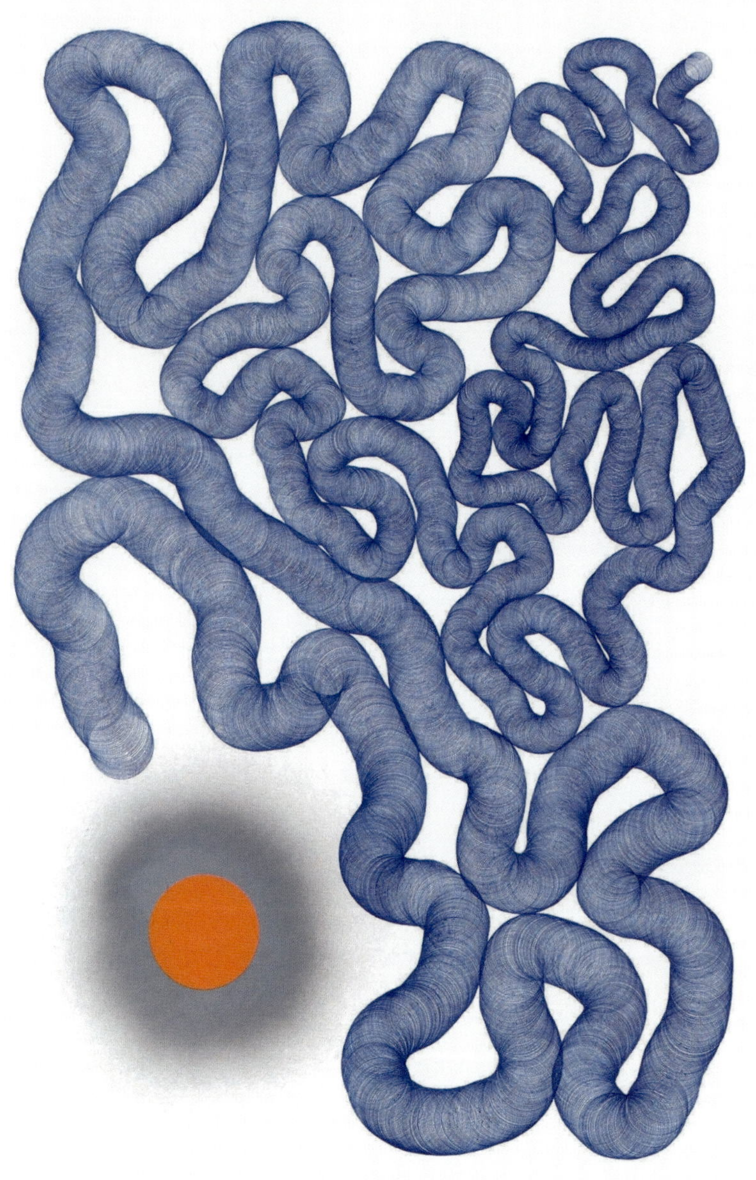

PP 13–15 David Ogle, *08019*, 2013, fluorescent fishing line, ultraviolet light, weather balloon, red halogen light, dimensions variable.

PP 16–17 David Ogle, *07008*, 2013, fluorescent cord, ultraviolet light, dimensions variable.

ABOVE David Ogle, *02024*, 2013, pen, ink, spray paint and collage on paper, giclée print on paper, 59.5 x 42 cm, edition of 30, plus 6 artist's proofs. Image courtesy the artist.

Notes from the Studio

Have you always had an interest in technology?

It seems that when any 'technology' reaches a level of ubiquity or domesticity it stops being referred to as 'technology' at all and fades into the background, becoming just another mechanism of everyday life. There is an inherent link between technologies and the idea of the future and also a natural link between technology and illusion. As Sir Arthur C Clarke, author of *2001: A Space Odyssey*, 1968, wrote, "any sufficiently advanced technology is indistinguishable from magic" and there is an element of trying to harness this in my work.

What appealed to you about the Sculpture Shock award?

The focus on specific sites was really the thing that most drew me to the award, as so much of my work is a reaction to an environment. This project seemed to demand an interrogative approach to the exhibition venues, which certainly tied in with the way I had been working and the way in which I see my practice progressing.

What was your inspiration for the Sculpture Shock commission?

To me there is something about underground spaces that has this sense of exploration, of seeking out something valuable, like a mine or a tomb. I wanted to consider underground light at its most precious and how living things are changed, blocked off from the sun, when they journey down beneath the surface.

Could you explain the process of creating one of your installations from drawing to realisation?

My installation works almost always begin as drawing on paper. In fact, the installations themselves are often attempts to further explore a process that has been carried out in two dimensions. Revealing an underlying process or set of operations that make up the work is key, and manifesting this as something that a viewer can physically or spatially experience is what progresses the work from drawing into installation. Thinking about the procedural properties of a two-dimensional work that I want to explore, I create a three-dimensional computer model of the specific space that I will be using and test out different approaches to realising the drawing in a sculptural form. This is then constructed within the space, replaying the system of the drawing across an environment.

You are currently working towards a PhD at Liverpool on a very sophisticated and ground-breaking area, namely the use of new media technologies in the cultural sphere. Is there is a fundamental paradox in your work in regards to your in-depth understanding of very sophisticated technological and scientific areas, and the very low-tech use of materials?

I find the critical debates surrounding new media and its cultural implications very interesting, particularly the ways in which established notions of space and materiality can be undermined. For a time I made work entirely digitally, producing interactive video installation works, but I often found that the computer imposes very strict parameters. The screen has become such a ubiquitous means of experience that it can cease to challenge a viewer. Our senses are actually more receptive to a physical confrontation in real-space. I feel that my work does reference technology, the grids, planes and strict mathematical ordering—but this is perhaps on a purely aesthetic level.

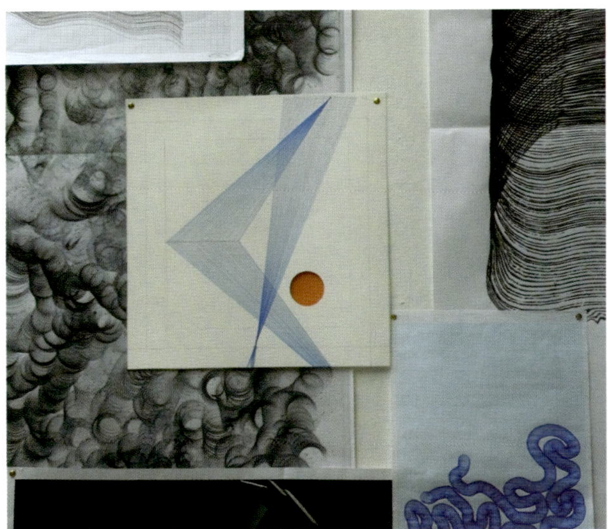

What impact do you hope to have on the viewer with your new commission?

Site-specific work puts the viewer into an environment that is unknown. When work is exhibited in a gallery, the space itself is always fulfilling its established function and I feel that this can cast certain preconceptions onto the experience of the work. Within a space previously inhabited for a different function, the installation of art objects strip the space of this previous role and it loses its utility, so it's not an industrial site but neither is it a gallery. It hangs precariously between the two. I think this tension is interesting for audiences, and can allow a unique experience of a site.

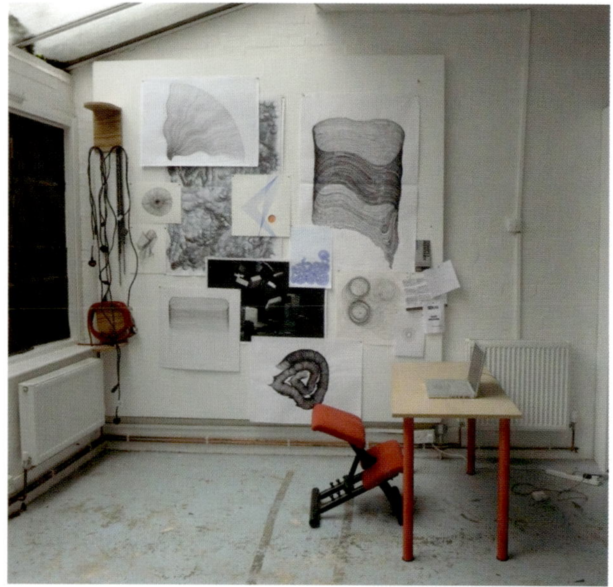

Your installations are all temporary. How do you feel about their impermanence?

I like the ephemeral nature of many of my works. I see them more as events or interventions than objects. As a set of procedures that are played out within the space, the work exists for a while and then it is destroyed. Then, in another place, at another the time, those same operations can be 're-activated', the work coming into being again. Each time the work is made anew, dictated by the surroundings in which it appears; the system, the blueprint or its making surviving after each of the works are demolished.

The transient nature of my work is central to their numerical titles. As numbers can increase infinitely, it shows each work as part of an ongoing system, cataloguing work that no longer exists. Perhaps the numbering allows a degree of detachment when it comes to dismantling a piece at the end of an exhibition. As my second solo exhibition, the title of my Sculpture Shock exhibition will be 00002.

Could you explain the importance of colour in your work?

There is a blue that I use in many of my installation pieces and I think that has partly been influenced by some of Yves Klein's writing. Discussing the different associative properties of colour, Klein wrote that in nature, blue represents that which is most abstract, hinting at the sea and the sky, entities that exist on a scale that defy physical comprehension. On a less lofty note, I tend to draw in blue ballpoint pen, so the colour further references the drawings that inspire the installations.

Who are the artists you most admire and which have had the greatest impact on your thinking and your work?

The work and writing of Sol LeWitt was a big influence when I first began working with serial systems and processes. The sets of instructions he used to create his wall drawings have had a big impact on the way I think about my own work. West Coast light and space artists such as James Turrell and Robert Irwin have also had a big impact, as well as younger light artists such as Carlo Bernardini who makes fantastic architectural light pieces. I am currently interested in Haroon Mirza. He makes kinetic sound sculptures from disparate sets of objects.

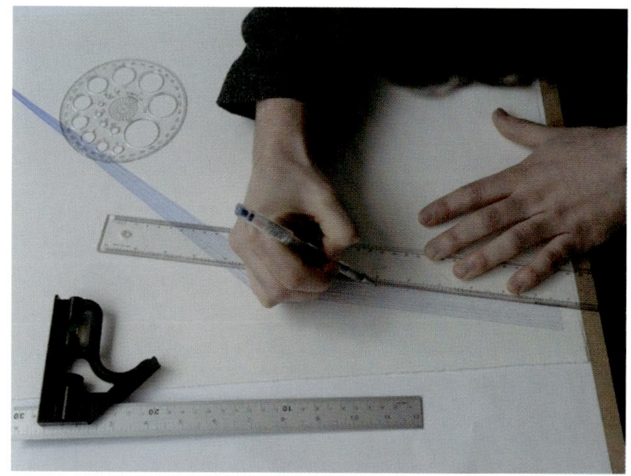

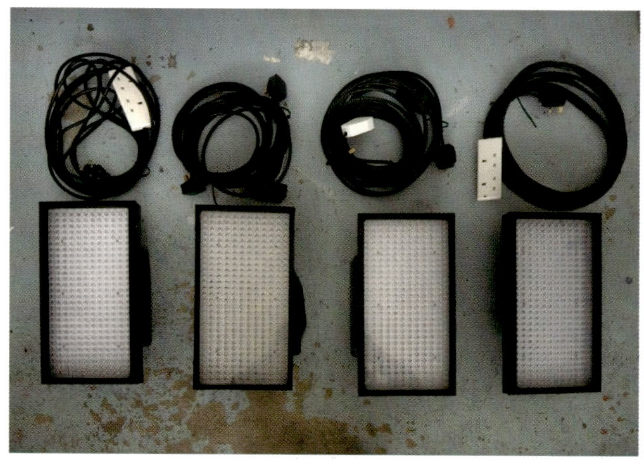

PREVIOUS PAGE AND ABOVE Work in progress during David Ogle's residency.

OPPOSITE TOP David Ogle, *Pink, Orange, Yellow, Green, 4*, 2013, plastic drinking straws, ultraviolet light, dimensions variable.

OPPOSITE BOTTOM David Ogle, *08019* (detail), 2013, fluorescent fishing line, ultraviolet light, weather balloon, red halogen light, dimensions variable.

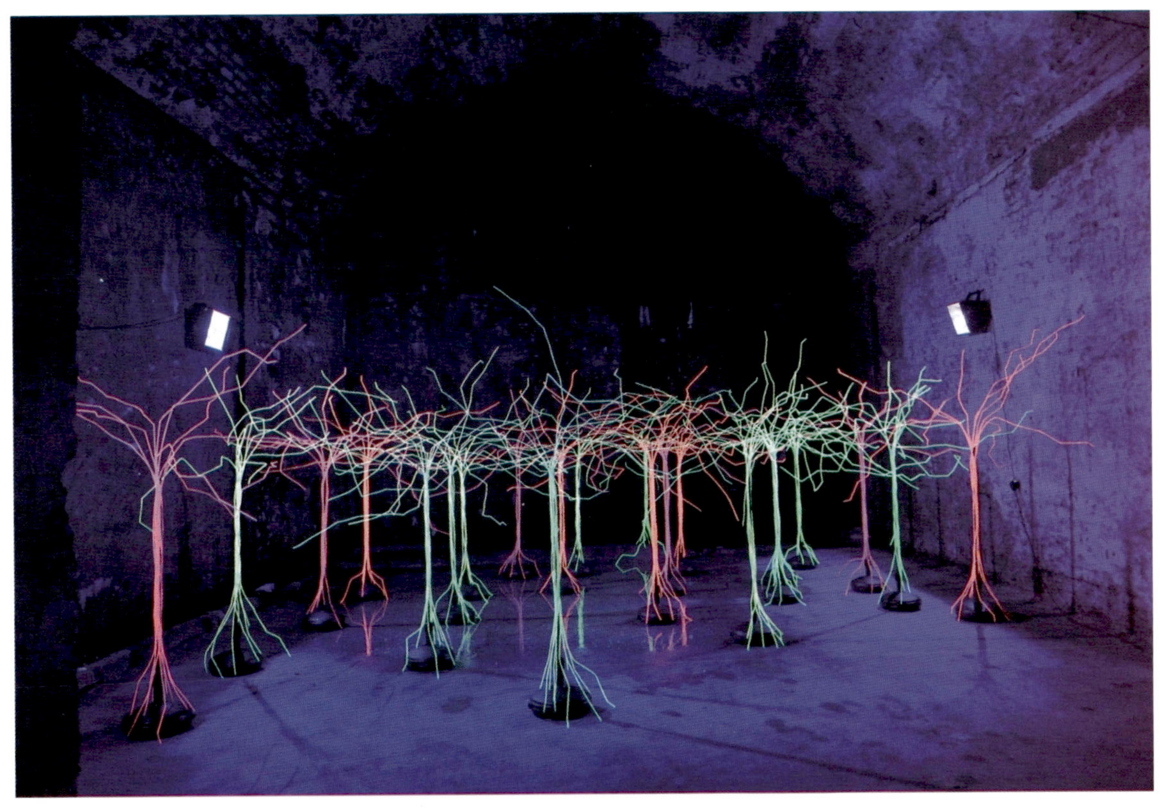

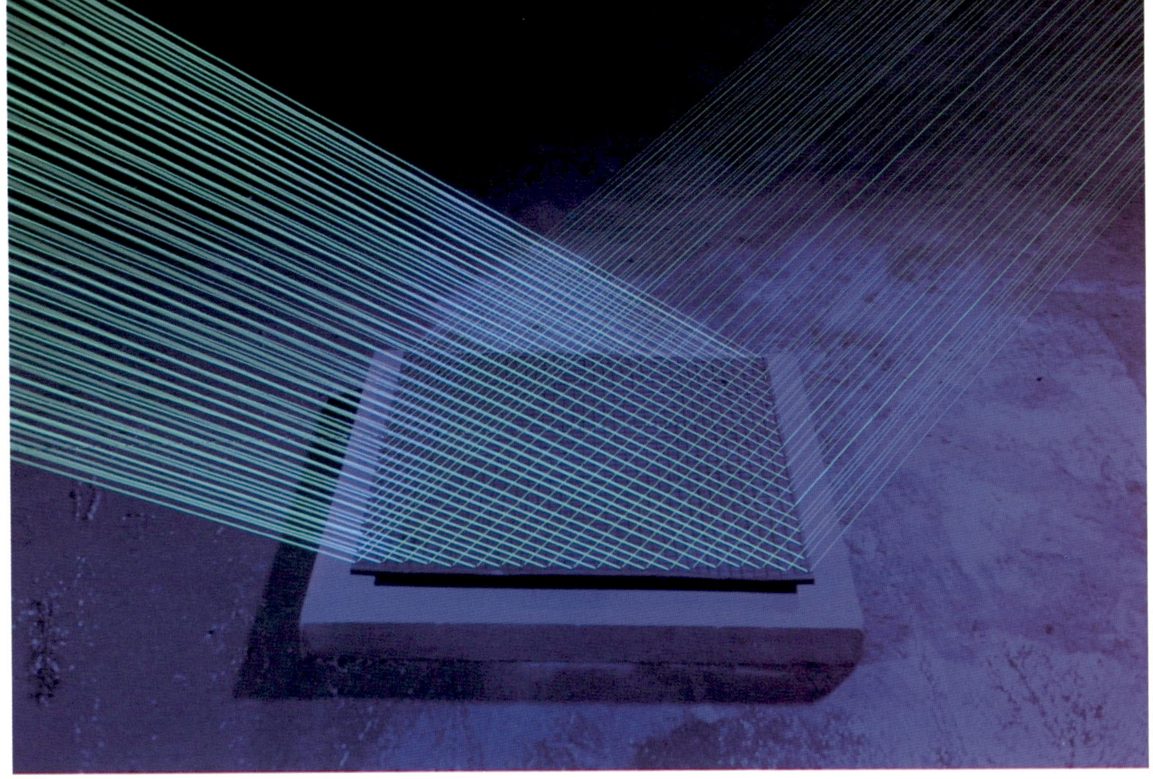

Patrick Lowry
The Horse Hospital, Bloomsbury, London

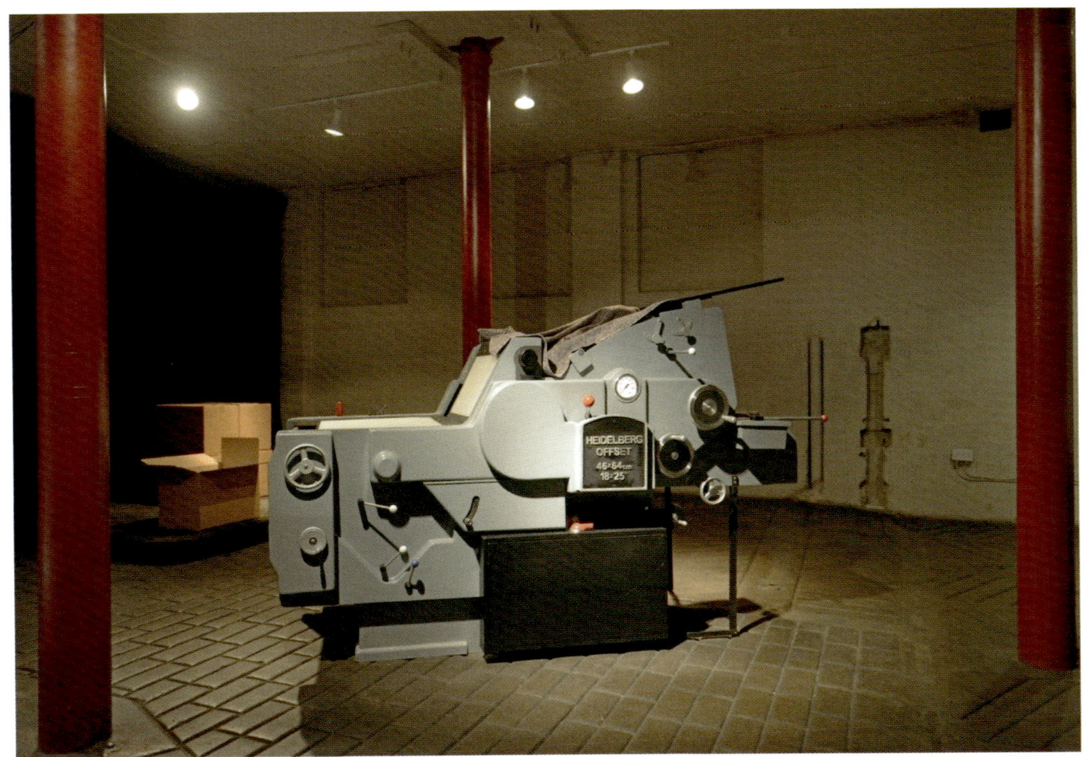

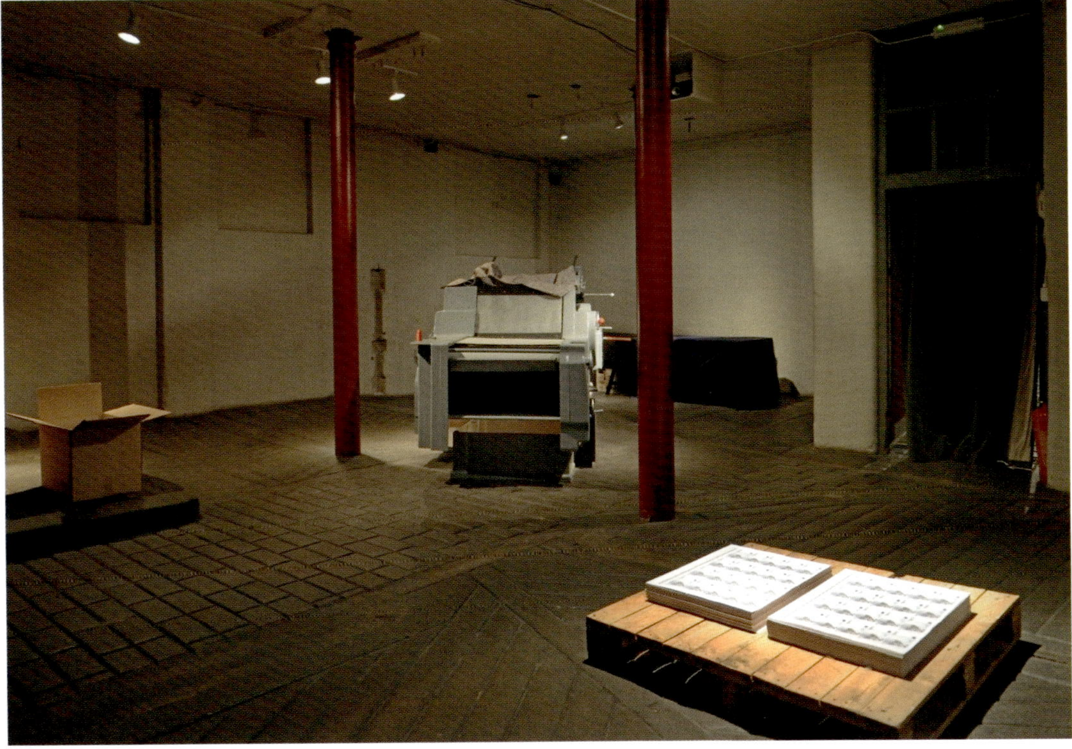

Patrick Lowry, *Quantitative Easing*, 2014, replica of the Heidelberg
Printing Machine, MDF, wood, acrylic, stainless steel, printed replica
Euros, pallet, money packs, cardboard boxes, dimensions variable.

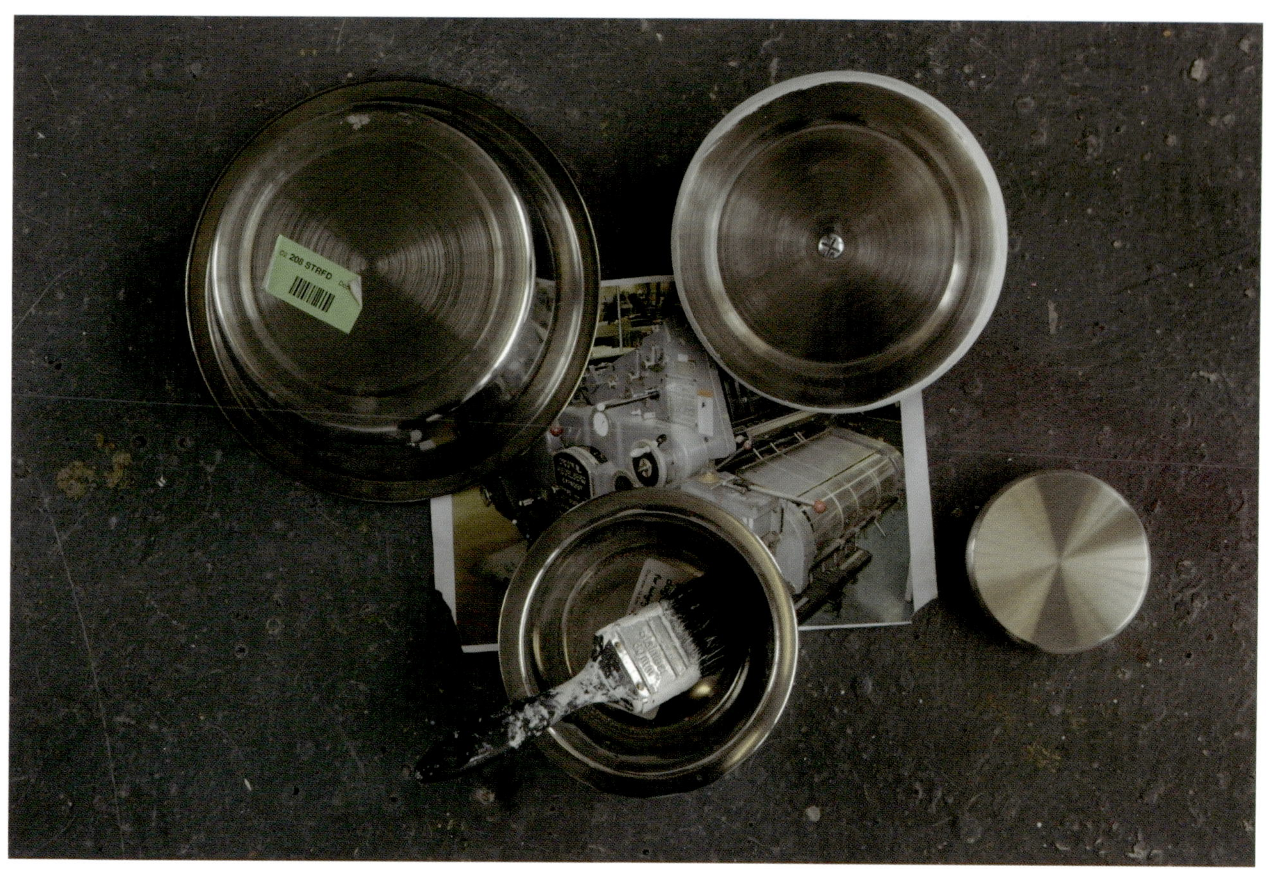

ABOVE AND OPPOSITE Work in progress during Patrick Lowry's residency.

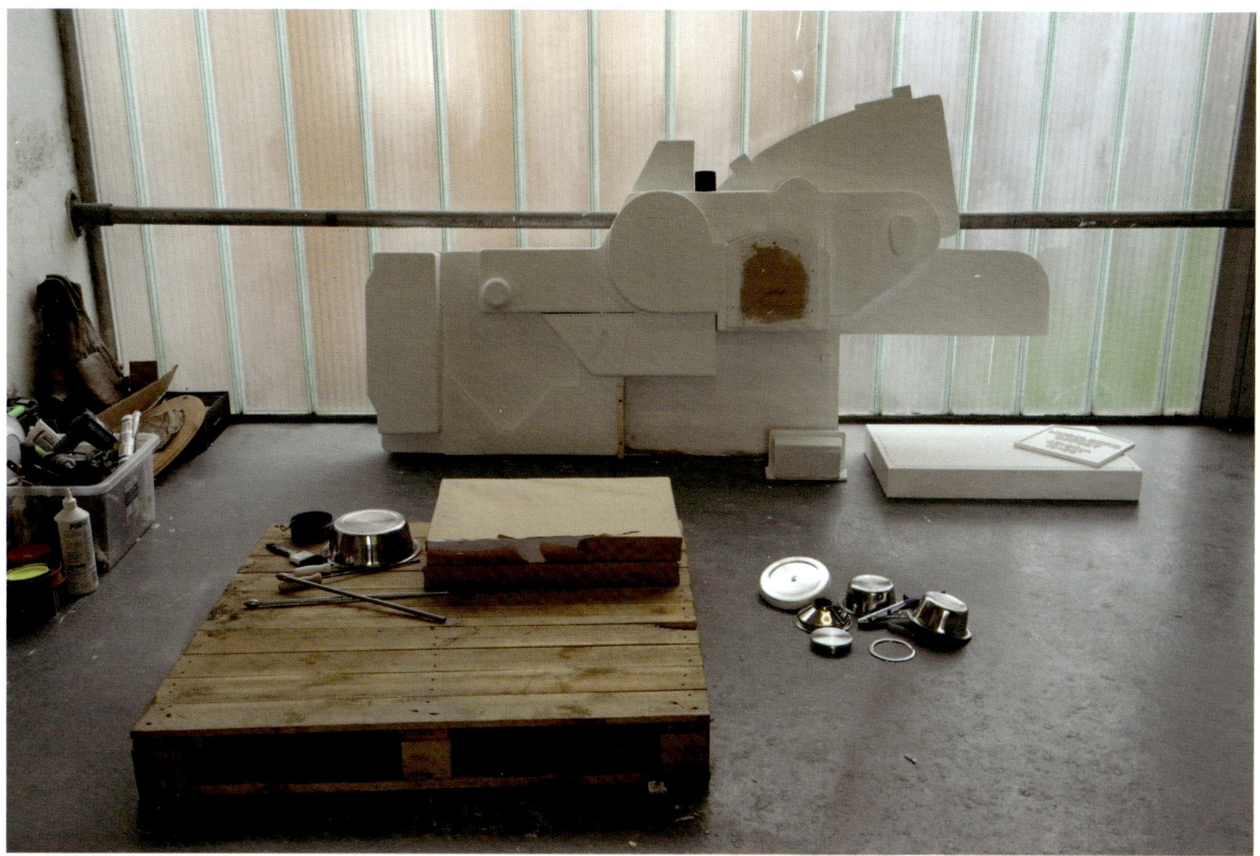

Notes from the Studio

What made you decide to become an artist?

Actually, I am doing the same thing now as I did when I was a child of eight. I was always drawing and making three-dimensional objects with bits and pieces I found. At school, I didn't manage to excel as my academic path was hindered by severe dyslexia. It was the art and design department that showed me the way towards something I enjoyed and was good at. I left school and started an Art Foundation course, but started to panic about being a fine artist. I thought it would drive me mad with its lack of boundaries and structure. So, I went on to do my first degree in product design at the Surrey College of Art and Design in 1971. I worked for ten years designing electrical equipment at Philips, which gave me parameters and a path. Ultimately, though, I hated the commercialism and the futility of it—new plastic boxes for the same old content. I left to set up my own design practice but doing this and having twins simultaneously proved to be bad timing. I rediscovered my artistic path by chance when I applied for a job in Cornwall teaching design on the Foundation course at Cornwall College. Being back in an art and design environment made me realise I needed to revisit my passion for art and I went on take my Masters at Falmouth College of Arts in 2003, where I am now a visiting lecturer.

Your work appears meticulously executed, so much so that it fools the viewer into thinking it is real. Is this craftsmanship essential to your work?

The work appears so, but appearances are deceptive. I am not aiming to make perfect functioning replicas, but to do enough to make the work believable as an entity in its own right. In fact, I am selective about what to include visually, even if this is not important to the functionality of the real thing. For *American Dream*, 2013, I made a replica of a 1950s American suburban home complete with a Chevrolet Bel Air parked outside. I have never seen a Bel Air but from looking at photographs and models I chose the aspects that made it believable—it is the impression of reality that counts.

I am not a highly skilled craftsman or maker—in fact, I find the making process very laborious (and often tedious). But it is an essential process for me as it makes me think through all aspects of the object/installation and its meanings and implications. The process of cutting, gluing, sanding and painting, and the analyses of the subject needed to replicate it, brings me closer to the subject matter and the commentary I am trying to convey.

What are your views on the debate around the artist's hand versus the use of fabricators?

Personally, I have always made my works myself by hand as I believe that the process of making somehow imbues the objects with some of the thought processes that I went through. I have never used 'real' manufactured objects, as they simply do not have the same visual or intellectual effect on the audience. Presenting the audience with the real object can quickly close down audience engagement: they know what it is so ask no more questions. The shift from initially believing they know what they are looking at to the realisation that the work is a facsimile makes them reassess and hopefully re-engage with what the work is about.

There is no right or wrong to using ready-mades or fabricated objects—it just depends on the message an artist wants to convey. I am dealing with the intricacies of illusion, which I must create myself otherwise there is no illusion, just bare reality.

What is the usual course of events leading to the creation of a new work?

The Sculpture Shock residency has turned my usual process on its head. I usually find the object or scenario and then locate a site that allows me to present it so that the message is clear.

For *Escalator*, 2006, I was meandering in Toulouse when I happened upon the construction of an escalator entrance to the underground system, which I had no idea existed. It seemed so out of context in the middle of a quiet tree-lined pavement with no other clues to what it was doing there. Some months later, I was thinking about making a work about the unquestioned decision-making of governments and local authorities, and how it resonated with the archetypal, but now fading, 1960s architectural statement of Cornwall's County Hall.

In terms of process, I make drawings—many drawings —that are not observational but technical. They contain measurements, details of construction techniques, materials. I make films of my subject matter—the audio of most end with, "Excuse me, Sir, you can't do that here", before jolting to a close. I take photographs from every accessible angle. I need to understand the thing I am replicating. This points me to what is important about its meaning and how I can convey my message through it.

Why is site-specificity so important to your work? Have you ever placed work in a gallery?

The site is the key. There are certain places that provide the perfect context to convey the message. I placed *Escalator* in the large, open foyer area of the Cornwall County Hall in Truro, installing it over a weekend when the building was largely empty. (I had permission, of course, to install an

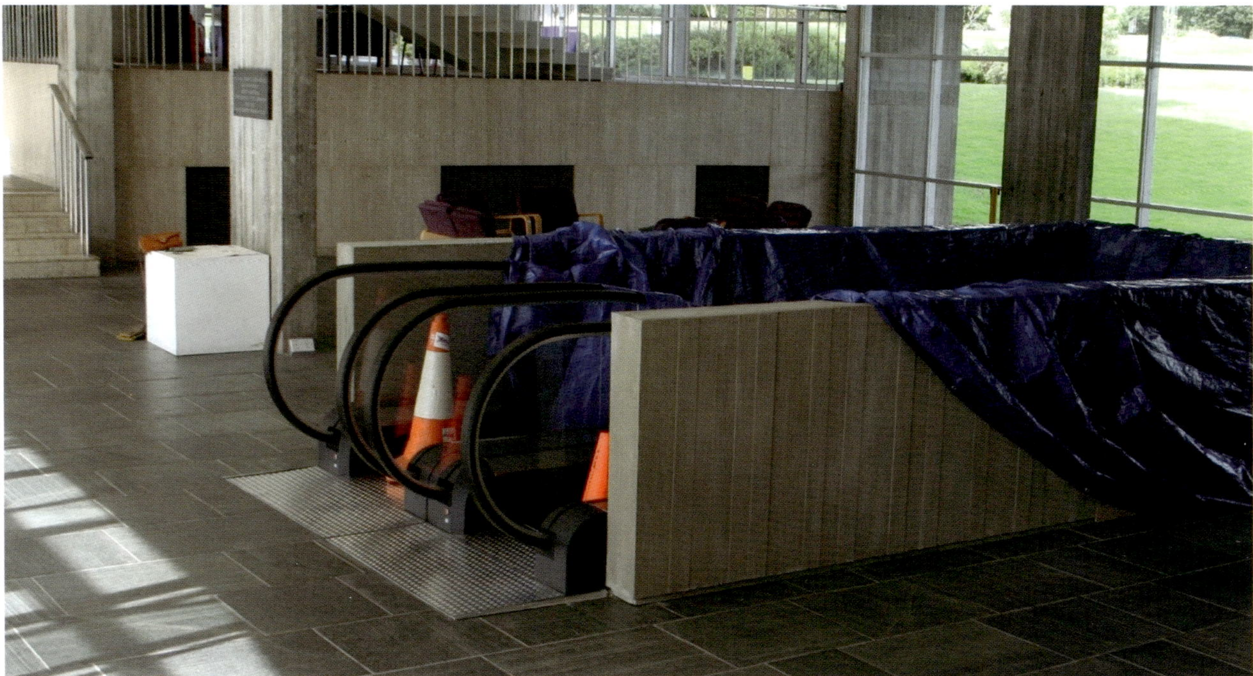

Patrick Lowry, *Escalator*, 2007, New County Hall, Truro, Cornwall, full-size replica of an escalator in chipboard, MDF, cast resin, wallpaper, cement, Fablon, tarpaulin, hazard cones, 100 x 272 x 488 cm. Image courtesy the artist.

'art exhibition'). It was the perfect location to comment on the invisibility of decision makers, the slow but steady descent of our economy, and the fabric of our society as I perceive it. The tarpaulins draped over the work pointed to the familiar and exasperating norm of public building works being abandoned midway or decisions never taken to their conclusion. I had to carefully consider what to do when invited to show this work in a gallery and had to substantially remake the work to establish a new narrative. *24 Hour Cash Machine*, 2009, on the other hand, was installed in the Leeds Metropolitan University Gallery and carefully placed in a discrete corner of the gallery. It worked well in this space as it was incongruous and yet such a familiar part of our lives that it confused the audience enough to question it and then their own relationship with the cash machine, with money which is seemingly on tap and our culture of desire, our obsession with spending.

Clearly your work engages directly with debates surrounding the simulacrum, the real and the copy. The history of art since Plato has largely been about representing the real, be it in naturalistic or abstract terms. The simulacrum subverts the relationships between the real and the copy, original and reproduction, image and likeness all of which affirm the status of the real. Meanwhile, the simulacrum—a copy

without a true original, an imitation without roots in the real—has been regarded negatively, until its adoption by postmodern and poststructural theorists in the late 1960s. For Baudrillard, simulacra blur the distinction between reality and reproduction as they produce a simulated experience of the contemporary world. As the world became (and remains) deluged with images, simulacra were (and are) employed by artists for different ends. Why do you employ simulacra?

As an industrial designer, I was not selling the technology of a product, I was selling the belief that the new product, which was more often than not just the old product repackaged, was better. I was selling a new reality again and again and the world was buying into that illusion, in fact, they were buying the illusion. Illusions increasingly form the reality in which we live. We are more and more physically detached from reality so what I attempt to do is to question this situation by presenting an object which looks real, but is not. Some viewers are happy to accept the Chevrolet as a real car as we are so attuned to recognising things through signs and images. For others, there is a jarring realisation that their eyes/mind are misreading the object and by extension the world.

I hope that initially the audience will believe that my work is the real thing. I am interested in the point at which realisation dawns that it is not. That is when the viewer starts to think about the meaning of the work. It is the moment that the brain shifts from acceptance to questioning, from one model of belief to another. I hope the audience experience that.

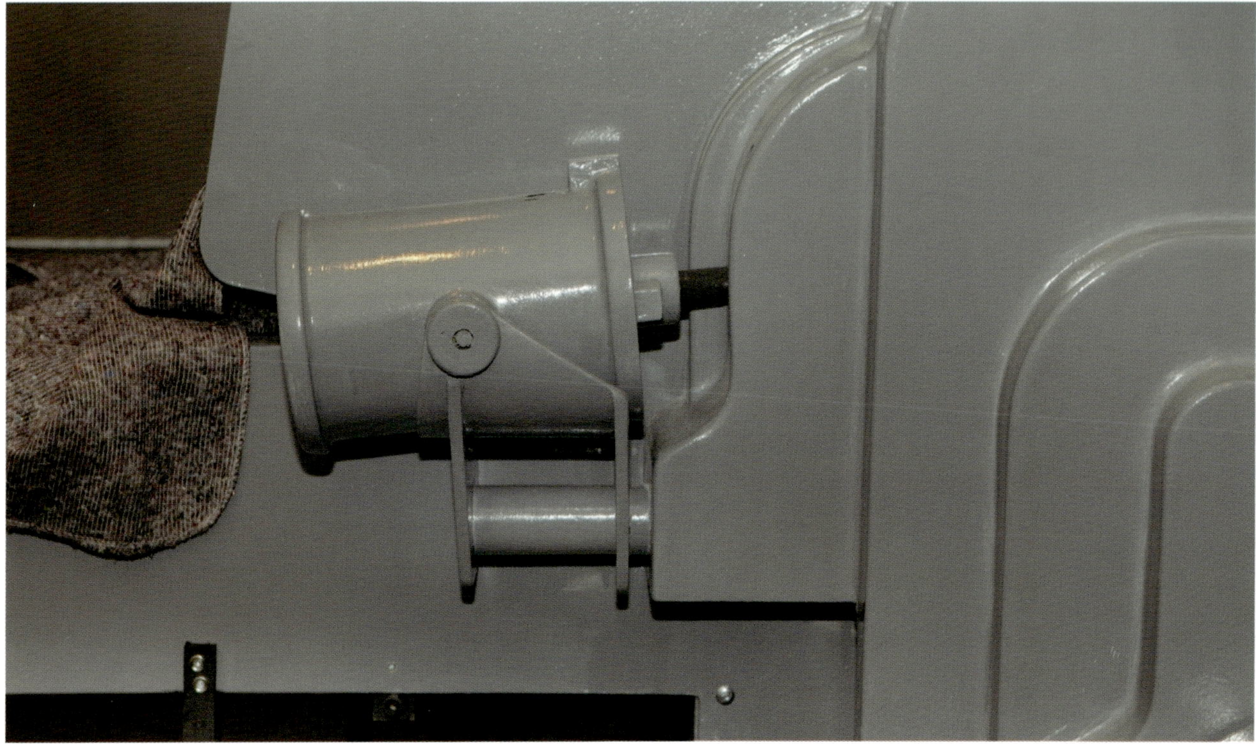

Patrick Lowry, *Quantitative Easing* (detail), 2014.

What are your thoughts around the subterranean in relation to your work?

For me, the subterranean conjures up images of the underworld, the black market world of forgery, fakes and counterfeit. Interestingly, the building itself is subterranean, but has this other overwhelming association with being a horse hospital. I intend to look beyond this and into other uses of the building, including from the 1920s to about 30 years ago when it was a commercial printers. I am deeply interested in the power structures surrounding the economic crash, the powerlessness of the individual and the dematerialisation of money. I am exploring the effect of cash becoming obsolete on our physical and aesthetic experience of the world.

Which artists have most influenced you and who do you most admire?

I'm not sure I have any direct influences and my interest in artists changes. Sometimes it might just be an individual work that catches my attention. There are a range of artists that I find myself revisiting, several of which don't work in three dimensions. I feel there is an overlap with Thomas Demand's work, both in content and process. He takes what appears to be the mundane and everyday but behind which there is something else. There is also Gerhard Richter. From the things I have read, when talking about his work, there is a refreshing uncertainty and contradiction. I'm always a bit suspicious of an artist that seems to be very clear about what they are doing; certainty is not the business we are in. Gabriel Orozco, Gavin Turk, Jeff Wall, Edward Hopper, Matthias Weischer, Fischli & Weiss, Peter Doge, Richard Wilson, all spring to mind as well, in no particular order.

Given the temporary nature of your work, how do you feel about photographic reproductions of your work?

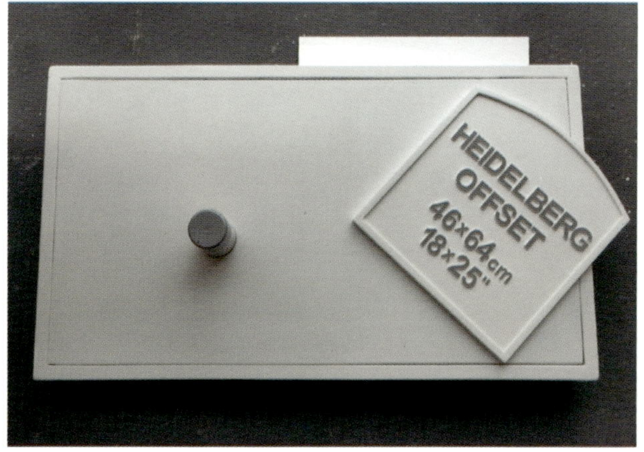

I do, of course, like people to physically engage with the work and that is its original intention. In reality, the majority of artists' work, not just mine, are only ever seen as two-dimensional reproductions, and I would rather that than it not being seen at all. Thomas Demand, whose work I find interesting, is of course exploring the whole question of the real and reproduced, starting with a found image, translating it into three dimensions and then finally back into a photograph. We never see the three-dimensional work in reality.

What was your message in *Crushing the Tate*, 2012?

The title of this work might at first seem to be making a derogatory comment, but it is not meant to. It refers to having to reduce the scale of the Tate stairs to be able to get even a single storey of the stairs into the small Bikini Gallery. The work was really about the art ecology and how small, independent contemporary galleries play an important part in the dynamics of the art world as well as big institutions like the Tate. I think at the time I made reference to it being like the plankton and the whale; the whale would not survive without the plankton.

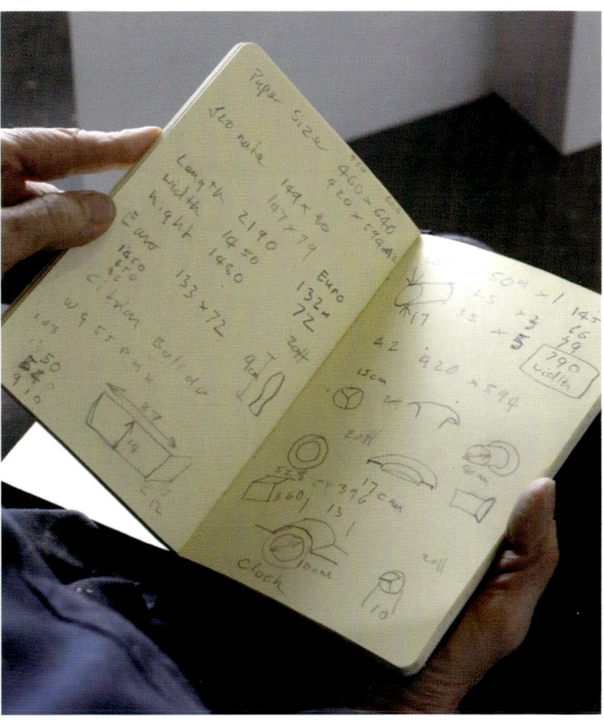

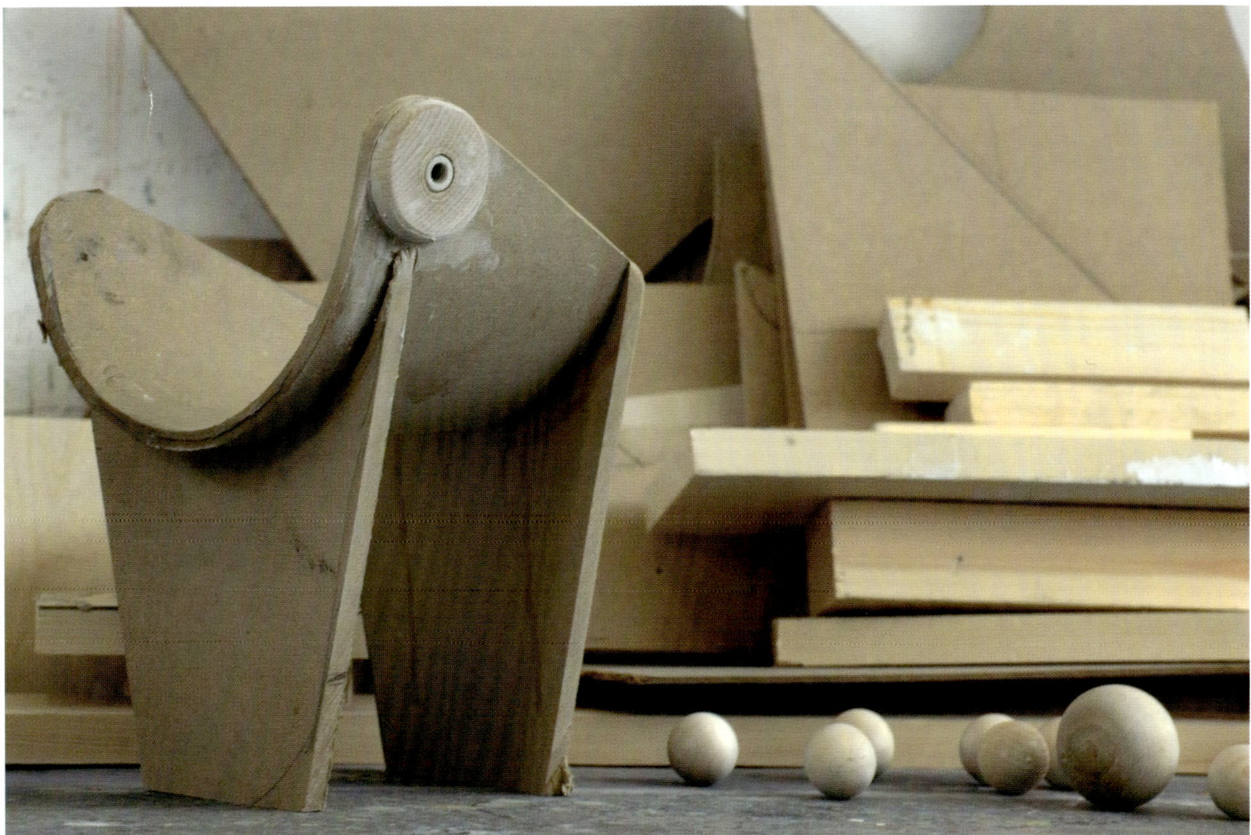

OPPOSITE BOTTOM AND ABOVE Work in progress during Patrick Lowry's residency.

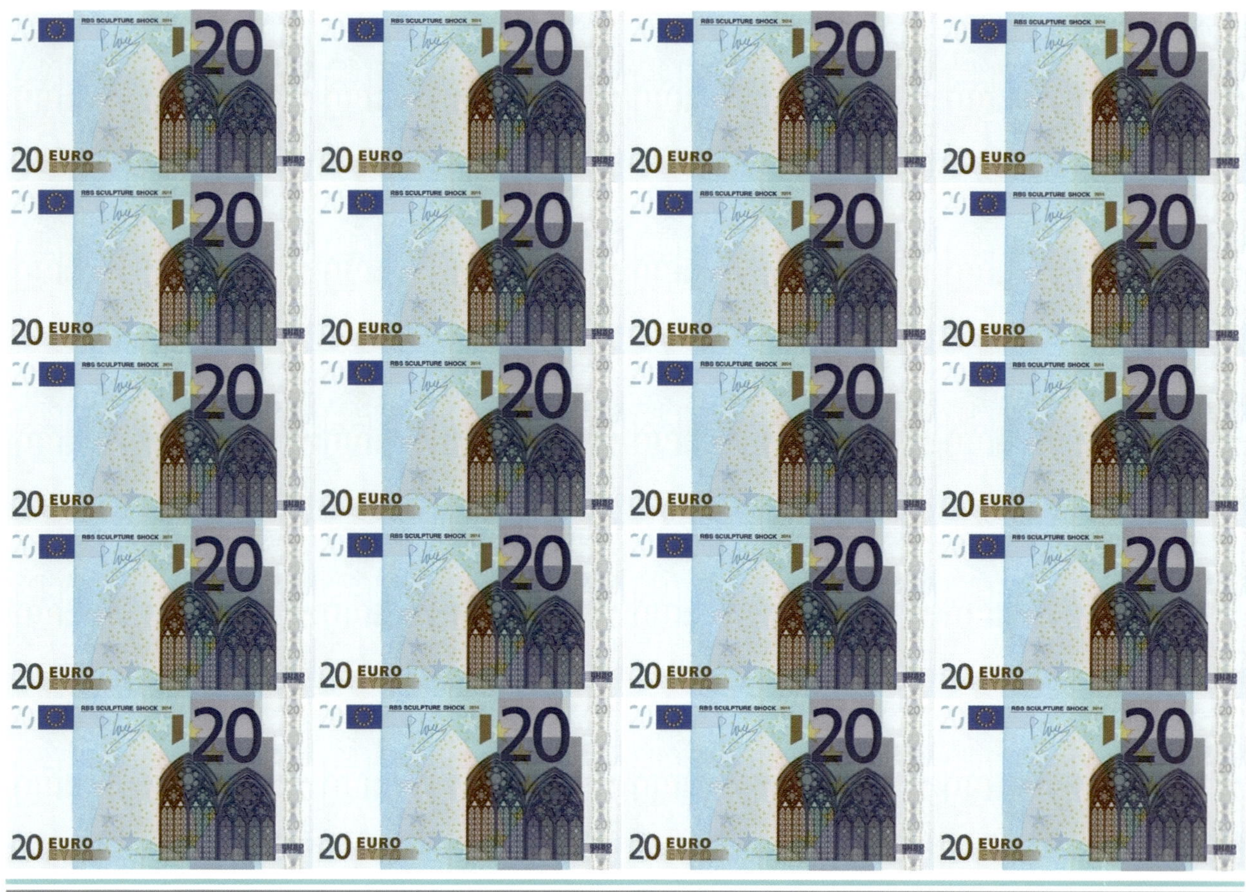

Patrick Lowry, *Quantitative Easing*, 2014, hand-pulled screen print on Southbank Smooth, 42 x 59.5 cm, edition of 30, plus 6 artist's proofs. Image courtesy the artist.

Patrick Lowry: *Quantitative Easing*, 2014—Sarah Kent

Sculpture Shock 2014 got underway with Patrick Lowry's installation *Quantitative Easing*, housed in the subterranean gloom of The Horse Hospital in Bloomsbury. Access to the space is via a steep ramp, a reminder that the premises were built (in the late eighteenth century) as a treatment centre for London's hard-working horses. Picking one's way down the steep incline, one can imagine their hooves slipping and sliding as they anxiously negotiated the unfamiliar descent.

After the closure of the hospital, a commercial printer turned the basement into a busy print shop, which continued operating until the 1980s. A concrete slab built to accommodate the heavy press is still in situ and it is this recent history that Lowry has chosen to address. You could be fooled, in fact, into thinking he has created a museum of social history. Occupying centre stage is a large Heidelberg offset press of the kind used in the print shop. Did the printers leave it behind because it was too heavy to move?

Rather than a trip down memory lane, though, this exhibition is a multilayered investigation of the smoke and mirrors world of contemporary finance. Despite being utterly convincing, the printing press turns out to be made from sheets of MDF painted grey to resemble steel. The pressure dial was created on Photoshop and its 'glass' cover is the plastic lid of a yoghurt pot; one lever is a footrest from a BMX bike, others are made from lengths of dowelling; the discs that crank the bed up and down are the bases of stainless steel food bowls found in Wickes. Thrown over the bed is a grey blanket of the kind used by removal firms; lift up one corner and, in place of the heavy rollers you expect to see, there is an immaculate void.

The duplicity does not end there. Apparently, the fake press has been printing euro bank notes, some of which are still drying while others are packed ready for shipment. Have we stumbled into a criminal underworld of forgers and counterfeiters? Things are not that clear cut. With central banks stimulating local economies by printing money—the quantitative easing of the title—and bankers generating millions by selling virtual commodities to imaginary buyers, the border between the legal and illicit seems remarkably elastic. Whether they like it or not, artists are sucked into this murky realm by producing work that, despite having no actual use, might one day become an investment opportunity.

Art has always dealt in illusion and, when nothing serious is at stake, being fooled is a delight; but Lowry's installation generates more than pure pleasure. He seduces us into considering the part played by illusion in other areas of activity, such as global finance, that have a profound impact on our lives— where our willingness to be duped becomes a political issue, rather than a self-reflective game.

Lynn Dennison
Brunel's Rotherhithe Shaft, London

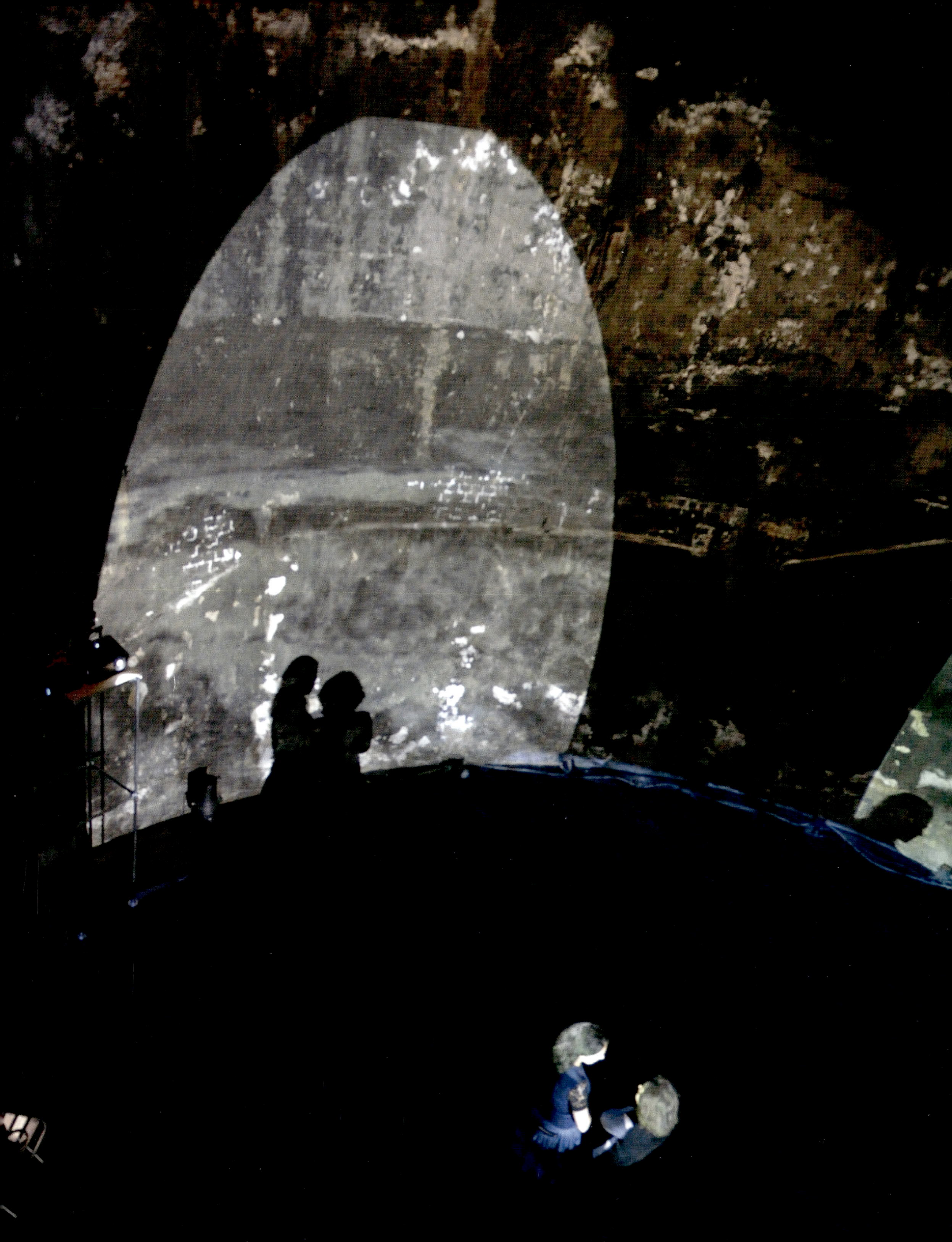

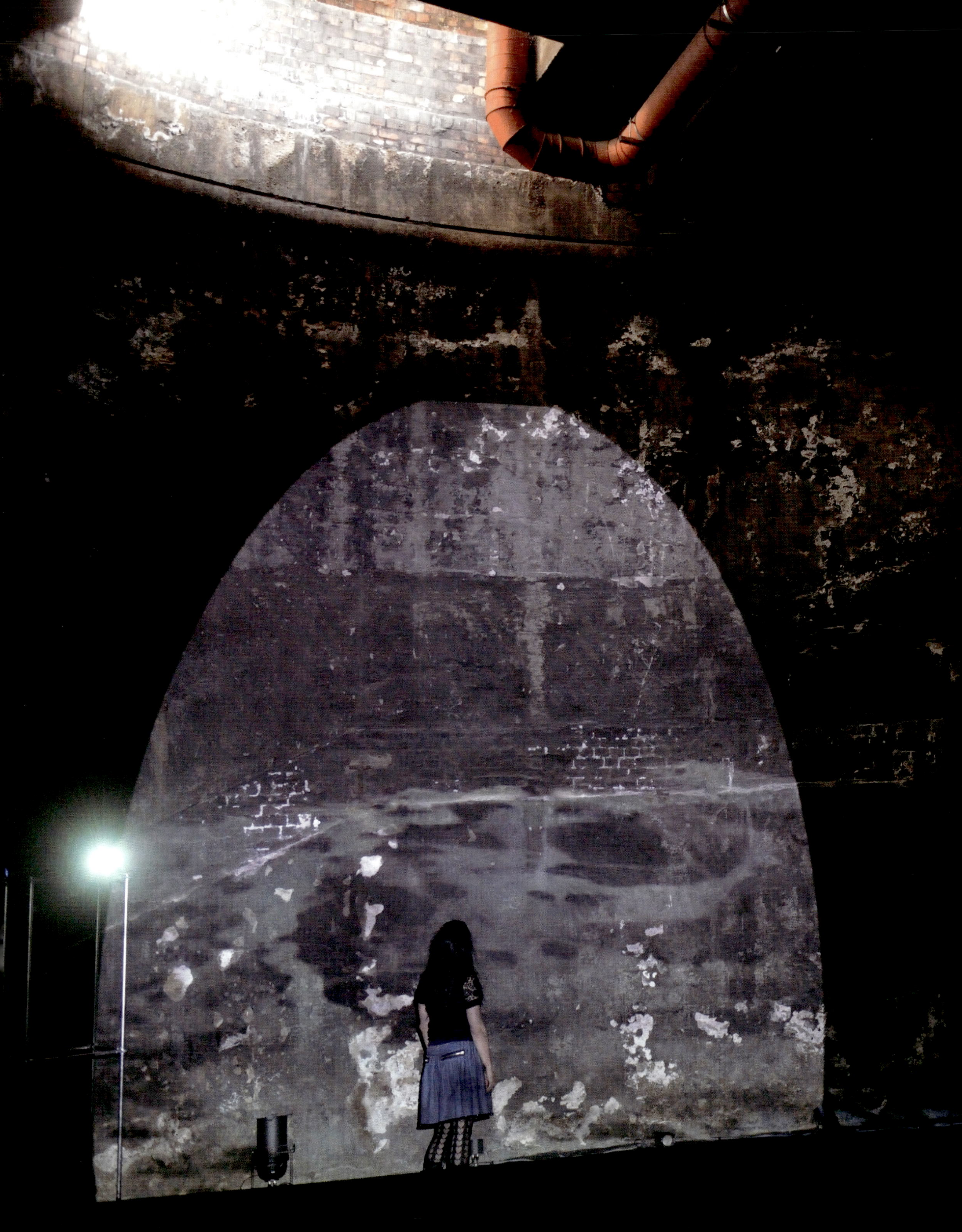

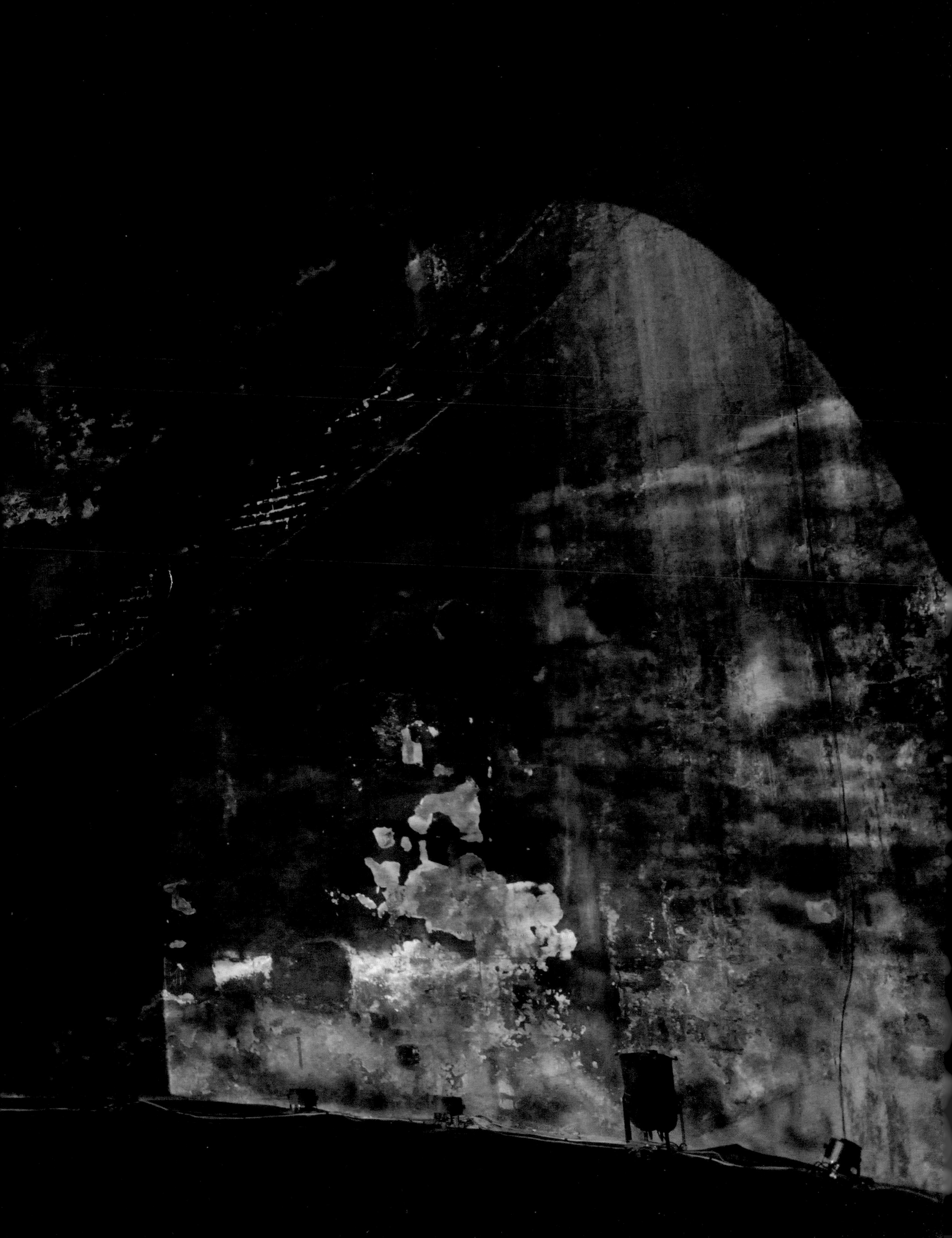

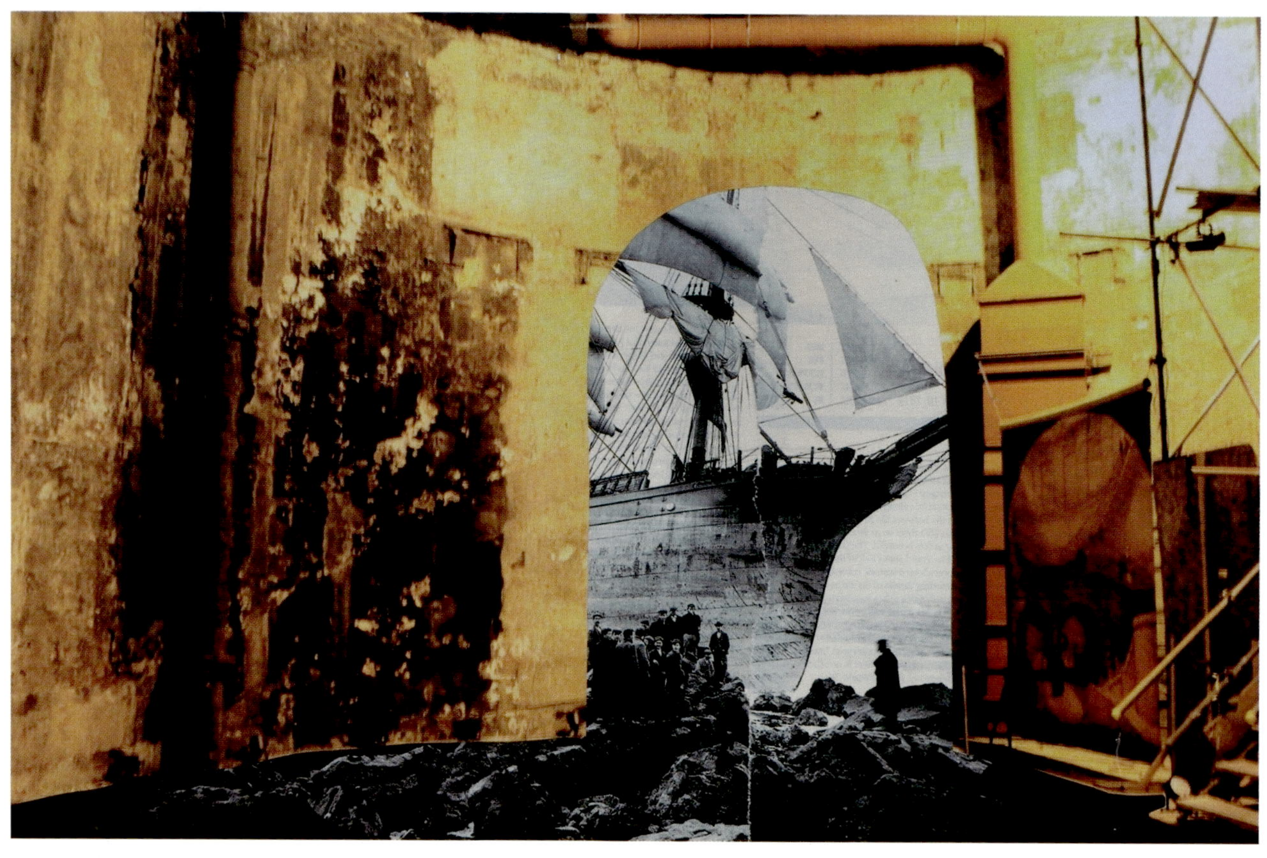

PP 33–35 Lynn Dennison, *Sweet Thames, run softly till I end my song,* 2015, installation comprised of projected images, accompanied by experimental music and voice performance by Leo Loebenberg as part of Museums at Night.

ABOVE Lynn Dennison, *Shipwreck*, 2015, giclée print on Southbank Smooth, 42 x 59.4 cm, edition of 30, plus 3 artist's proofs. Image courtesy the artist.

Notes from the Studio

**What made you decide to become a sculptor?
When did your interest in the site-specific develop?**

Well, I actually started my career as a painter after having completed a Fine Art BA at the Slade School of Art. After about eight or nine years working as a painter, I started to introduce three-dimensional shapes into my work. Gradually these three-dimensional pieces took over from the two-dimensional pieces, and in the end the paintings became studies for the sculptures, and sculpture became my main focus.

My interest in the site-specific really developed from my desire to introduce the moving image into my sculptures. I went back to university and did a Masters at Central Saint Martins and that's when it really began. I had started off in a white cube gallery environment, in which I placed objects and then projected onto them—I felt this created more of a theatrical scene that the viewer stood outside of and looked at. During the course of my Masters I started to think about how I could make this experience into something more immersive that the viewer could be surrounded by completely. The forms I was projecting onto became less about something I was making myself and became more of an interaction with the space I was projecting into. In fact, the first piece of site-specific work I did was for our interim show at V22 in Bermondsey.

Who are the artists and photographers that you most admire and which have had the greatest impact on your thinking and your work?

Diana Thater has had an impact on me, not only due to the imagery she uses to explore the relationship between humans and the natural world and the difference between untouched and manipulated nature, but also in the way she uses the space that she is exhibiting in, covering windows and light sources with coloured gels so that the viewer is aware of the space they are in. The existing architecture is important to her; it is not just a venue to exhibit her work. I think that dualism has been very influential to my work. There is also John Stezaker's collages and films—his fascination with an idea of a liminal or in-between space, of "the slender margin between the real and the unreal". James Casebere, who creates models of environments and then photographs them so that they appear to be real spaces, until a closer look reveals them to be fabrications, makes this 'edge' visible. One of the first things that got me interested in immersive spaces was the Sublime Object research project at Tate Modern between 2003 and 2010, in particular Olafur Eliasson's *The Weather Project*, 2003, and Miroslaw Balka's *How it is*, 2009. Both these artists create immersive environments that change the viewer's

perception of their surroundings, which is something I attempt to do with my own work. Some photographers have also influenced my work, including Noemie Goudal, who places large photographs, often of landscapes, in abandoned and decaying urban settings. Also, Jitka Hanzlová, who explores the relationship between nature and culture.

Do you agree that "video art has a distinctive interdisciplinary quality" as John G Hanhart said? How do other disciplines play into your practice?

Yes, I would definitely agree. There seems to be a lot of space for other disciplines to interact with film and media arts. I sometimes use ideas from literature in my work. For example, in Virginia Woolf's *To the Lighthouse*, 1927, she describes the water metaphorically seeping into the house and submerging the furniture, which influenced my work *Shipping News*, 2013.

I use collage to work out what I want to do in a space. Because I come from a painting and a sculpting background, both of which are very hands on, when I suddenly found myself editing video clips on a computer, I really missed the more tactile elements of the creative process. My painting often contained elements of collages so it was almost a natural progression that, when it came to working out what I wanted to do on a three-dimensional plane, I did so with two-dimensional collages.

I will also be collaborating with experimental composer and Royal College of Music postgraduate student, Leo Loebenberg, to create an innovative composition using vocal techniques, generating effects both from natural voice and pedals, which will respond to both the site and my work within it.

Your work is particularly informed by Michel Foucault's theory of heterotopias (*Des Espaces Autres*, 1967), which posits "a sort of simultaneously mythic and real contestation of the space in which we live". Please elaborate on why this (and any other) theory is important to your work.

Foucault's ideas around space are broad, but I am drawn to his sixth principle of space: the idea of one space where several others converge, and where the juxtaposition of several supposedly incompatible sites meet in a single, real place. It is this idea of bringing together different worlds that do not normally coexist into a single environment, making possible simultaneously both the real and the unreal. By juxtaposing images of rural spaces into constructed manmade environments I hope to bring into question our relationship with the surrounding world.

The idea of nature and culture converging has also been suggested by Bruno Latour, who maintains that modernity creates two separate poles: nature/science and culture/society. In Foucault's, *Nous n'avons jamais été modernes*, 1991, he suggests that, as hybrids such as global warming and deforestation increase, it is no longer possible to keep the idea of nature and culture separate, so we need to rethink these distinctions. He said, "The unthinkable non-place becomes the point in the Constitution where the work of mediation emerges. It is far from empty: quasi-objects, quasi-subjects, proliferate in it."

I think there are some parallel concerns between my work and Robert Smithson's, especially with his non-site works because, like him, I am bringing one site into another. There is a certain degree of ambiguity as to where the new site has come from: although it's suggested it's never fully disclosed. The journeys he undertook were central to his practice as an artist, and his non-site sculptures often included maps and aerial photos of a particular location, as well as the geological artefacts displaced from those sites. I also consider walking to be a very important part of my process and I use my recordings of this process in my work. We both share an interest in the sublime and the picturesque, and his ideas about Olmsted's Central Park and the layering of history and human intervention in the site is something I have also explored for a recent collaboration in a work about Greenham Common.

Our experience of the landscape and nature's potential to be a violent and destructive force is at the heart of your practice. What do you hope to inspire in your audience by using this subject matter and what experience do you hope it will provoke?

My preoccupation with nature's power to be destructive, and our inability to contain it, stems from my interest in the sublime and trying to recreate this experience. I am hoping that by bringing the landscape into unexpected places, the viewer will look again at their surroundings. There are so many glossy representations of nature that don't seem to have much to do with the real thing. The idea that nature is just beautiful to look at is, for me, disregarding its potential for destruction. Storms, floods and earthquakes wreak havoc, often with little warning. It is not only this fear of our world becoming a hostile environment that I explore in my work, but also an anxiety that may be closer to home, the struggle to reconcile ourselves with the natural world around us. Kathleen Jamie asks in her book *Sightlines*, 2012, "... what is it that we're just not seeing?", suggesting that somehow in our dealings with nature there is a disconnect. By questioning

our responses to landscape and creating situations that challenge our expectations of the surrounding world, I am trying to discover a connection.

Water is a repeated theme in your work. Why does it hold such resonance for you?

I suppose it is the sublime element of a vast and dangerous sea or mass of water that resonates for me, but I am also interested in the romantic ideas surrounding the idea of water and the sea in particular. The idea of a world under the sea has long held a fascination for me. I grew up spending a lot of time by the sea and spent many days in and around the water fantasising about these things. It still fascinates me that there are underwater towns and cities such as Dunwich in Suffolk. The power of the water to cover our world in that way is both fascinating and frightening. I use water as a metaphor for memory and the passing of time, as if things are buried beneath it, but I also use it as a surprise element—cascading down a set of stairs or filling up a building.

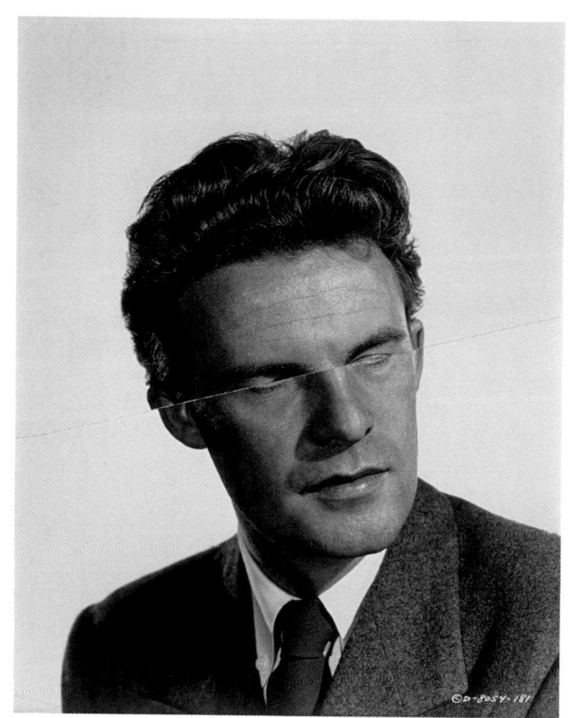

ABOVE John Stezaker, *Blind I*, 2006, photographic collage, 23.2 x 18.7 cm. Image courtesy the artist and The Approach, London.

OPPOSITE Work in progress during Lynn Dennison's residency.

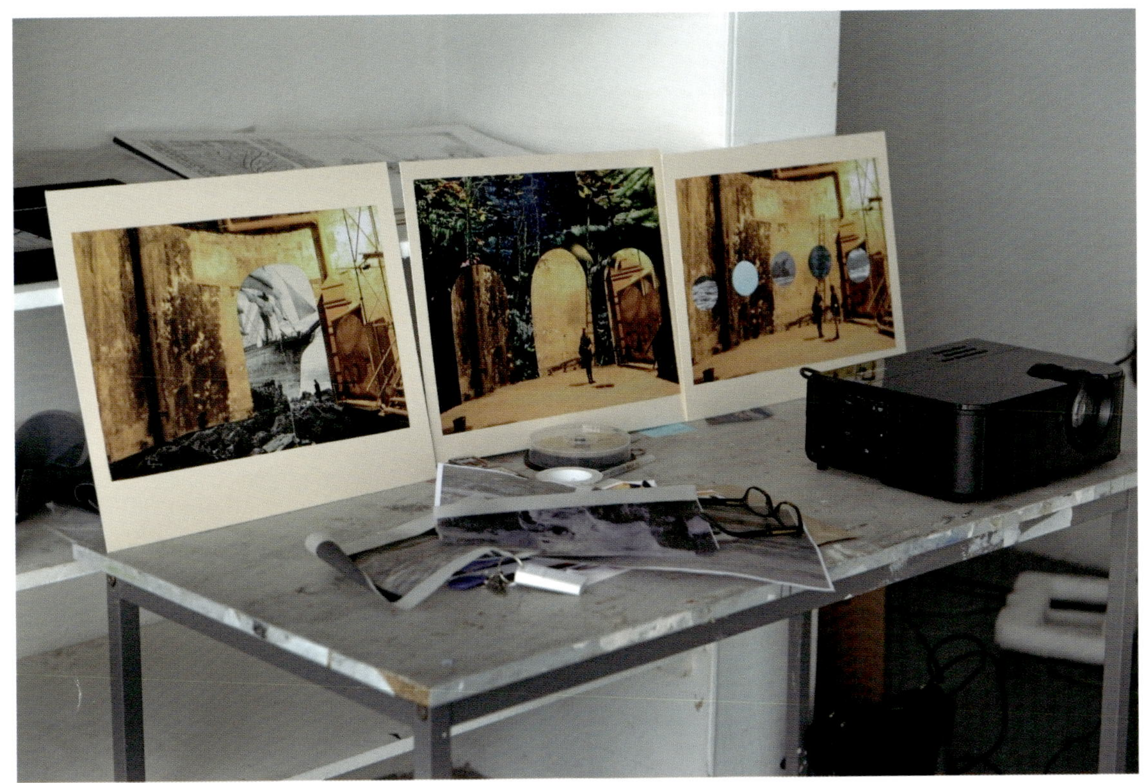

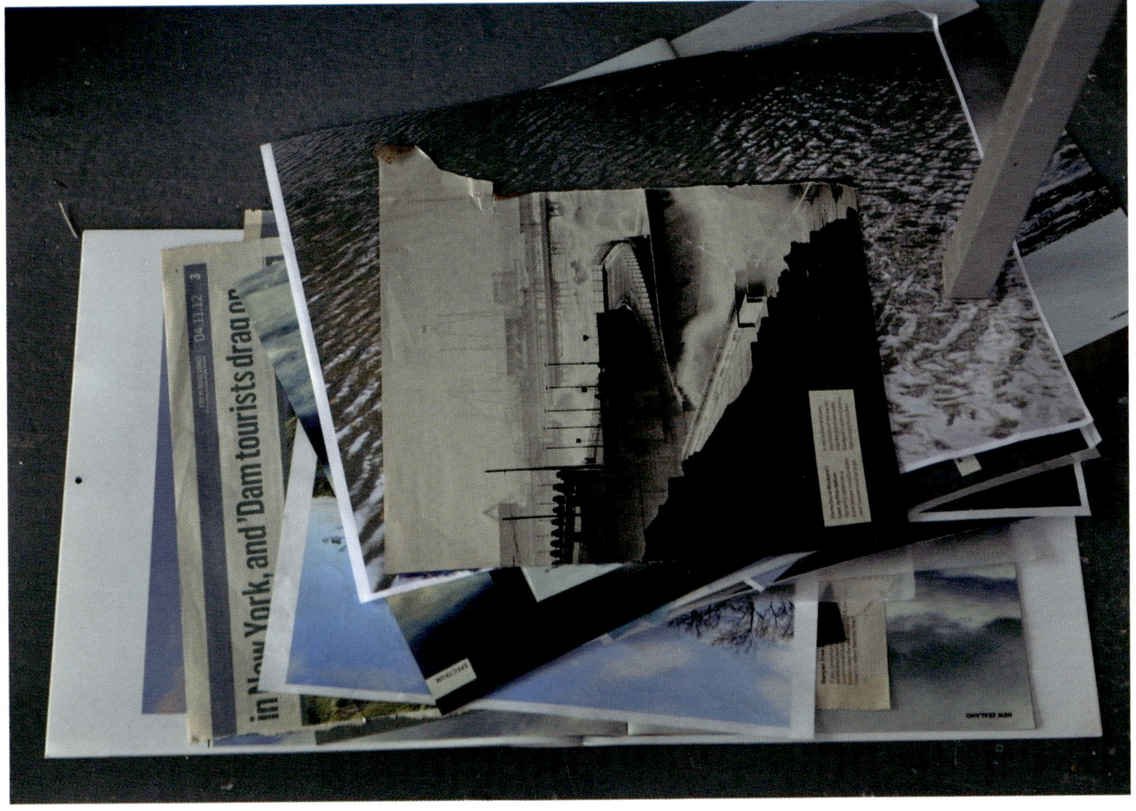

Lynn Dennison: *Sweet Thames, run softly till I end my song*, 2015—Dave Beech

Nature is shrinking, but the signs of nature and the natural are multiplying, replacing and supplanting real 'nature'.

Henri Lefebvre[1]

The transition from agriculture to industry, from rural living to urbanisation, brings a chronic shrinkage of nature, and, at the same time, a proliferation of images of nature. Advertising sells cars, deodorant, detergents, air travel and financial services by associating products with spectacular mountainscapes, natural springs, animated swarms of petals, montages of sea, desert, sky and forest, and lush green fields. The TV schedule is peppered with documentaries of everything from deep sea creatures to storm chasing, printed textiles are almost synonymous with pictures of flowers, and nature is treasured in the backgrounds to millions of selfies, postcards, jigsaw puzzles, greetings cards, and website stock images.

Lynn Dennison's new work for Sculpture Shock, *Sweet Thames, run softly till I end my song*, divides up the surface of the Rotherhithe Shaft, an impressive underground monument to Brunel's engineering prowess, with large video projections of the river looking like a calm sea. Nature is restored to the industrial setting, here, but it is not only nature that has been reduced to an image: at The Brunel Museum heavy industry itself survives only as a sign. Buildings, bridges and tunnels continue to be constructed on an ever-increasing scale, of course, but the classic opposition between industry and nature, captured by Adorno and Horkheimer's concept of the "dialectic of Enlightenment", has been replaced with ecological crisis and ecodesign. If Dennison's work is a eulogy to nature, a paean to the river under threat, then it is equally a eulogy to its old adversary, the industrial.

The transition to industrialisation is mirrored in a fetishism of nature: the sentimental love of nature in modernity is an effect of the Industrial Revolution and an expression of it, insofar as it results from the rift between city and county, progress and tradition, work and leisure, that capitalism unbuckled. Romantic artists such as Friedrich, Constable and Wordsworth, on the cusp of industrialism, modernised culture by drawing on the semiotics of nature. Realism opposed elite cultural codes of meaning by asserting that "the forms of Nature speak directly". At the end of the eighteenth century, coinciding therefore with the period of the bourgeois revolution, nature appeared as the uncoded code of emotion and feeling. Not only could a painting of leafless bushes in the snow signify death in an apparently immediate, unlearned way; the experience of nature itself, in hillwalking, hiking and mountain climbing, for instance, became one of the central modes with which the bourgeoisie learned to feel deeply.

Nature was the centrepiece of the modern concept of aesthetic experience. Whereas the classical theory of beauty had modelled itself on the bodies of beauties and secondarily on artworks that replicated their proportions, the revolutionary bourgeoisie turned to nature as the basis both of its theory of judgements of taste and its theory of the sublime. Nature is the utopia specific to industrialisation. This is why, like Dennison's videos, nature was projected into the very heart of modernity by radical Romantics, both as a corrective to its instrumental, calculative and exploitative industry, and as a confirmation of its democratic, subjective and expressive freedom. One of the first things that William Morris says about industry in a future socialist society, in his essay "A Factory As It Might Be", is that the factory should be surrounded by vast, beautiful gardens. Each room, we might add, should look out to the river or have the river run through it.

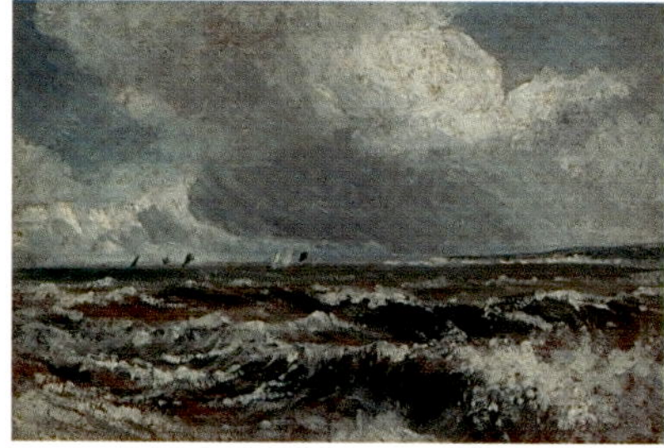

John Constable, *Seascape With Boats on the Horizon, Brighton*, 1824, oil on brown paper board, 11.5 x 17.5 cm.

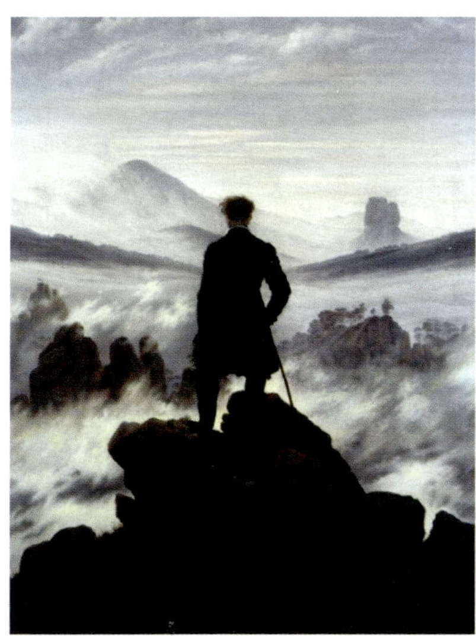

Caspar David Friedrich, *Wanderer above the Sea of Fog*, c 1818, oil on canvas, 94.8 x 74.8 cm.

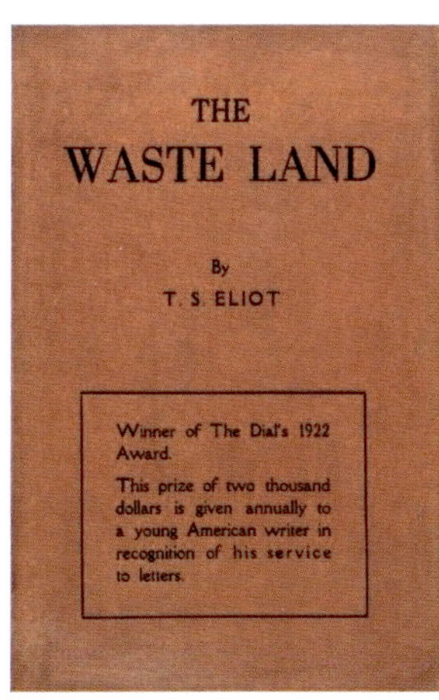

Cover of TS Eliot's *The Waste Land*, 1922.

1   Lefebvre, Henri, *The Urban Revolution*, 1970, Robert Bononno trans, University of Minnesota: Minneapolis, 2003.

Landscape painting has traditionally inserted simulated windows into domestic rooms so that the interior can be blessed with views unavailable through the actual windows. Dennison's digital installation is scaled-up, like the spectacle of an aquarium in which visitors stand face-to-face with sea creatures. Facing the wall, looking at the river, the viewer is momentarily a figure in a Caspar David Friedrich painting, turning her back to the world in order to face nature and thereby to feel. One of the most profound legacies of Romanticism is the belief that this encounter is the paradigm of feeling, or at least of refined aestheticised feeling. It is the experience of nature modelled on the experience of Greek statues ripped from their original architectural, cultural and religious setting. The modern love of nature is the result of a cut, which is both a spatial dislocation from nature and a framing of nature dislocated. Putting nature in a dirty industrial setting, albeit one as refined in its own terms as the Rotherhithe Shaft, is to experience that cut as an embrace.

In the era of regeneration, Brunel's shaft seems as endangered as the Thames. The shaft itself will remain in place but its setting is likely to be gentrified, as no area of London appears to be immune from this monetising and cultivating process. The industrial is to be nothing but a tourist attraction and its architectural relics are bound to be repurposed for the leisure of the incoming tide. Dennison's lapping water of the Thames will be followed up, it might be assumed, with a flood of fashionable events. Modernisation eats itself, naturally, and at the moment between one crisis and another it is only proper that we should contemplate, reflect and try to feel something. Regret, perhaps, or hope, might be acceptable responses, but then so is anger, fear, love, resignation or delight. Aesthetic experience, heightened by the yoking of industry and nature, is a realm of freedom only if we can feel pleasure in the vicinity of threat. The sublime was an aesthetic experience invented by the bourgeoisie in its revolutionary phase in order, primarily, to address the pleasure felt by those protected from the deadly effects of nature or the unnatural deaths of others.

Dennison's work is not sublime. Can nature be sublime in the era of ecological disaster? Nature is no longer conceived primarily as simultaneously the source of life and harbouring the forces inimical to human life; nature today is conceived primarily as a victim. The closest we come to a contemporary sublime is the image of total ecological collapse that brings all human life to an end in a narrative in which technology reaches a limit in its destructive exploitation of the world. Nevertheless, *Sweet Thames, run softly till I end my song*, despite the title being taken from a line in TS Eliot's "The Waste Land", is not a modernist grievance against modernity. Nature, here, is not a ruined, barren place. The river is soft, relentlessly soothing or even happy. Dennison has created an oasis.

Sweet Thames, run softly till I end my song is utopian in Henri Lefebvre's sense, which he ascribes to parks and gardens: "they refer to a twofold utopia: absolute nature and pure facticity". He explains, "they suggest an absolute and inaccessible nature—grottos, wind, altitude, the sea, islands—as well as facticity—the trimmed and tortured tree that serves as pure ornament". Absolute nature is made possible by pure facticity: only when nature is cut off from use and other meanings (food, farming, real estate) and is therefore conceived as pure facticity (water, field, hill) can it be fully enjoyed aesthetically, that is as nature in the abstract. Utopia, therefore, is the experience of dislocation, like Greek statues which appear freer and more beautiful when they are carried off from the Parthenon to the museum. Nowadays the cut of utopia doesn't require chisels and a fleet of ships, only a video camera. Utopia has been let loose: nowhere is everywhere, and it still calls on us to make the world anew.

Hidden Depths—Sarah Kent

Artists are among the most resourceful people on the planet; resourcefulness is one of their most important attributes. Confront them with a problem and most likely they will find a way to overcome or circumvent it and, in so doing, will act as role models encouraging the rest of us to think on our feet, be brave, adapt and thrive.

In his book *Man's Rage for Chaos*, 1967, Morse Peckham argues that art plays a vital role in human survival; by frustrating our desire for order and disrupting our preference for the familiar, it keeps us alert, aware and on our toes, ready to respond to changes in real life. "The drive to order", he writes, "is also a drive to get stuck in the mud"; but art "serves to break up orientations, to weaken and frustrate the tyrannous drive to order, to prepare the individual to observe what the orientation tells him is irrelevant, but what very well may be highly relevant."[1]

In 2013, the Royal British Society of Sculptors (RBS) inaugurated Sculpture Shock, an annual competition designed to further this notion of art as a disruptive, but necessary, form of exploration. Over the next three years they challenged artists to respond to unorthodox venues that, unlike the white cube galleries where art is normally shown, have strong characteristics of their own including dark interiors, crumbling walls, dripping ceilings or trains rumbling overhead.

The winners were each given three months in a free studio space to develop their ideas followed by a pop-up exhibition at the allocated venue. The project was a deliberate provocation; the point of the exercise was to coax artists out of their comfort zones so as to engage with an unfamiliar and often difficult site, and, by encouraging them to focus on the creative process as much as the end product, to stimulate innovation.

Sculpture Shock artists were, of course, not the first artists to infiltrate London's hidden corners; there have been many inspirational forerunners. The idea took hold in the late 1980s in response to a serious financial crisis. The British economy was in dire straits. Black Monday, 19 October 1987, saw a huge fall on the stock market and five years later, almost to the day, came Black Wednesday when the pound fell to a record low.

The few dealers brave enough to promote contemporary art were going bankrupt, so graduates emerging from art schools had no hope of showing their work in a commercial gallery. So they took matters into their own hands.[2] Robin Klassnik set an example by inviting artists to show in his studio in London Fields. In 1987, Richard Wilson filled the interior with a lake of used sump oil, whose black surface acted as a mirror that magically doubled the space. Later, Charles Saatchi bought *20/50* and the piece is still installed in his Chelsea gallery.

London was full of empty buildings and, in 1988, Damien Hirst persuaded the Port of London Authority to lend him a derelict warehouse in Docklands to mount Freeze, a show of work by him and 13 fellow graduates from Goldsmiths. Two years later, they staged both Gambler and Modern Medicine in a disused biscuit factory in Surrey Quays, Docklands.

The huge scale of these premises and the lack of potential buyers encouraged artists to take risks by thinking big and using unorthodox materials to create site-specific works. Michael Landy created a large-scale installation of market stalls covered in artificial grass, while Anya Gallaccio left a ton of oranges to rot in one exhibition and a 32-ton block of ice to melt in another. Damien Hirst housed tropical butterflies in a shop just off Oxford Street and others mounted exhibitions in disused banks, offices, factories, betting shops, schools and swimming pools.

The exploration of London's underground spaces followed some time after. In 1995, Artangel commissioned American theatre director Robert Wilson and

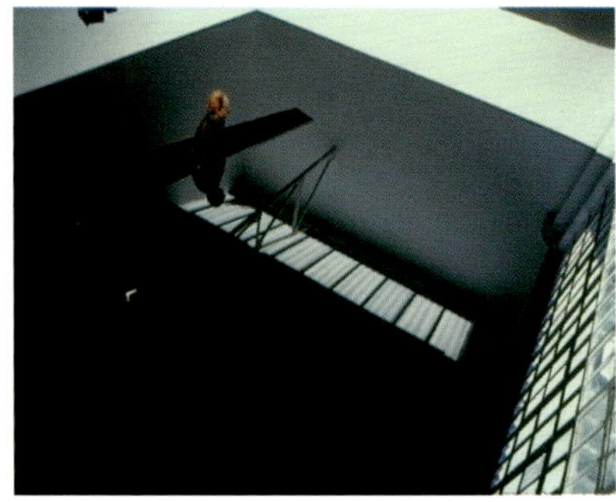

Richard Wilson, *20:50* (installation view), 1987, Matts Gallery. Photograph by Edward Woodman.

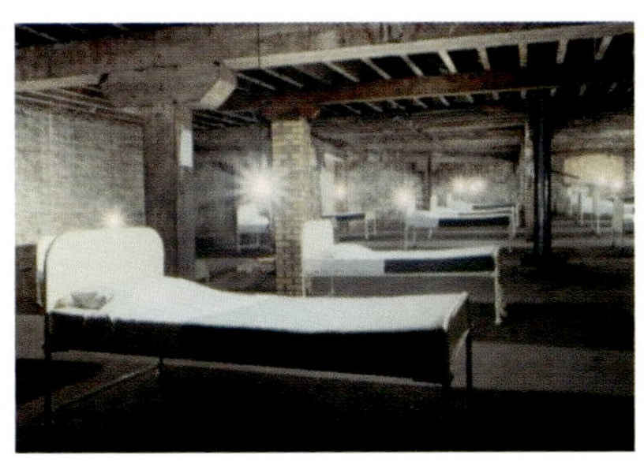

Hans Peter Kuhn and Robert Wilson, *HG*, 1995, The Clink Street Vaults, London. Commissioned and produced by Artangerl. Photograph by Stephen White.

sound artist Hans Peter Kuhn to create *HG* for the cavernous underground vaults of the Clink, once a Medieval prison on the south bank of the Thames.[3] A series of tableaux inspired by the centenary of HG Wells' *The Time Machine* took viewers on a disquieting journey back through time. As you wandered past a dinner party apparently abandoned in 1895, rows of old hospital beds, a mummified cat and a mouldering corpse, the noise of a train hurtling through the claustrophobic space further jarred your senses.

Four years later, John Berger and Simon McBurney led visitors down 122 steps to the platforms of the disused Strand underground station, 30 meters below Bush House, then home of the BBC's World Service. Using recordings of major world events, they created *The Vertical Line* going back in time; the enveloping darkness prompted Berger to think back 25,000 years to another subterranean space, the vast Chauvet Caves in southern France, where our distant ancestors painted glorious images of stampeding herds on the limestone walls.

Sculpture Shock's subterranean programme therefore has forerunners that span thousands of years, from prehistoric cave paintings to recent Artangel commissions. The ongoing fascination of RBS's project comes, though, from the way it brings to light unexpected spaces concealed beneath the fabric of the city, and instigates a dialogue between their former use and their present state of dereliction.

David Ogle, the first winner of Sculpture Shock's Subterranean category, works with light, a medium especially appropriate for underground spaces. He thinks of his installations as drawings in space rather than sculptures and produces detailed drawings on paper, which he translates into what might be described as three-dimensional diagrams in light. His inspiration comes from West Coast artists like James Turrell and Robert Irwin, who specialise in exploiting the ability of light to transform an environment, and on the abstract wall drawings of Sol LeWitt who invited others to carry out his precise instructions.

The Subterranean venue lay beneath the railway lines converging on Waterloo station. Access is via a dingy alleyway covered in graffiti by competing street artists. Dark, cold and dank, the vaults themselves are scarcely more inviting; trains rumble overhead and water dripping from the ceiling forms puddles on the floor—not a congenial place in which to linger or exhibit art, you might think.

Therein lay the challenge, of course, and rather than showing pre-existing work, Ogle concentrated on transforming the experience of the space itself. His goal was to animate the gloomy interior using minimal means, but he spent nine days installing an exhibition that was scheduled to last only four.

Made from fluorescent drinking straws, a colony of dendritic organisms glowed ethereal red and green, like some enchanted forest bathed in artificial light. This unnatural glade reminded me of the tubular worms that cluster round hydrothermal vents on the floor of the Pacific Ocean and thrive in waters sulphurous enough to kill other life forms. Is it too fanciful to regard the vault as the urban equivalent of that dark seabed and imagine Ogle's creatures as a species uniquely adapted to this hostile environment?

The second room was bathed in ultramarine light, reminiscent of International Klein Blue, an intense colour developed by the famous French artist. "Klein wrote that in nature, blue represents that which is most abstract, hinting at the sea and the sky, entities that exist on a scale that defy comprehension", Ogle explains. "Also on a less lofty note, I tend to draw in blue ball point pen so the colour further references the drawings that inspire the installations." Drawn with ultraviolet light, four triangles traversed the space, seeming to rest on the coloured air like flimsy sheets of glass or transparent wings gliding on invisible up-currents. Had an angel passed this way?

The main vault was bathed in red, blue and purple light that dramatised the space. It seemed to hold its breath like a stage awaiting a theatrical event; beamed along clusters of fine wire, shafts of green light sliced through the space from ceiling to floor. They hit their target with the precision of the celestial beams that impregnate the Virgin Mary in paintings of the Annunciation.

Hanging low in the distance, meanwhile, a weather balloon glowed orange. Reflected in a puddle of water, it was reminiscent of the sun setting over a lake and draining the light from the sky as it sank towards the horizon. Memories of landscape and the nuances of natural light opened one's mind to the wider world beyond this sunless place.

In 2014, the winner of the Subterranean category was Patrick Lowry, who worked as a product designer for ten years before returning to college to study for a Masters degree in Fine Art. As an industrial designer he was, he says, "selling the belief that the new product, which was more often than not the old product repackaged, was better. I was selling a new reality again and again and the world was buying into that illusion.... Illusions increasingly form the reality in which we live."

Built-in obsolescence is one of the motors that drive capitalism, alongside the belief that the new is always an improvement on the old and makes the world a better place. This dangerous hypothesis is driving humanity to the brink of disaster, yet our craving for the new continues undiminished and our belief in the power of new technologies to solve the world's problems remains undimmed. So the dance of death goes on.

As an artist, Lowry continues to deal in illusions—not to lull us into submission as consumers, but to wake us up to our folly. Installed in Leeds Metropolitan University in 2011, *24 Hour Cash Machine* was an ATM that did not dispense any money. Close inspection revealed that, instead of the real thing, this frustrating object was a convincing facsimile. Its purpose was to provoke thought about our reliance on ready supplies of cash to fund the instant gratification we regard as normal in our fast-moving lives.

The venue chosen for Subterranean in 2014 was The Horse Hospital in Bloomsbury, built in the eighteenth century for the treatment of London's overworked horses. After the closure of the veterinary facility, the space was turned into a busy print shop, which operated successfully until the late 1980s. Lowry focused on this more recent period of the building's history and, descending the ramp to his exhibition, one got the impression that the printers were still in situ, but had just stepped out for a break.

Standing on the concrete slab built to accommodate its enormous weight was the Heidelberg offset printing press and piled up on the floor around it, apparently hot off the press, were stacks of euro bank notes, some still drying, others packed ready for shipment. Had Lowry uncovered an illicit operation producing counterfeit bank notes? "For me the subterranean conjured up images of the underworld, the black market world of forgery, fakes and counterfeit", says Lowry. Things were more complicated than that, though.

If you lifted up the grey blanket thrown over the bed of the printing press, you discovered that, in place of the heavy rollers that power the bed, there was nothing but a void. The machine was a lightweight fabrication expertly cobbled together from sheets of MDF painted to resemble steel, and additional bits and pieces were made from dowelling rods, plastic lids, metal bowls and a bike pedal. We were not in the realm of old fashioned forgeries so much as the parallel universe of modern banking, a virtual world of illusion and make believe.

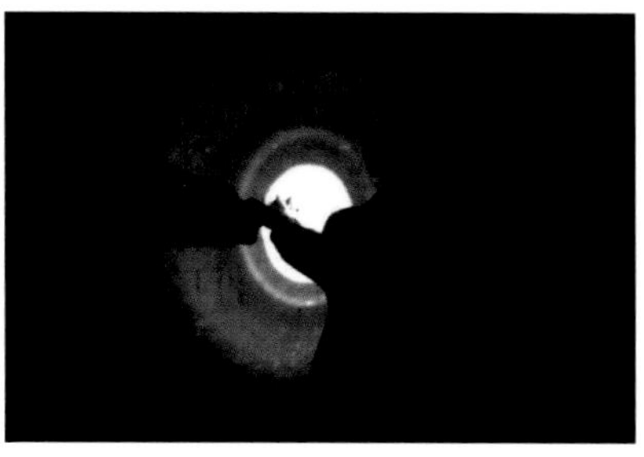

David Ogle on day one of eight installing his work in the tunnels under Waterloo railway station.

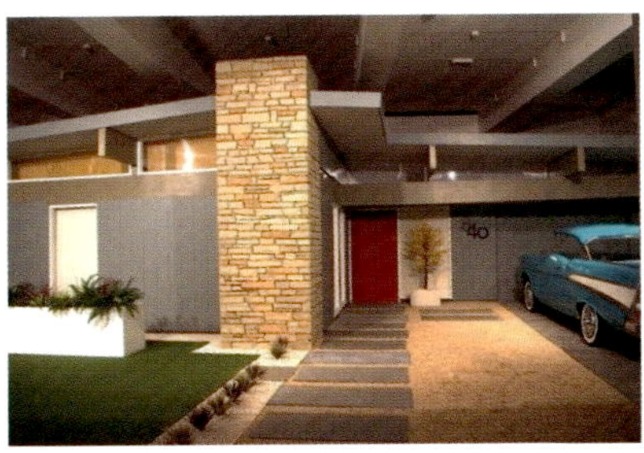

Patrick Lowry, *American Dream*, 2013, full-size replica of the facade and garden of a 1950s American suburban home complete with a 1957 Chevrolet Bel Air of plywood, wood, Perspex, fibreglass, artificial plants, gravel, 1,400 x 800 x 100 cm. Photograph by Steve Tanner.

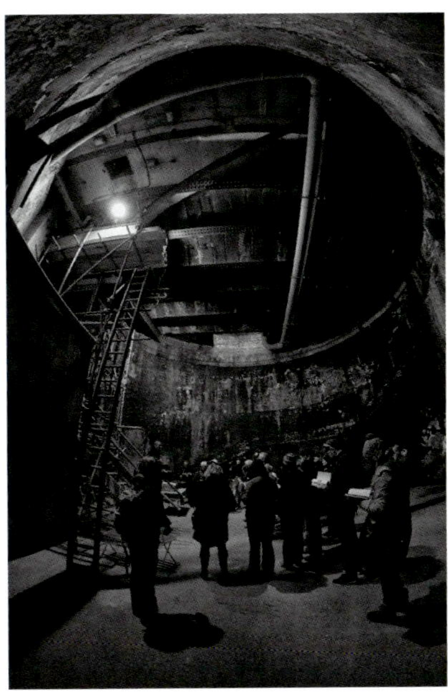

Sir Marc Isambard Brunel and Isambard Kingdom Brunel's Rotherhithe Grand Entrance Hall, The Brunel Museum, London. Image courtesy Aidan Cusack.

The fake bank notes symbolised quantitative easing, a means used by the Bank of England to stimulate the economy after the banking crisis of 2008 had sent it into a tailspin. Increasing the money supply is not an illegal measure, of course; nor is the game of international banking played on the net by financiers selling imaginary commodities to nonexistent buyers and making a fortune in the process—all of which fascinates Lowry. "I am deeply interested in the power structures surrounding the economic crash", he confirms, "the powerlessness of the individual and the dematerialisation of money."

His exhibition was a house of cards; its success rested on his ability to persuade viewers to suspend their disbelief and accept the illusions he created, while acknowledging the deception. We are adept at playing such games, of course, and we enjoy them. We buy into the myths propagated by advertisers, politicians, gurus, media moguls and financiers, even when we know they are suspect. "I hope that initially the audience will believe that the work is the real thing", Lowry explains. "I'm interested in the point at which realisation dawns that it is not. That is when the viewer starts to think about the meaning of the work. It is the moment that the brain shifts from acceptance to questioning, from one model of belief to another."

The pleasure generated by Lowry's sculptures comes from our enjoyment of his sleight-of-hand wizardry. We like being duped! Deep down, do we not admire the bankers' audacity and equate their powers of invention with the skills used by artists to create illusions? Lowry encourages us to consider this proposition, which, if true, would reveal the capitalist world to be pirouetting around an axis of lies, myths and illusions—while the rest us gawp from the sidelines.

The third venue for the Subterranean section of Sculpture Shock was the Grand Entrance Hall of the Rotherhithe Shaft, a site of major historical importance. Begun in 1825, the ambitious project was the brainchild of Marc Isambard Brunel and his son Isambard Kingdom Brunel. Linking Wapping and Rotherhithe, it was to be the first underwater tunnel constructed anywhere in the world, previous attempts having been thwarted by flooding.

First, a ventilation shaft was needed and Marc's ingenious design quickly became a *cause célèbre*. He built a circular brick tower resting on an iron hoop, which under the weight of the 1,000-ton structure, sliced through the soft ground like a pastry cutter. People soon came to watch the tower sink a few inches each day until it reached the desired level and could be stabilised. Work on the tunnel could then begin and, after endless delays caused by flooding, it opened in 1843. Initially built for horse drawn carriages, it was adapted in 1869 to accommodate steam trains. In 2010, the tunnel became part of London's overground network and was sealed off from the shaft, leaving the Grand Entrance Hall free to be used as an arts venue.

The 2015 winner of Subterranean was Lynn Dennison. Titled *Sweet Thames, run softly till I end my song* after a line in TS Eliot's "The Waste Land", her installation was reached via a scaffolding staircase that led visitors 50 feet below the streets of South East London. A video projection flooded the space with a rippling expanse of deep water, while waves crashing onto the shore were projected onto the circular walls.

Visitors were engulfed in the sight and sound of water and I imagine panic levels rising. "I like the idea of creating a space which is simultaneously real and unreal", says Dennison; given that throughout the tunnel's history, flooding had been an issue, her inundation seemed extremely plausible. "I often let the site dictate what the work will be", she explains. "The history and geography as well as the colours, shapes and architectural details of a place are all part of the work."

The project was also inspired by a passage in Virginia Woolf's novel *To The Lighthouse*, 1927, in which she describes water metaphorically seeping into the house and covering the furniture. Other influences include Olafur Eliasson, who in 2003 filled Tate Modern's Turbine Hall with the yellow light of an artificial sun (the installation proved so popular that people came to sunbathe in the artificial glow)[4] and Polish artist, Miroslaw Balka who, in 2009, invited people to spend time in the pitch-black interior of a container installed in the Turbine Hall.[5]

Sweet Thames, run softly till I end my song reminded me, though, of Bill Fontana's installation *River Sounding* at Somerset House in 2010. Having recorded the sound of water at numerous spots along the river, the American artist relayed them through speakers located in the cellars of the building. But rather than imagining some future disaster, his installation recreated the actual past. The river once flowed into the vaults of Somerset House and Admiral Lord Nelson regularly docked his ship in this convenient location.

The circular shape of the Rotherhithe Grand Entrance Hall made it feel as much like a tower as a shaft and Dennison's projections created the impression that the walls were perforated by windows overlooking the sea. The swell still seemed threatening, but if you imagined you were watching from the safe vantage point of a lighthouse, it felt thrilling rather than dangerous. This duality—fear of nature's awesome power and wonder at its beauty—is a key component of the sublime, an experience of interest to Dennison. "It is the sublime element of a vast and dangerous sea or mass of water that resonates for me", she says. "My preoccupation with nature's power to be destructive, and our inability to contain it stems from my interest in the sublime."

In 2014 she projected a video of surging water onto the staircase of the De La Warr Pavilion at Bexhill on Sea. The shipping forecast detailed weather conditions in the coastal waters round our island, while sea water appeared to cascade from one floor to the next. Depending on one's degree of paranoia, *Waterfall* could be seen as a poetic meditation on the beauty of the waves lapping against the shore a few feet from the Pavilion, or a warning about our inadequate coastal defences in the face of rising sea levels.

Our attitude towards nature, and to Dennison's installations, shifts according to circumstances. Since more and more of us live in cities and experience the natural world mainly through mediated images or highly managed parks, gardens and golf courses, our ideas are severely skewed and easily manipulated. Once perceived as something to be controlled and tamed, these days nature is more often perceived as a victim needing protection from excessive exploitation. Recent increases in the frequency of terrible storms and devastating floods have once again reminded us, though, of nature's ability to wreak havoc despite our efforts to contain its incursions.

The strength of Dennison's work lies in its ambiguity. She invites us to consider our relationship with the natural world in general, and water in particular, without telling us what to think. This stems partly from her own ambivalence; she is fascinated, after all, by towns such as Dunwich in Suffolk that were swallowed up by the sea. Paraphrasing the French philosopher Bruno Latour, she concludes that "as hybrids such as global warming and deforestation increase, it is no longer possible to keep the idea of nature and culture separate and we need to rethink these distinctions and recognise the relationship between nature and culture."[6]

Sculpture Shock was only funded for three years, but in that time many short-lived installation and permanent works of art were created that would not otherwise have been made. For the artists who accepted RBS's invitation, the implied challenge to leave their comfort zones behind encouraged them to

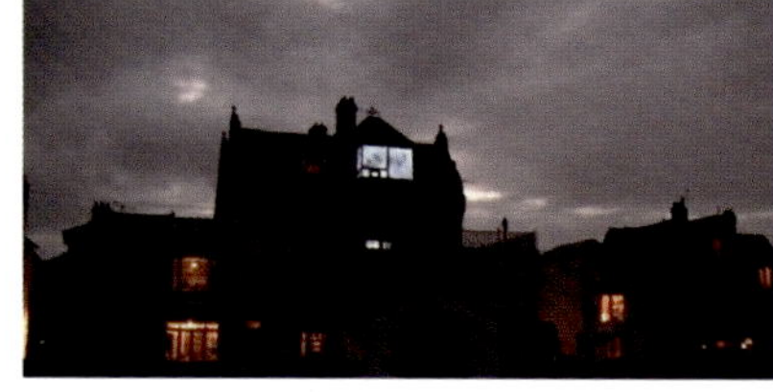

Lynn Dennison, *Lookout Tower*, 2013–2014, installation with video projection, dimensions variable. Image courtesy the artist.

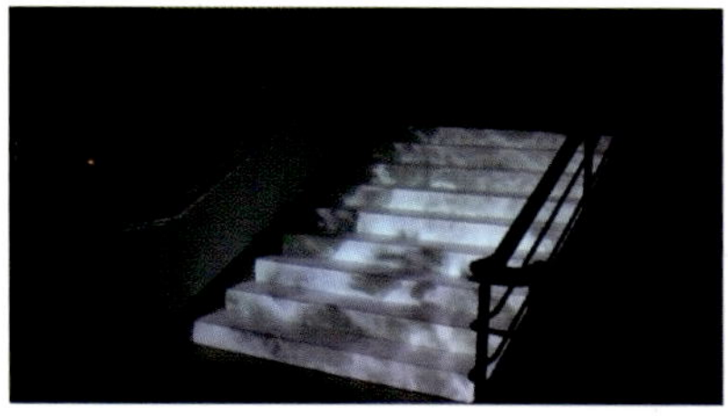

Lynn Dennison, *Waterfall*, 2014, installation with video projection, dimensions variable. Image courtesy the artist.

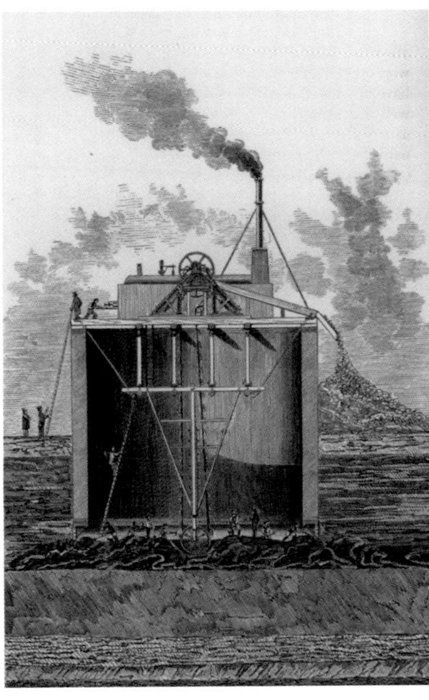

Illustration showing cross section of the sinking shaft from the guidebook to The Brunel Museum, 1826.

be more adventurous and take more risks; in other words, to allow the sort of conditions to flourish that foster major achievements. If enlightened sponsorship of this kind is an inspiration, so was the response of the artists. And in this regard, Sculpture Shock has created an enduring legacy.

1 Peckham, Morse, *Man's Rage for Chaos*, New York: Schocken Books, 1967, preface, p xi.

2 For more information on this period see Kent, Sarah, "Groundswell", *London From Punk to Blair*, Joe Kerr and Andrew Gibson eds, London: Reaktion Books, 2003.

3 For more information on Artangel commissions see Lingwood, James and Michael Morris, *Off Limits: 40 Artangel Projects*, London: Merrell Publishers Ltd, 2002.

4 For more information on Olafur Eliasson see May, Susan, *Olafur Eliasson—The Weather Project—(Unilever Series)*, London: Tate Publishing, 2003.

5 For more information on Miroslaw Balka see Sainsbury, Helen, *The Unilever Series: Miroslaw Balka*, London: Tate Publishing, 2009.

6 Latour, Bruno, *We Have Never Been Born*, Cambridge, MA: Harvard University Press, 1993.

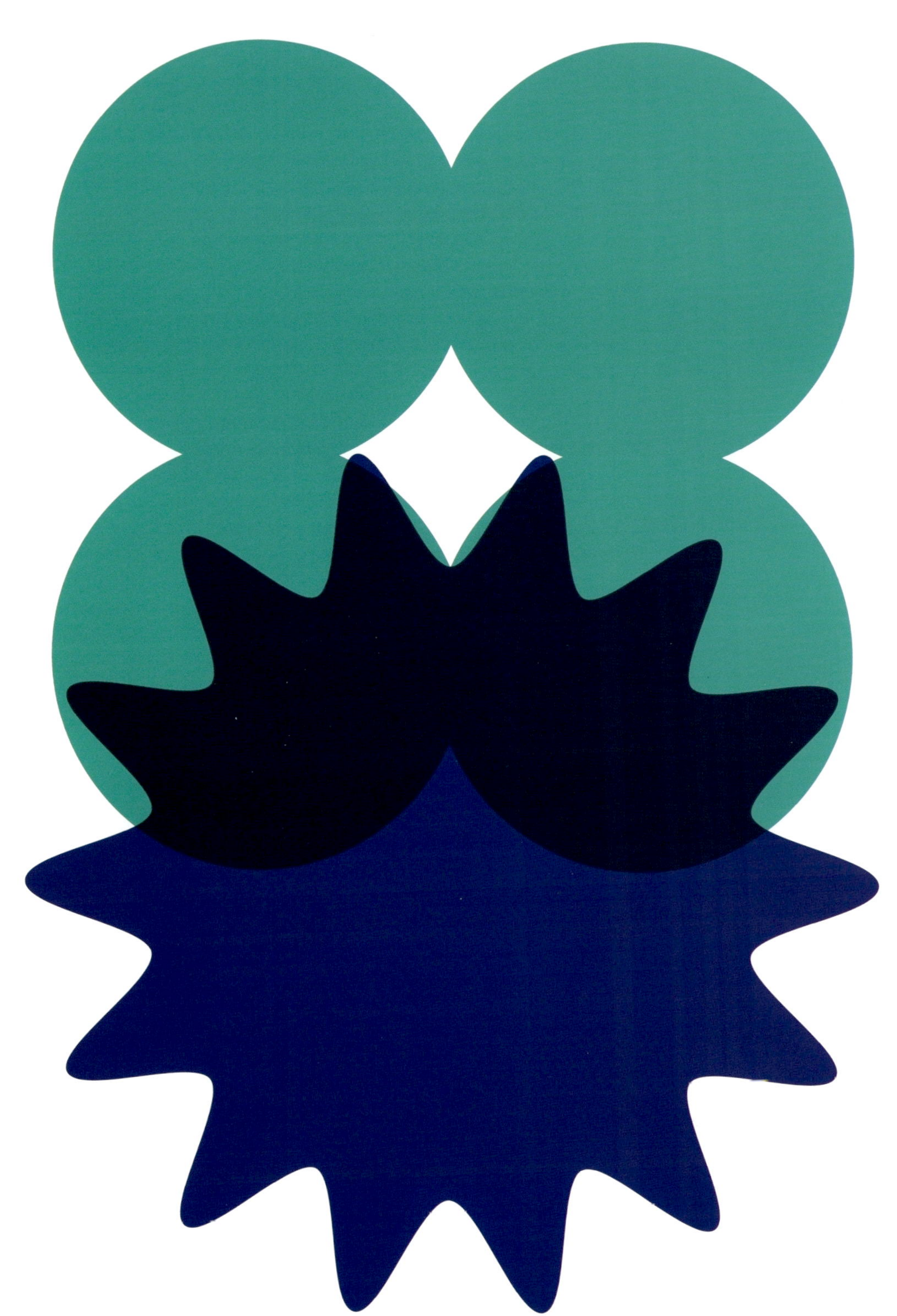

Ambulatory

Amy Sharrocks
Public spaces in the Royal Borough
of Kensington and Chelsea, London

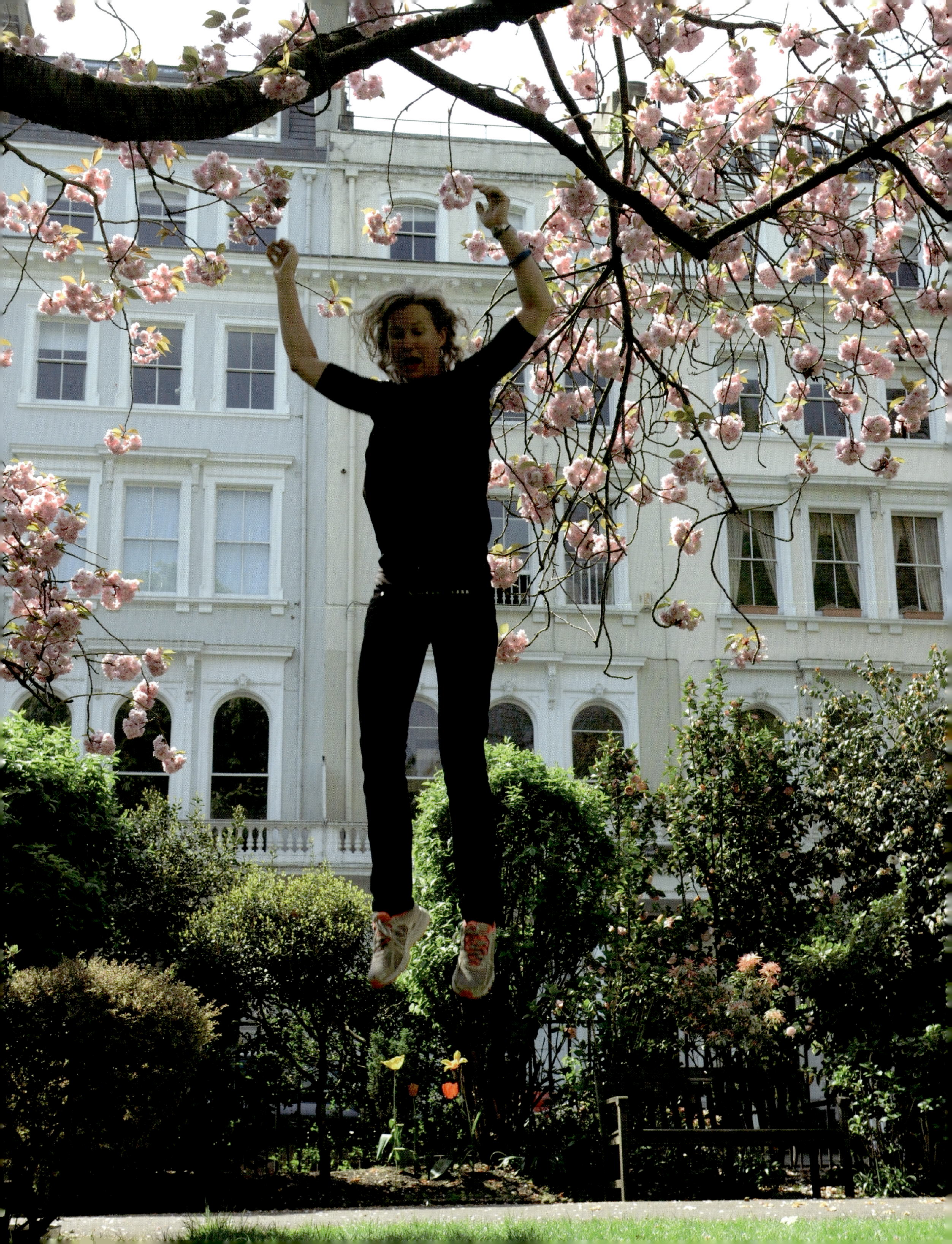

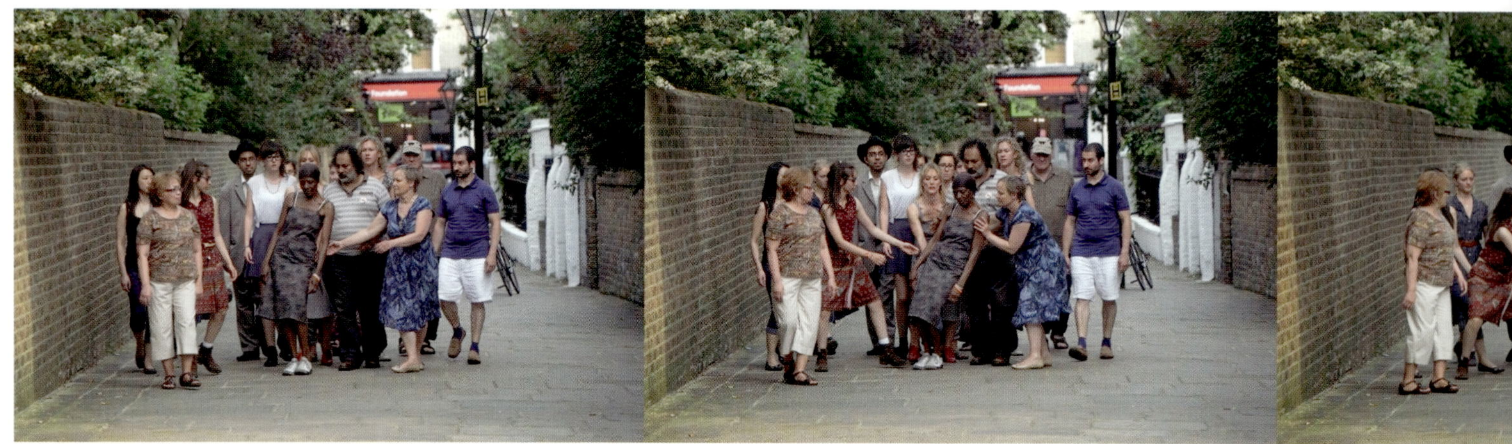

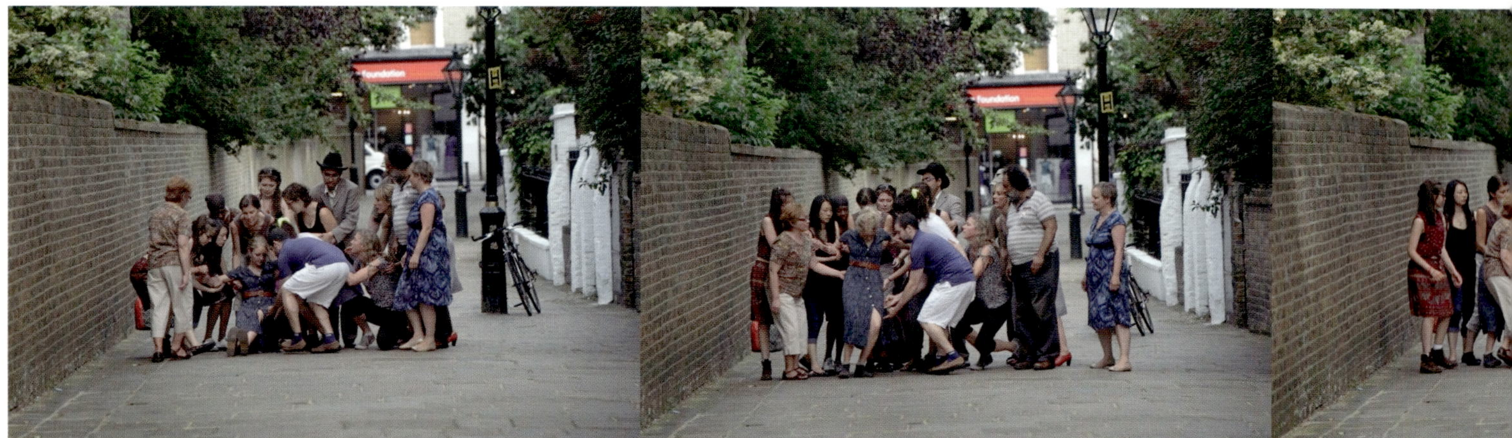

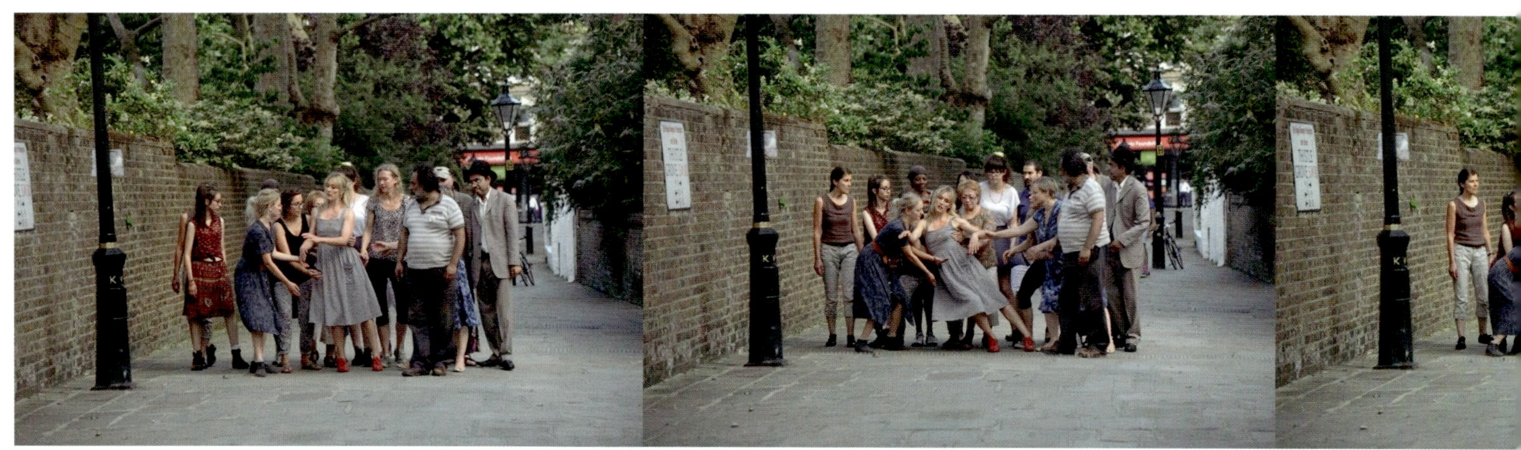

PREVIOUS PAGE Amy Sharrocks, *London Falling*, 2013, Cornwall Gardens, London, live artwork, one in series, duration 15 mins.

ABOVE AND OPPOSITE Amy Sharrocks, *A Time To Fall*, 2013, Thistle Grove, London, live artwork, duration 6 hrs.

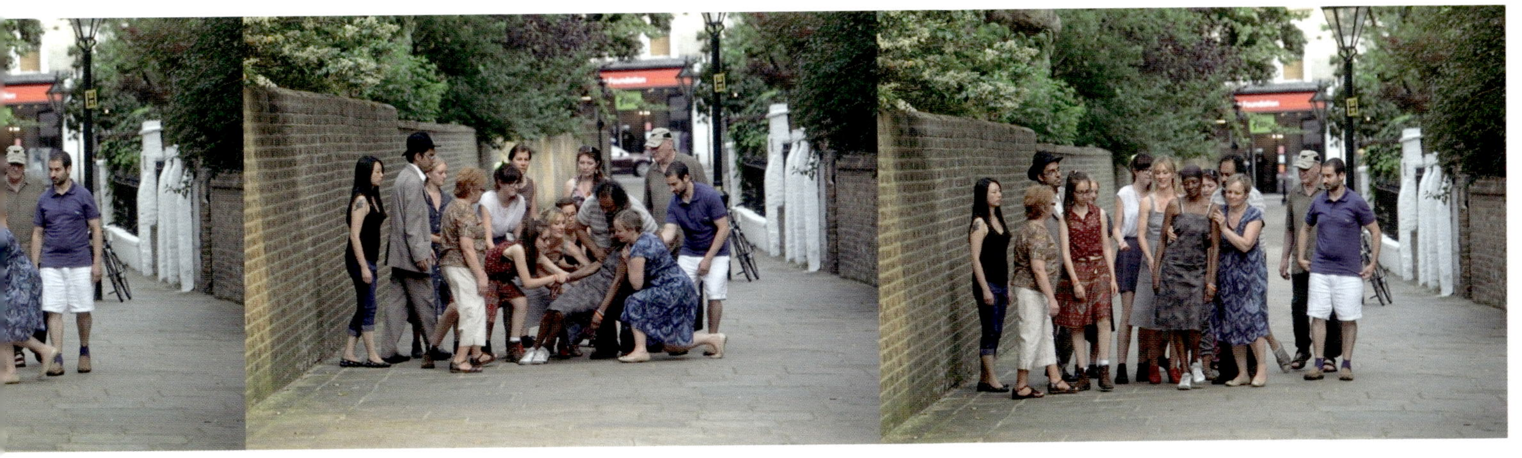

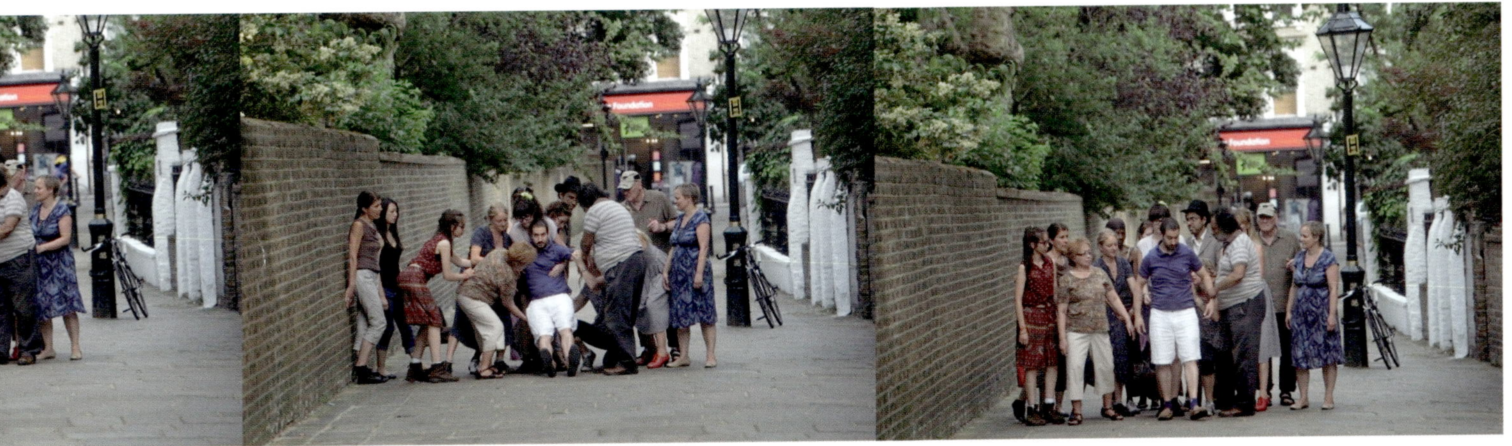

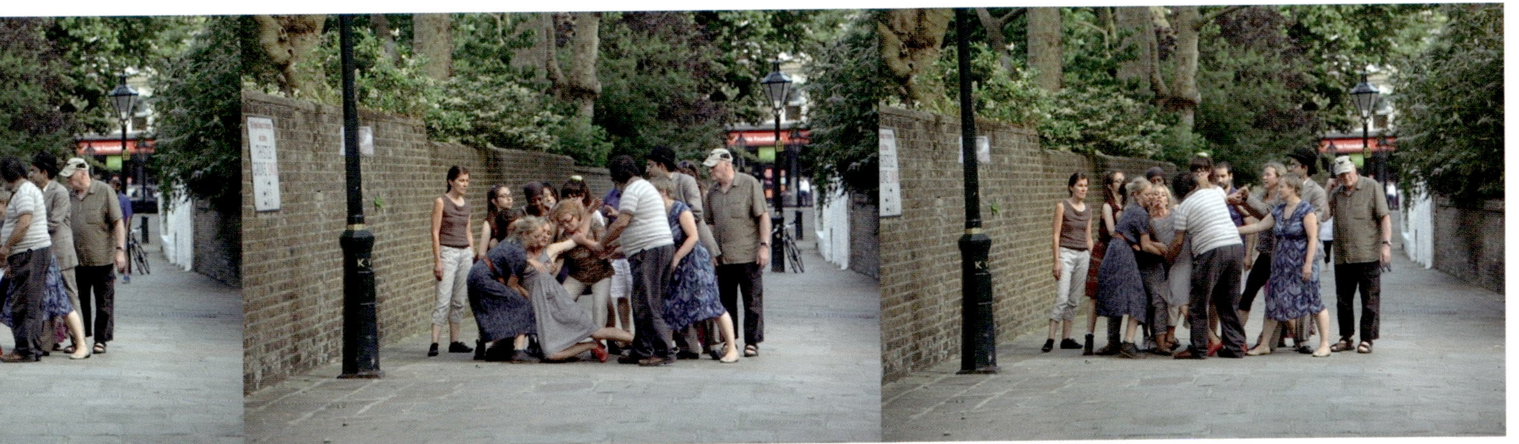

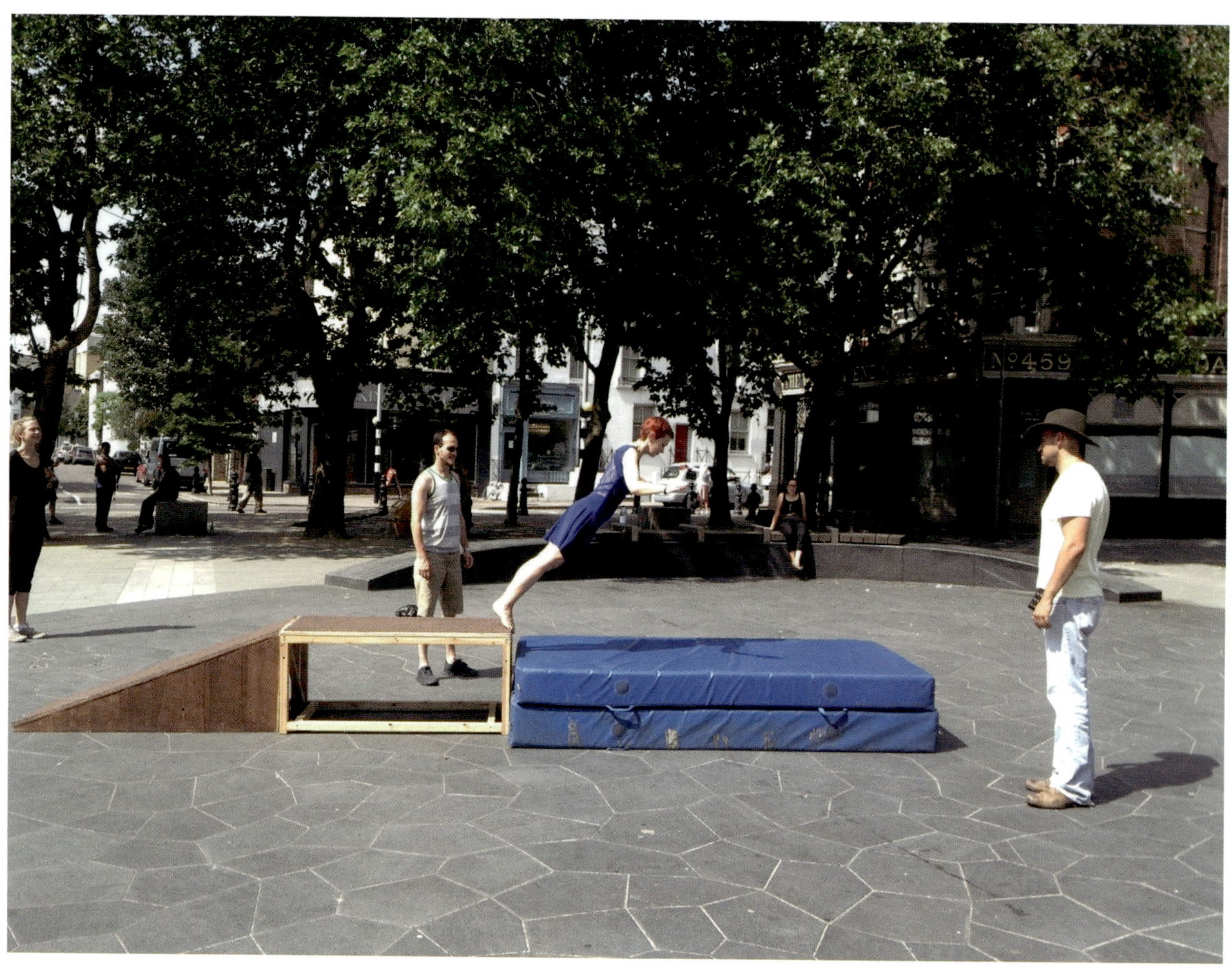

Amy Sharrocks, *Invitation to Fall*, 2013, World's End Place, London, live
artwork, duration 6 hrs, dimensions variable. Photograph by Iris Long.

Notes from the Studio

What excites you most about live art/performance as a genre?

The delicacy of each moment. The shifting, fluid possibilities of each minute. What could be more thrilling? How each person involved can alter the piece, the power it gives to each participant to shape and grow the work. I enjoy offering the gift of co-authorship with each live piece. The focus needed. The hugeness of the power of live art: the transformative possibilities inherent for everyone. How much I learn each time; that each piece takes me beyond what I know already.

What made you want to undertake a Sculpture Shock residency?

I trained as a sculptor, and I have always thought of my work as much as sculpture as live art. Each piece is sited, has a clear shape, is fashioned by hand and experience—I think about the architecture of a moment as a shape that can be moulded. People often like to label work clearly as one thing or another, yet I have always recognised a dual understanding in a work. I am glad in some ways also for the weight of the tradition of the Society—a weight it confers on the live work, live art, because it may be ephemeral and is often described in terms of its fragility—this seemed to appreciate its power. I like that it can skip round you, but still hit you like a sledgehammer.

Could you explain the process of creating one of your works from the germination of an idea to its realisation?

Sometimes ideas can come very quickly, in that glimmering moment before you are fully awake perhaps—a bit of a eureka moment—and then it is a question of trying it out, effecting the plans, making it and seeing what happens along the way. This was a residency however, and I wanted to start from an empty space (the gift of this beautiful studio) and see what developed. I knew I wanted to start from the beginning, from nothing. I had ideas of working from a seed or a fall. So I literally started with nothing. I chose to use the time to think all about falling, because it seemed to be the very first step—even before the very first step in fact—that before a walk there is a fall, a flop, a drop.

You are often asked where the artwork resides. You say that it lies "in the architecture of a moment that is made between people", in situations which you facilitate. I sense that this belies the conceptual strength of your ideas. What is more important to you, concept or execution?

Concept. No, execution. No, no, wait. Concept. No, execution; I believe in rigour. I believe in months of work and research that you can throw up in the air at the drop of a hat for a moment that was born, well, of a moment, and a situation that arose with that one person, in that one place, at that particular time. Which might have been different a second later. It may be my concept that each work springs from, but it is utterly malleable in the execution by the person who meets me. And thank goodness for that. I believe that we have all fed into every moment that we have now, and that ideally, we can be alive to all those possibilities and memories, and draw on them to shape the moment. But each moment is otherwise shaped by someone else, and it would be a poor exchange not to let them in. I'm not in this just to get my point across. It is of course everybody's right to squander time as anyone sees fit.

How do you feel about the intangibility of your work? In what ways are traces of your work left for people who did not experience the live work?

Occasionally I long for some solid mass to exit my studio into the world, that I could point to and say, "Look at that! I did that!", but it always seems a little grandiose. I have no less grand claims—I want to change people's lives, explode their minds with the possibilities of things, change their days and ways—but I don't make grand claims for things, but for people.

What traces have your favourite artworks left in you? If they are really great, have they changed your ideas about the world.

There's always traces left of a work—there are a lot of photographs, but I reckon you mean something different. For the people who weren't there, there's the story your friend tells you the next day, the conversation you have had that might stick with you, there's the idea that occurred to you—perhaps while you were thinking of something else—there's your response to the photo you saw, the feelings generated in you by looking, talking, almost being a part... maybe you'll take part next time, eh?

I am a bit weirded out that I have a growing number of websites. I have a slight horror of being formulated, so I make sites (yes, intangible, virtual sites) for the works, not for me, but sooner or later I will have to own them under one banner perhaps.

I get my joy from people's responses. People contact me and tell me wonderful things. Sometimes they wait a long time on the off-chance they can make a piece, and I am so thankful for the time and effort people offer. Sometimes it's not easy to leave the house, but some people cross the countryside, spend hours getting there. Someone once drove from London to Cambridge to

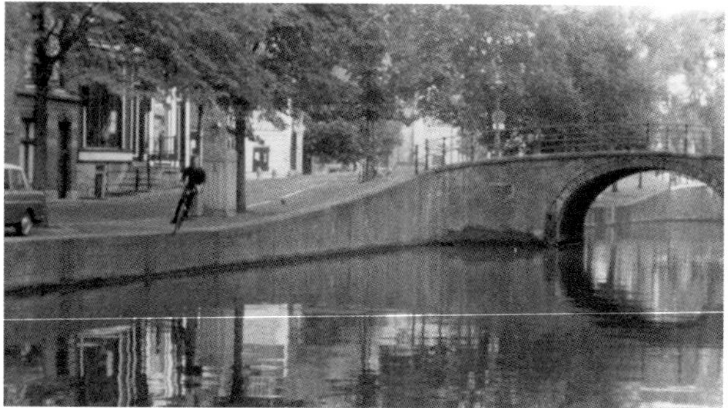

drift with me, and people came from miles and miles (Northampton, Whitstable, Brighton) to donate water to the *Museum of Water*. I am pretty proud that three people have written poems after joining in in different works of mine.

And I love word of mouth—from one person to another, in huddles of excitement perhaps, or dreamy memories? What could be better than to be on somebody's lips, the voice in their ear: "You wouldn't believe…", "I did the most…", or even, "I still don't know what to think…". And it always begs the return question, "What did you do?", "How did you spend your time?"

The first time I visited you in the studio, you had a book of etchings by Elisabeth Frink in your bookcase, and nothing else. As an extremely emotionally receptive artist, how did you react to working in the studio where such a great sculptor once worked?

I gathered stories about her for a while. My dad said he had met her once, and shook her hand and been amazed at how strong her handshake was—she would do, wouldn't she, being a stone mason—but I felt for a while that I could feel her handshake. I like a cool, strong woman, uncowed.

That book came from my mother's studio, and was a gift from my sister, so I guess I was taking Elisabeth Frink in—into my story, making my own connection with her and the other women in my family and seeing how we got on together. I had a slight sense that I was trying to get on her good side too. She'd been kind enough to let me in. I am very thankful to her (and very pleased to borrow her vacated space). I like that idea of leaving space for someone. What a gift it's been for me.

During your residency for Sculpture Shock you are creating a series of works that examine falling. How have the boundaries of the work changed during the residency?

I'm not sure there were any boundaries to the work, that's one of the things that has been most interesting. As you said, I started with nothing, and have been entirely open to everything. I have welcomed every suggestion, every sketch, every gift that I have been given since the start, and tried to be as open as possible to any one of their prompts. And not only people. I have looked at nature closely for three months, noticed the changing of the seasons, chased after each moment and stage, each tree and flower. I have lurked in parks for weeks on end. I have made sculptures and films, live works and my first performance piece. A dance, of sorts! I couldn't be more surprised! I have used my body and other peoples' as material. I've used us all as research. But we have also been co-conspirators, co-authors, colleagues and supporters. Now we will be dancers and participants too.

You have a pronounced interest in literature and the significance of words. How have you applied this to your *Season for Falling*?

Concept. Execution. Words.

Who are the artists you most admire and which have had the greatest impact on your thinking and your work?

Rembrandt. TS Eliot. Sophie Calle. Luce Irigaray. Susan Hiller. Adrian Piper. Orlan. Baudelaire. Bas Jan Ader. Yayoi Kusama. Yoko Ono. Martin Creed. Shakespeare. Anne Norman. Leon Kossoff. Marina Abramovic. Lone Twin. Roni Horn. Paul O'Kane. Cornelia Parker. Sarah Lucas. Arte Povera. Richard Long. I think that's enough? I like a lot of specific pieces: the canned shit and fistfuls of plaster by Piero Manzoni, Alighiero e Boetti's *Airplanes*, Baldessari's *The backs of all the trucks passed while driving from Los Angeles to Santa Barbara…*. The Merzbau. *The impossibility of death in the mind of someone living*. I am part of a marvellous artist's group, full of extraordinary and strong women artists, whom I admire. I am enjoying the way we are impacting on each other.

MISTAKE

COLLAPSE   *MIS-STEP*

UNDO   *CASCADE*   *MISCONSTRUE*   *FLOW*

LOWER   *SPLINTER*   *DIVE*   *LOSE FOOTING*   *RETURN*   *CRUMPLE*

LET GO   *SHATTER*   *PLUNGE*   *BE PRECARIOUS*   *BE FLUID*   *BEFALL*

GO DOWN   *SWAGGER*   *CRASH*   *DE-STABILISE*   *UNRESTRAIN*   *VEER*

SUSPEND   *STAGGER*   *LEAP*   *MAKE UNSAFE*   *RELEASE*   *DRIP*

UN-BALANCE   *SHUFFLE*   *TRIP*   *DEGENERATE*   *RE-ORIENT*   *PAUSE*

COME DOWN   *STUTTER*   *TUMBLE*   *UNDERMINE*   *RE-BALANCE*   *DROOP*

DESCEND   *TEETER*   *FLOUNDER*   *DECREASE*   *PROGRESS*   *FLOP*

DROP   *TOTTER*   *SPIRAL*   *DISTURB*   *ADVENTURE*   *LAPSE*

KEEL   *STUMBLE*   *OVERWHELM*   *DECLINE*   *VENTURE*   *SINK*

TIP   *PLUMMET*   *SHRINK*   *REGENERATE*   *EBB*

REDUCE   *FREE FALL*

SHIRK   *FLY*

UPSET

FAIL

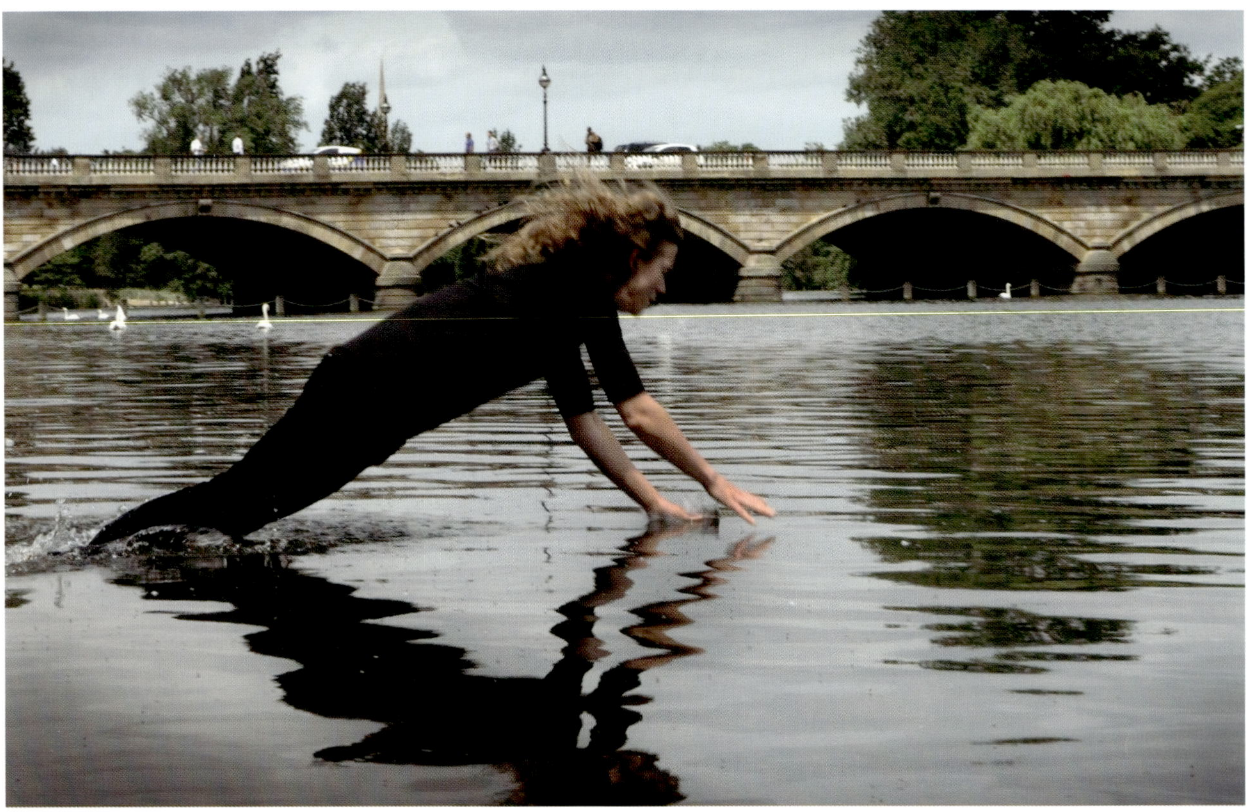

Ambulatory

ABOVE AND OPPOSITE Amy Sharrocks, *Serpentine Fall*, 2013, The
Serpentine, London, live artwork, one in series, duration 2 mins.

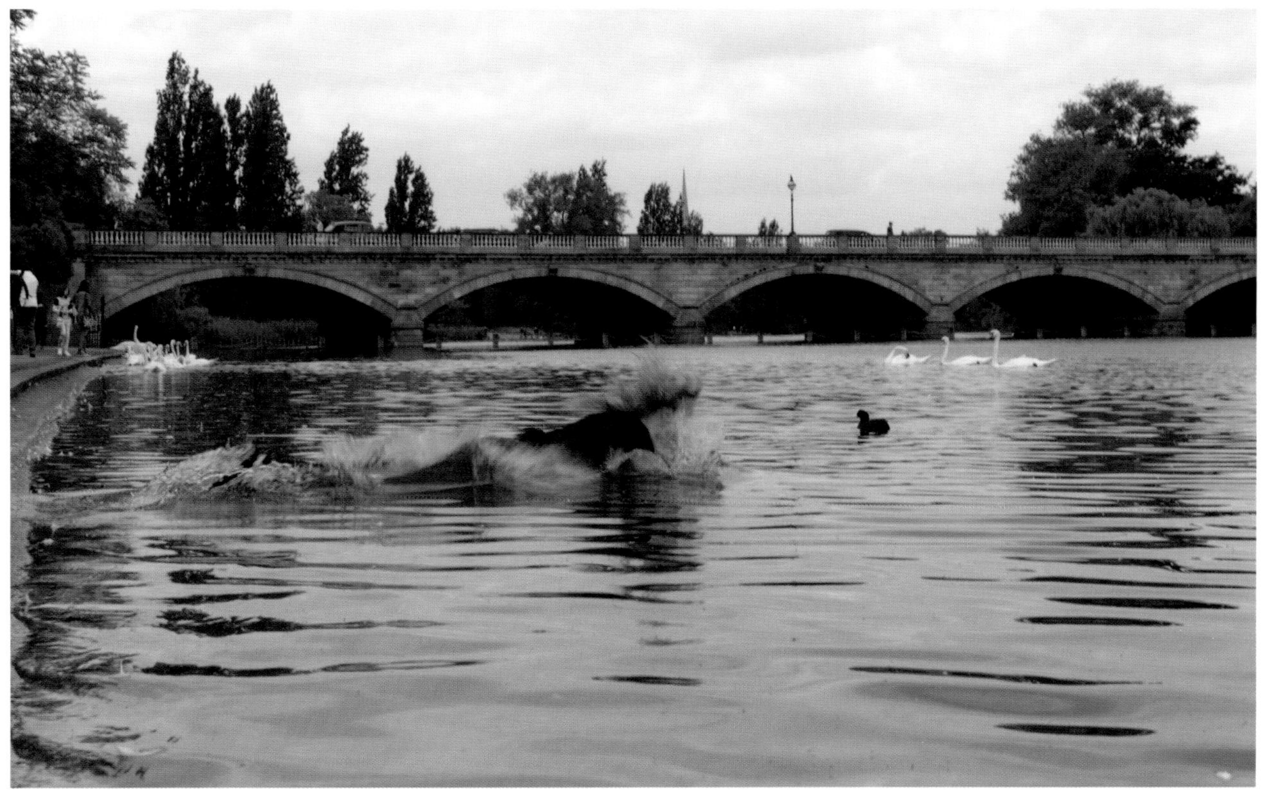

**Alexander Costello
Canal barge on the waterways of North East London**

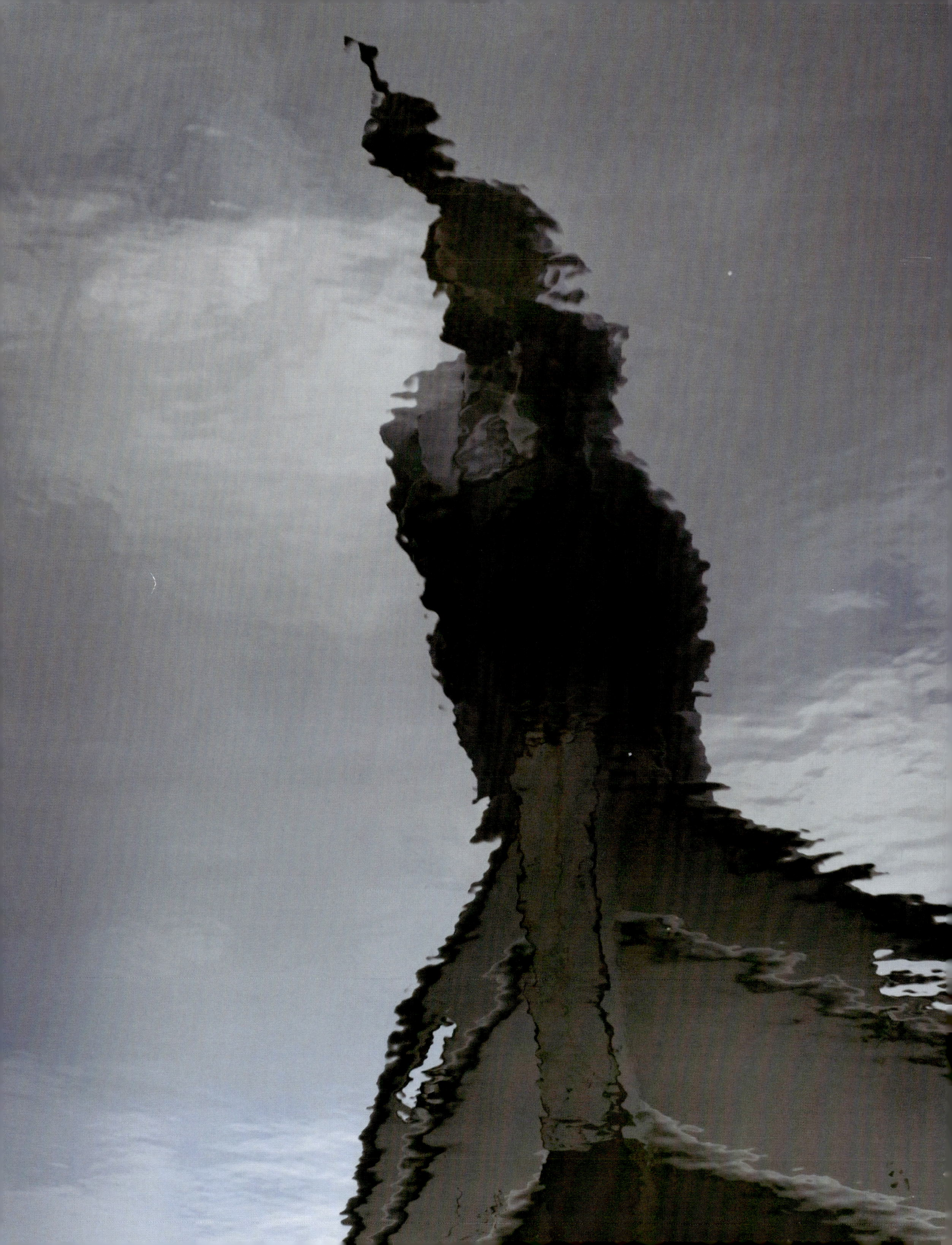

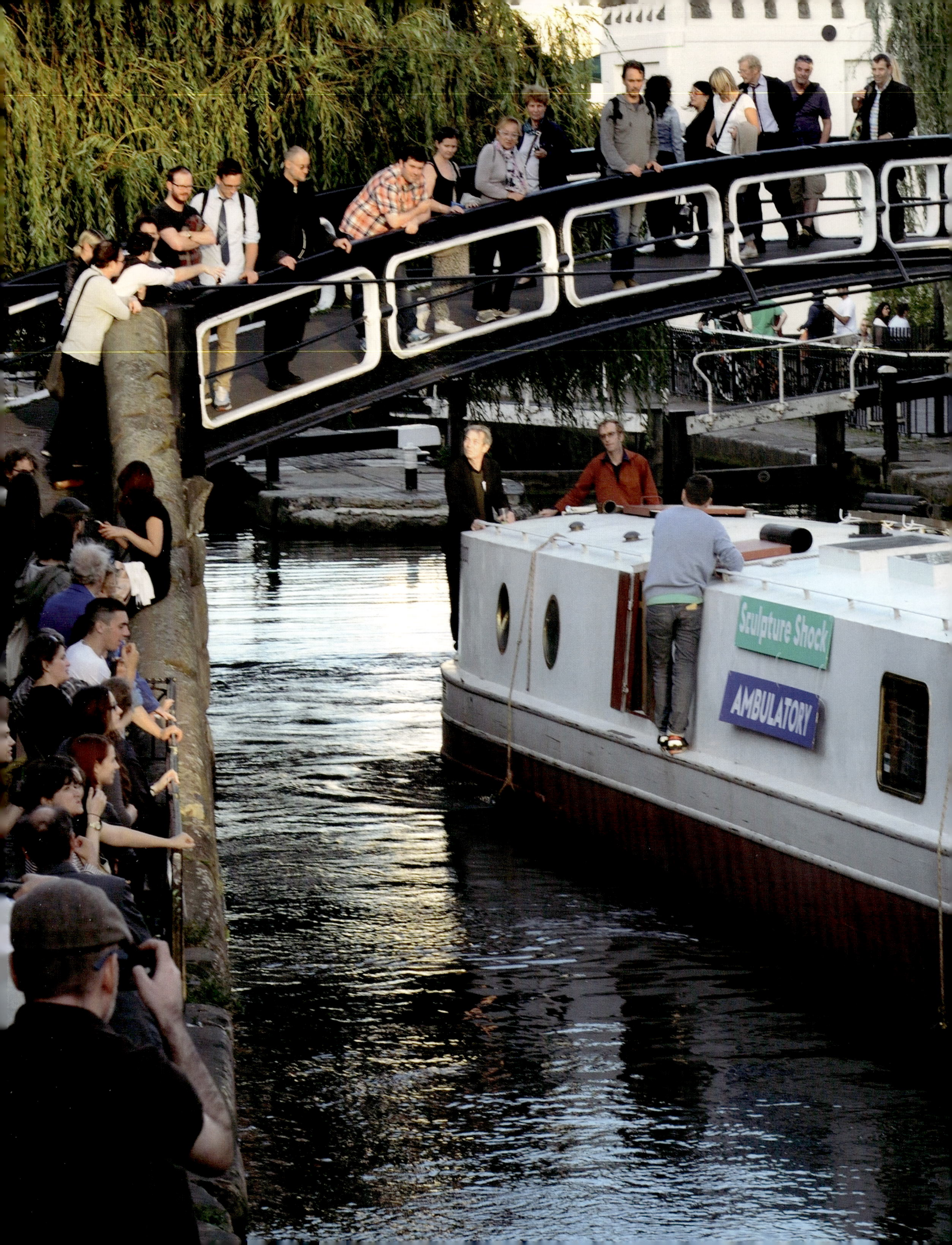
Sculpture Shock
AMBULATORY

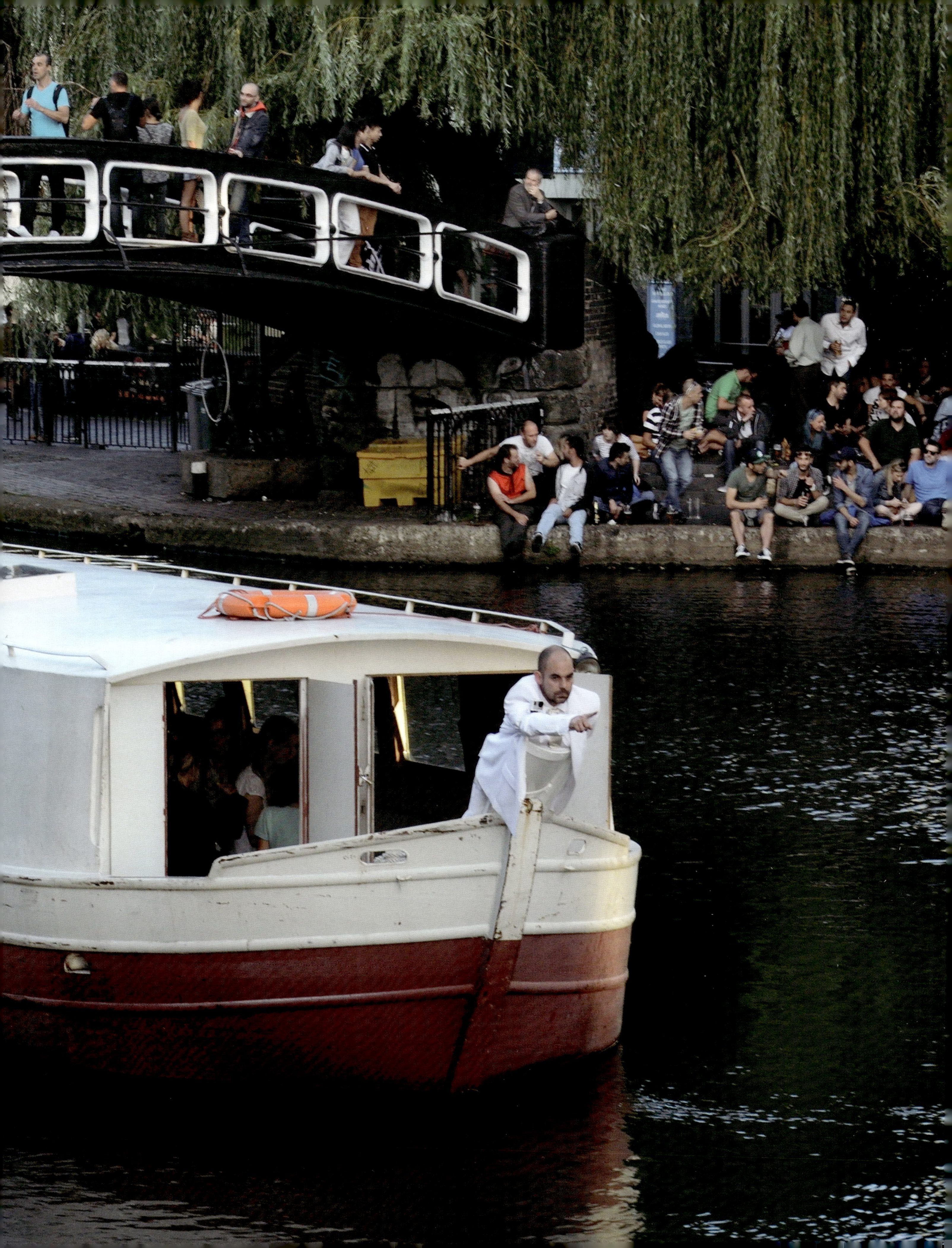

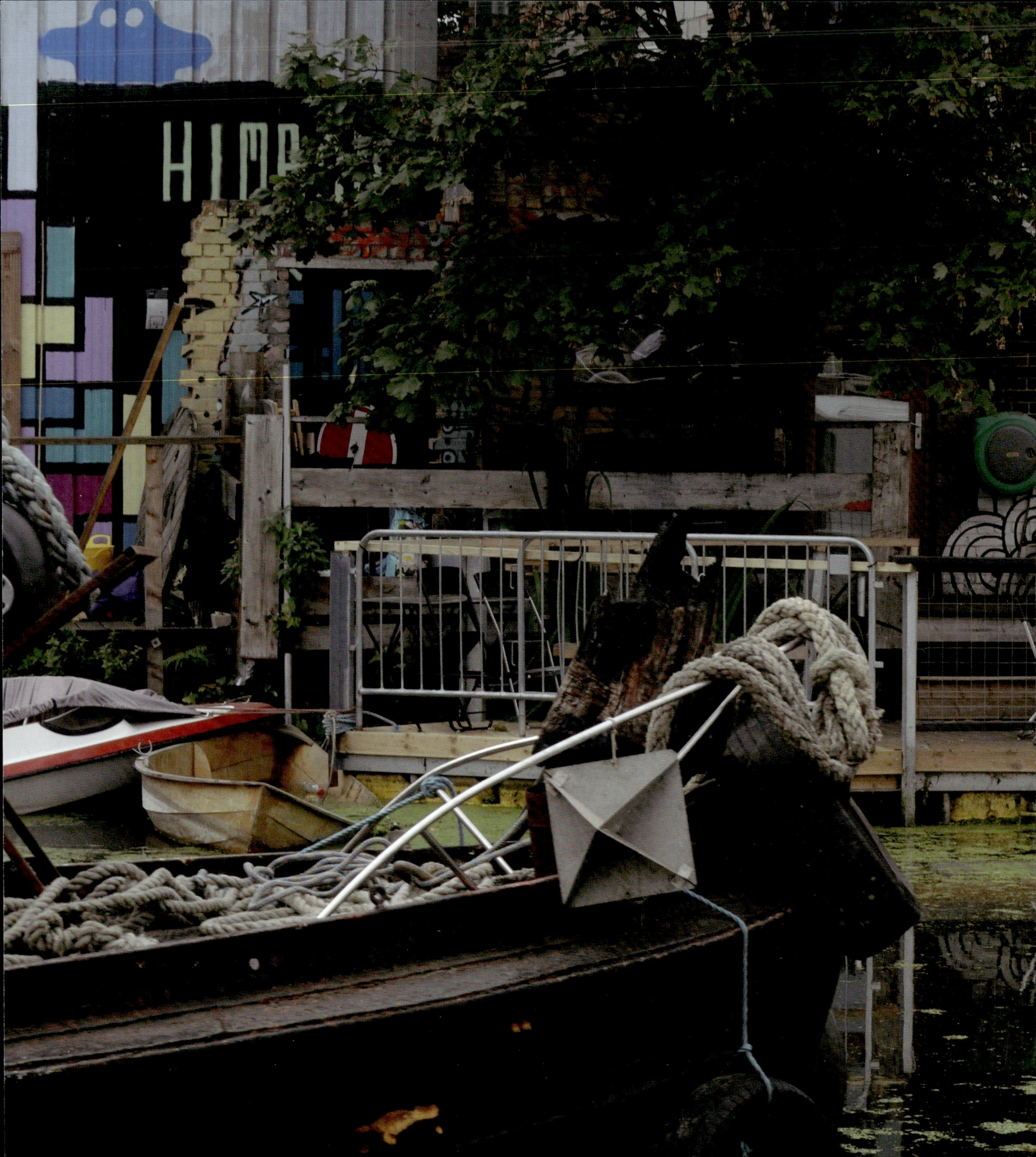
HIMA

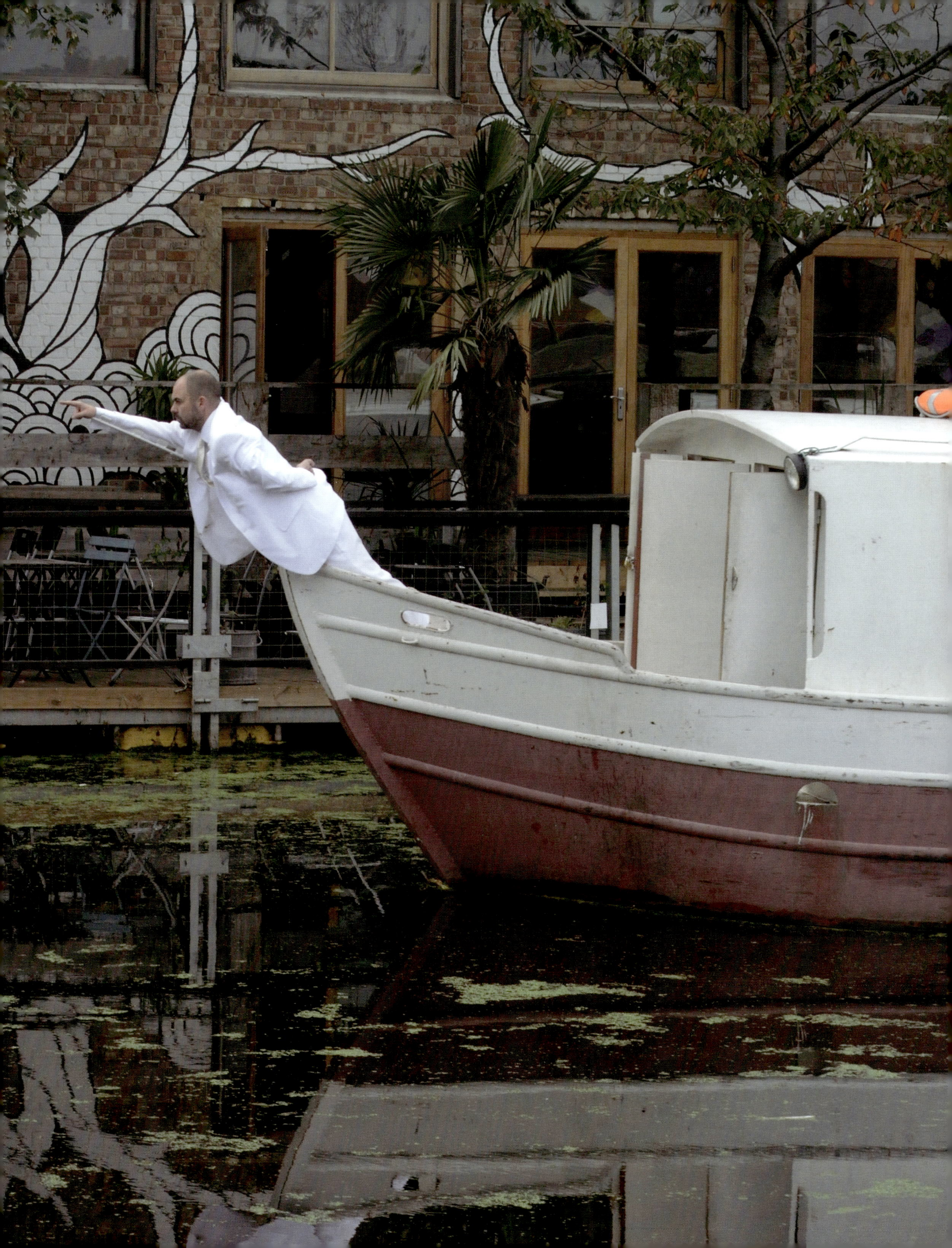

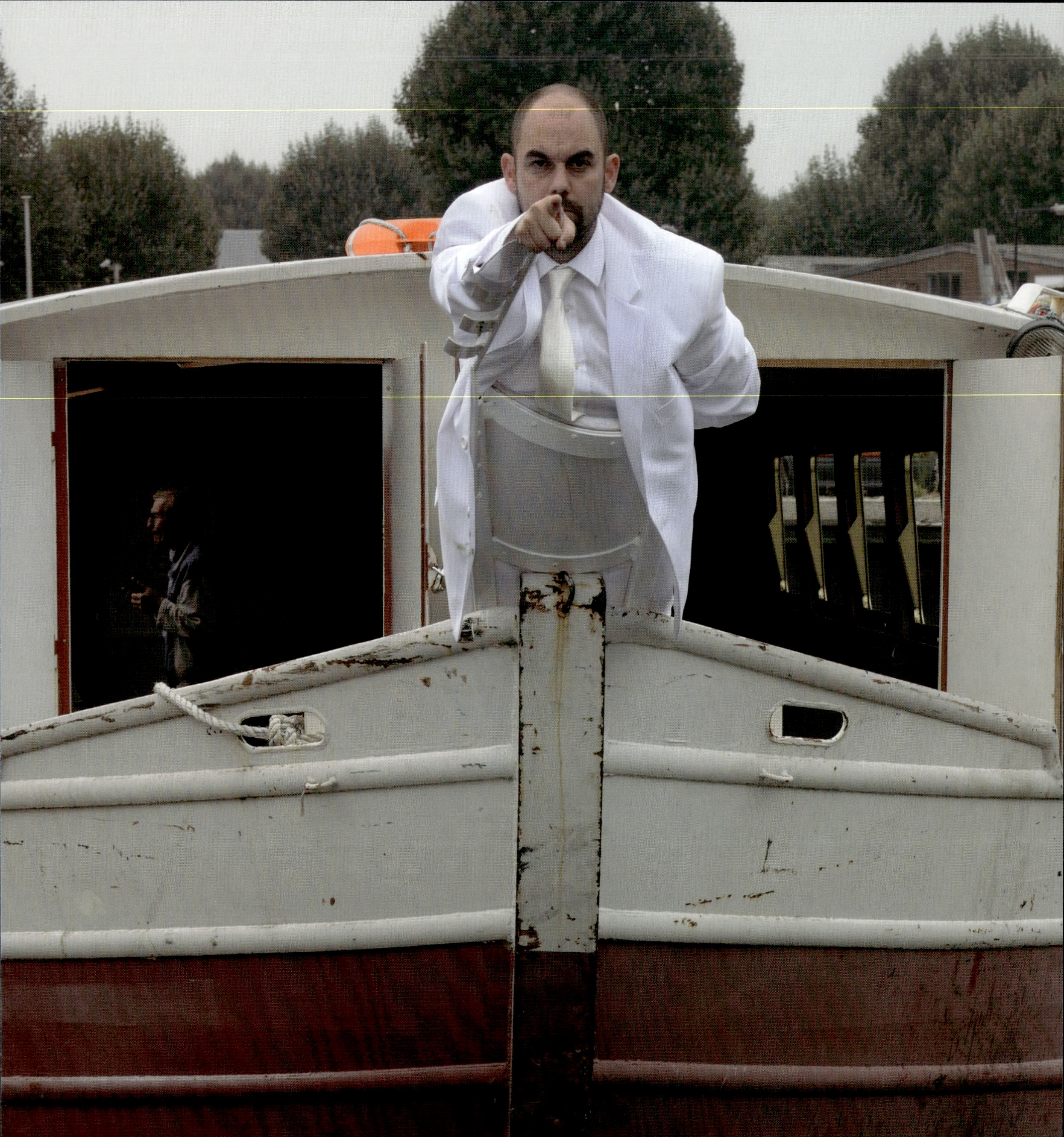

Notes from the Studio

How important is the written or spoken word to the conception of your works?

The faults, oddities, devices, misinterpretations and slippages that exist in language are the unconscious, subliminal foundations to ideas that find themselves re-presented in my more solid visual work.

Who are the artists you most admire and which have had the greatest impact on your thinking and your work?

Big hitters for me are Manzoni, Baldessari, Tati, Prince, McLean, WC Fields, Bas Jan Ader, Salvatore Scarpitta, Laurie Anderson, Beckett, Abramovic, Yves Klein, Robert Rauschenberg, de Chirico, Pettibon, Bukowski, Herman Hesse, Kurt Vonnegut, Fontana....

Your Sculpture Shock residency is called *Making Progress*. What do you perceive as 'progress'?

I don't actually know what progress is supposed to be, what it looks like or what we should be doing with it, but the idea of it dominates how we value and locate ourselves today. I suppose getting somewhere with something, wherever that is or whatever it looks like, and coming to terms with what happens, was always going to happen. This is not to be confused with making things better though. There is nothing better than being inside the moment of making; time spent pushing at things, teasing confidence with doubt, and just keeping going. Because of that, endings interest me as well as the anticipation of the next thing. There is always the next thing.

In the wider social (Western) context, progress often skips hand in hand down the street with proactivism, the mighty slayer of inertia, and as such is perceived as something positive for society. I am uncomfortable with this perception, as much as I am also uncomfortable with progress being linked to the importance of accountability, when accountability concerns a race to the bottom. Steve Aylett said that, "progress accelerates downhill". I am happy to know that and keep it in mind. As such, progress concerns ideas to do with 'moving forward', be it as an individual or society, which is perhaps a flawed consensus. Who is progress for? This a very important question to ask.

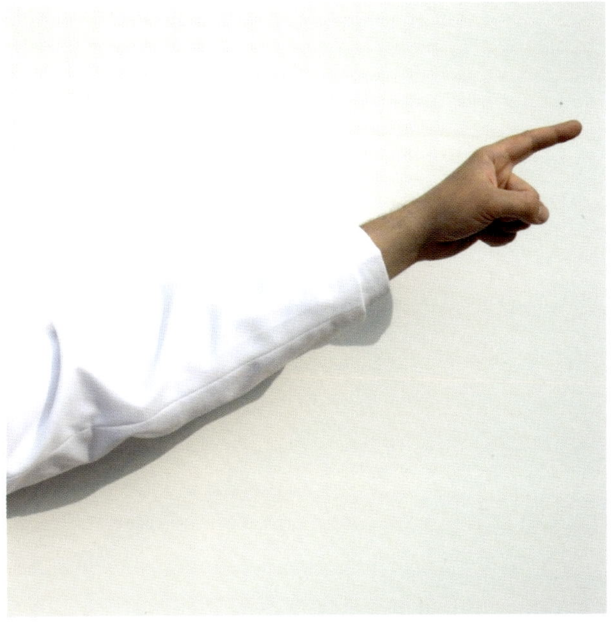

You said that the film *The Bed Sitting Room* based on the play by Spike Milligan and John Antrobus provides the context for your residency. Can you elaborate on this?

The world has been destroyed by a nuclear war, which lasted only two and a half minutes and only a few survivors remain. The landscape is a desperate environment of cutlery, mud and rubbish. There is nothing to look forward to. Dudley Moore and Peter Cook appear as the police, floating over the heads of the survivors in a hot air balloon and insist that everyone keeps moving—moving forwards —as if that is what is required and is the necessary default position, in the given circumstances. The fact that it means absolutely nothing goes unquestioned. The world is a tabula rasa. Despite having the opportunity to start again, the survivors cling on to their perceived, ingrained and oppressive social norms and aim for and rely on the same mundane things like a Tesco, a bank, etc, when rebuilding their world. The absurdity is that having been given the world, they cling to their ideals and habits of progress.

Humour and the absurd are cornerstones of your work. What do you hope to achieve by using these 'tools' and how do they help convey your message?

Humour is where the circle of seriousness and gravity comes to an end. Deadpan is at that fine point, and it is the means of entry and engagement with my work. All art is funny, and as such should always be taken seriously. Humour is a way of communicating something that is both funny and critical, an unwelcome observation or the

pp 61–66 Alexander Costello, *Making Progress*, 2014, four-day performance on a canal barge travelling at 3 mph with the artist wearing a white suit and tie; sound installation of voice repeating "Keep Moving Forward" on a loop in the interior.

ABOVE RIGHT Work in progress during Alexander Costello's residency. Photograph by Tobias Hussey.

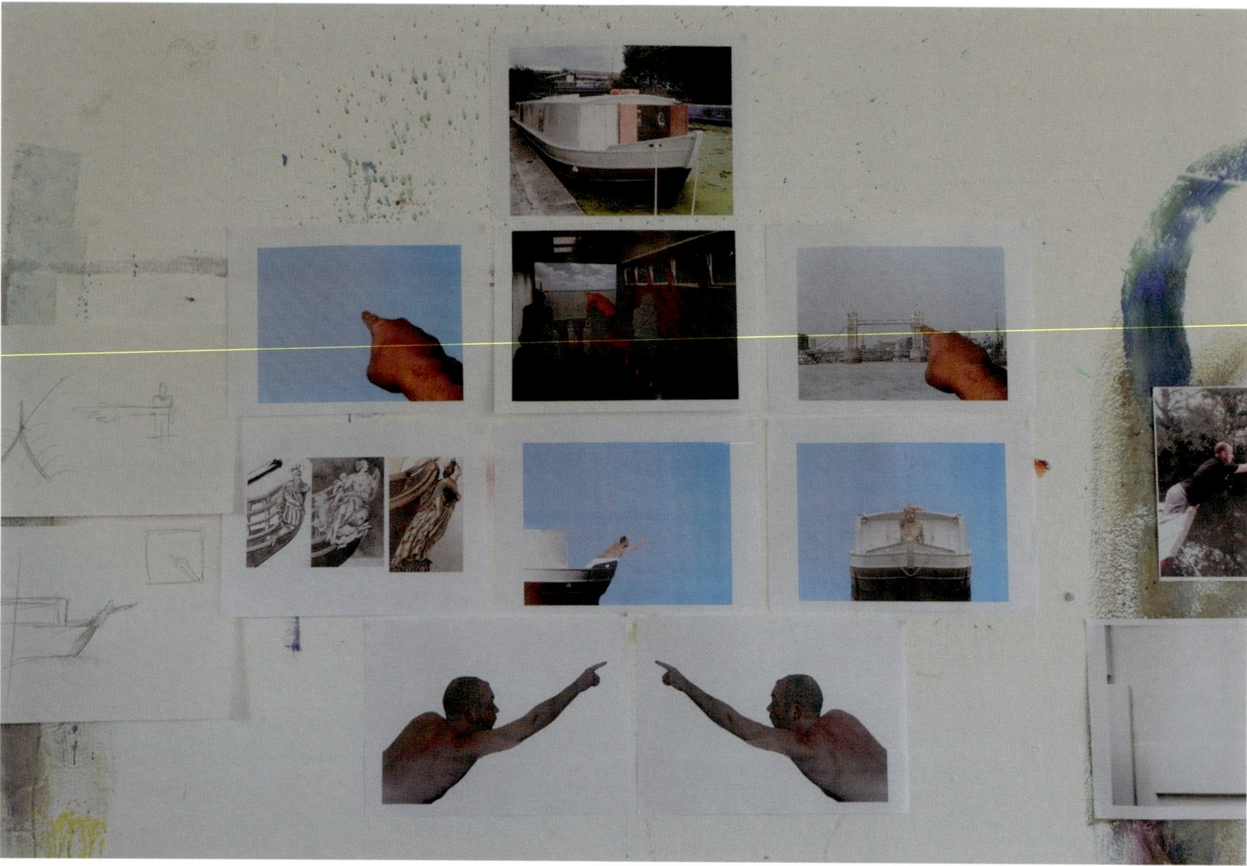

Work in progress during Alexander Costello's residency.

uncovering of an embedded but dysfunctional social norm. Utterly ridiculous in delivery, utterly serious in content.

What impact do you hope your work to have on the viewer? What is the importance of public spectacle to you?

I do not expect people to immediately understand what I am doing or what the point of the work is, but I do hope to create strong images that lodge a future thought in their heads. Sometimes people need some thoughtful respite in order to progress.

How important is site-specificity to your work? To what extent do you tailor your pieces to a particular 'public landscape', as you put it?

The 'public landscape' is like a live canvas and backdrop to my performance and video work. All my work is a response to people or places that punctuate the brusque contingencies of the everyday. I choose to respond, either by challenging these experiences or reflecting on them. I suppose there are two types of artistic process I engage with. The work you make as a process of making one thing after the other, where work itself generates ideas for new work and development. The other is making work in response to the site-specific, whether it is a space, an incident, an object or environment. The site-specific is often a peopled space and experienced differently, person to person. As such, there is a greater chance to interact, interrupt, subvert and play with it through the types of interventions I design.

How do you feel about the impermanence of the performance components of your work in contrast to the more lasting nature of the text based, video, object-making, drawing and painting elements? Are these intended as the documentary part of the piece, standalone works, or perhaps both?

One of my firm beliefs is "It's not about the thing. It's about all of it and doing things." Everything informs everything else. As such, my performance work does not need to be anything else it is not. As an impermanent medium, I'm all right with it occupying the very moment it is supposed to, as that is the moment. In fact, it lends itself well to making sure that "What something is is exactly what it is, and what it was always going to be."

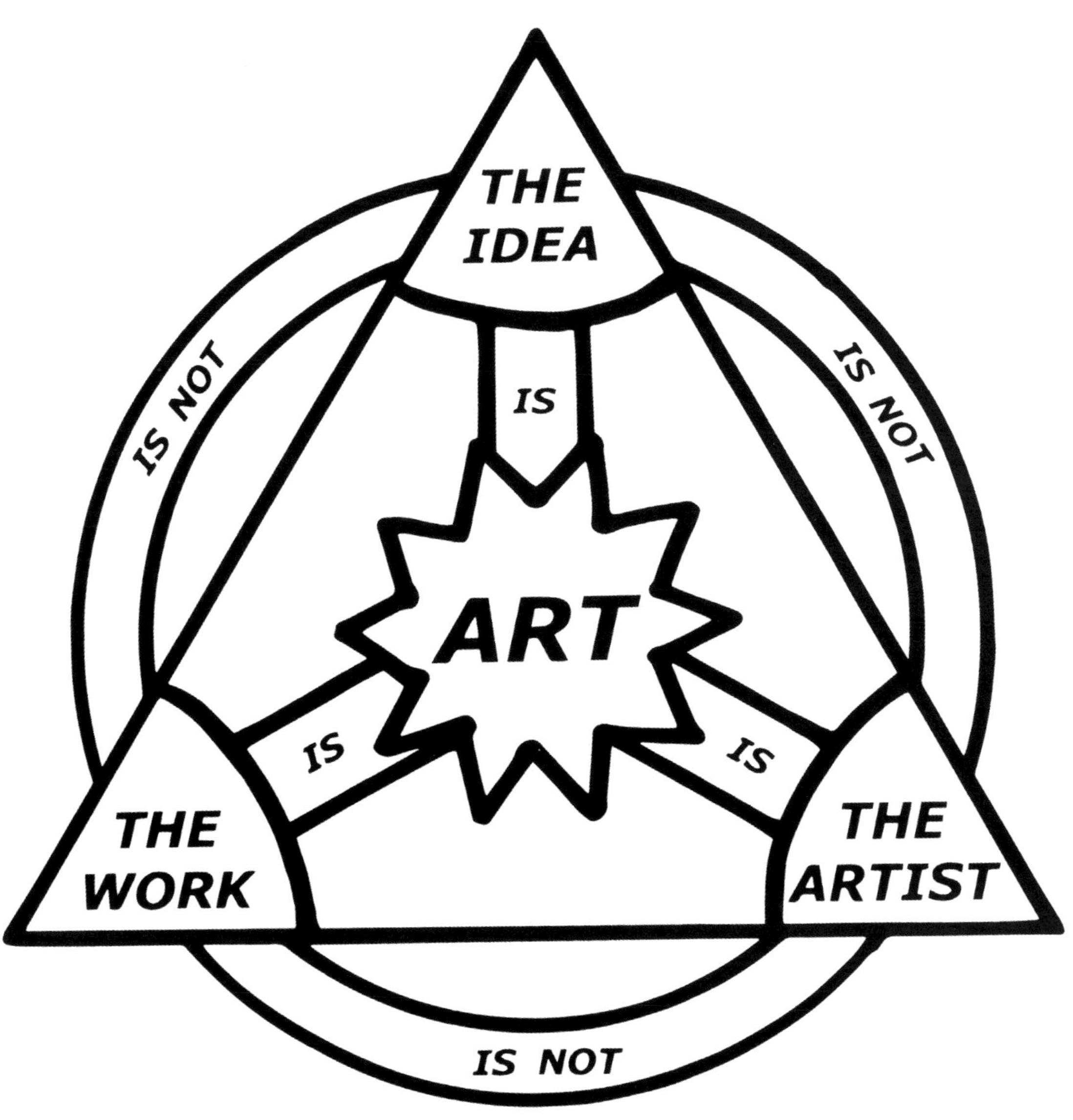

Alexander Costello, *Art is...*, 2014, hand-pulled screen print on Southbank Smooth, 42 x 59.5 cm, edition of 30, plus 6 artist's proofs. Image courtesy the artist.

Alexander Costello: *Making Progress*, 2014—Sarah Kent

A white barge was to be seen floating slowly along the Regent's Canal; nothing unusual in that. If you looked closely, though, you could see a figure standing motionless in the prow pointing ahead as though urging the vessel to maintain its forward momentum.

This was neither a carved wooden figurehead nor the skipper navigating shallow waters, but the artist Alexander Costello performing *Making Progress*, a four-day journey aboard a barge that doubles as the Fordham Gallery.

For the occasion, he wore a white suit that blended in with the fabric of the boat, so that he could easily be mistaken for a fixture. Copious sleeves hid the steel structure made by the artist to support his arm during the journey; this made his ability to sustain such an awkward and absurd pose over many hours seem little short of miraculous.

"I've never not performed", Costello tells me. "As a boy I was a chorister standing still for hours on end and, later, I became the front man for a band. It's nice to be alive; I like the endurance aspect of being in the moment— feeling the doing, experiencing things in the now. Whatever happens, happens. I like testing myself and asking, 'How am I accountable?'"

Attached to his pointing arm, a video camera provided live footage to a screen below deck so that passengers could share Costello's privileged view of the canal and its banks as the boat glided inexorably forwards into the future. They could also watch people on the towpath responding with surprise, hilarity or dismay as they caught sight of the artist pursuing his apparently pointless task with such determination and focus.

"That's exactly what it was", agrees Costello, "a poor sod persisting in nothingness. The whole point of the performance was this steady nothing—in all its metaphorical glory!" This remark brings to mind Samuel Beckett's play *Waiting for Godot*, in which two benighted fools, Vladimir and Estragon, persist in waiting for the arrival of someone called Godot even when their vigil appears increasingly fruitless. The more time they commit to waiting, the more they feel the need to continue. "Beckett is massive", affirms Costello. "Even when people are offered a fresh start, they still want and expect the things they are accustomed to."

On the one hand, the journey was like any other; it passed the time pleasantly while ferrying passengers from A to B; and like many performances, Costello's offering was light hearted, humorous and transitory. But while passing the time, like Beckett's play, it had the potential to stir up the dark silt that lies beneath the beguiling surface of performance and encourage consideration of more serious issues.

Travelling along the canals of North London from Camden Lock to Tottenham Hale, the barge passed through King's Cross, Haggerston, London Fields, Hackney Wick and the Olympic Park—areas transformed beyond recognition by the ambitious programme of regeneration embarked on in preparation for the London Olympics of 2012. In the process, the empty warehouses, derelict factories and small businesses that once lined the canal banks had been refurbished or replaced by blocks of luxury flats that invite the well-heeled to elbow out poorer residents.

Some saw the development as a much-needed improvement; others viewed it with disgust as wanton vandalism. Costello deliberately chose the route and the title, *Making Progress*, to provoke questions about the concept of progress— what it means and its intended and unintended consequences. Does the notion of progress spur us on toward a desirable future or, in the vain pursuit of unattainable goals, does it encourage the destruction of things we should

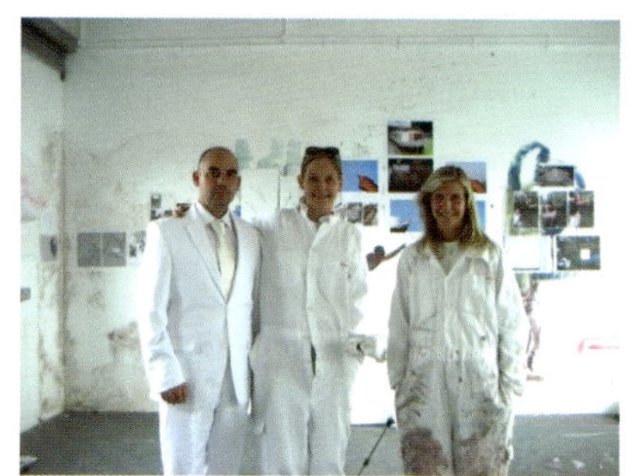

From left to right: Alexander Costello, Claire Mander and Nina Wisnia performing a studio visit in white overalls provided by the artist during his residency.

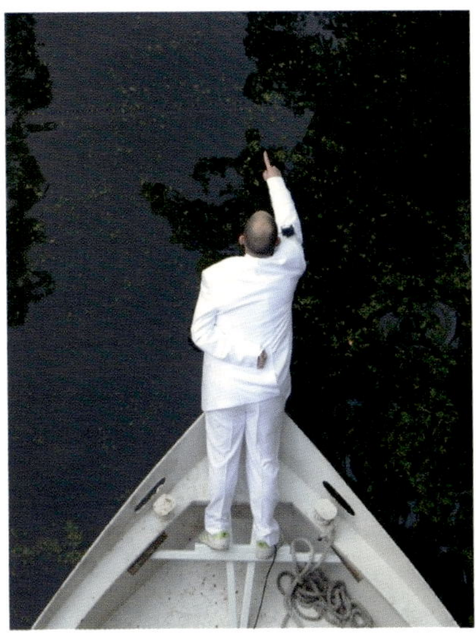

Alexander Costello, *Making Progress*, 2014.

hold dear? Where are we heading individually and collectively, and what would constitute a worthy ambition, a meaningful journey or a useful life?

"As a teacher I'm expected to subscribe to the notion of 'making progress'", explains Costello, who is a teacher as well as an artist:

In life we're always on a journey—going forwards rather than retreating—but some people need more time to get started and, in the education system, late developers are written off.... At university I made sure I achieved something every day, but things soon became strained. I didn't want to force the work, so I taught myself to do nothing, to enjoy the nothing (the empty canvas)—to let things gestate and allow the work to happen. I'm interested in processes. If I know where I'm going—if the idea is already in my head—its no good to me. If I'm too much in control, whatever made it interesting in the first place no longer exists.

Does he believe that art can change anything? "Yes", comes the emphatic reply.

This project is ridiculously silly, but also very important vis-à-vis social politics. We're encouraged to equate progress with making things bigger, better and faster, but this acceleration leads to homogenisation, which generates conservatism. And who orchestrates change? Big corporations.... Like the slipstream off the end of my finger, progress always remains just out of reach, so I'm encouraging people to question what 'making progress' actually means, and the silliness is the doorway. At one time I tried to be funny but it didn't work, partly because that wasn't the point, partly because the desire to entertain encourages mediocrity. So now the audience has to take me as I come. I'm interested in ideas; I like hard work, something rich and nourishing, a real chew.

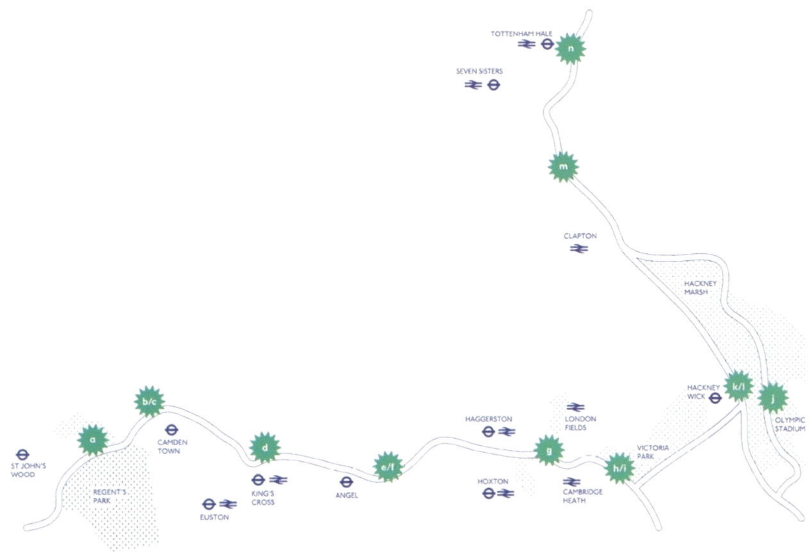

Map of the route followed by the Fordham Gallery canal barge during the four-day performance of *Making Progress*.

William Mackrell
No 9 bus, Aldwych to Hammersmith, London

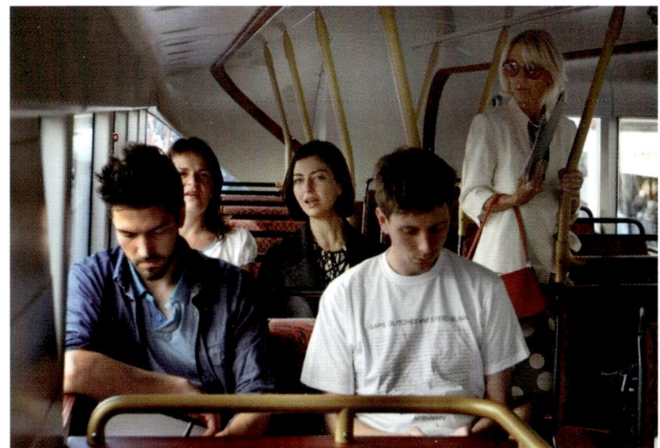
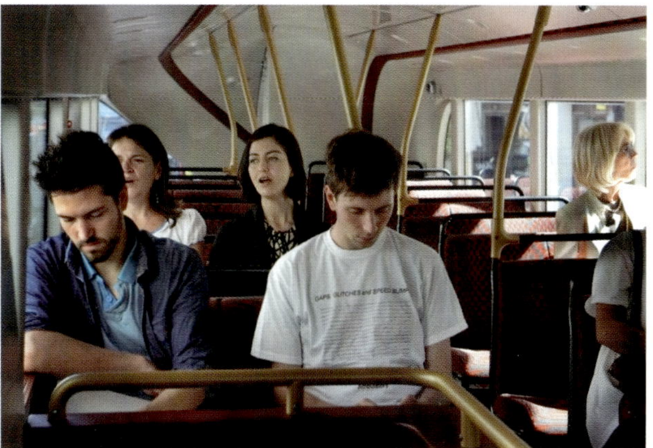
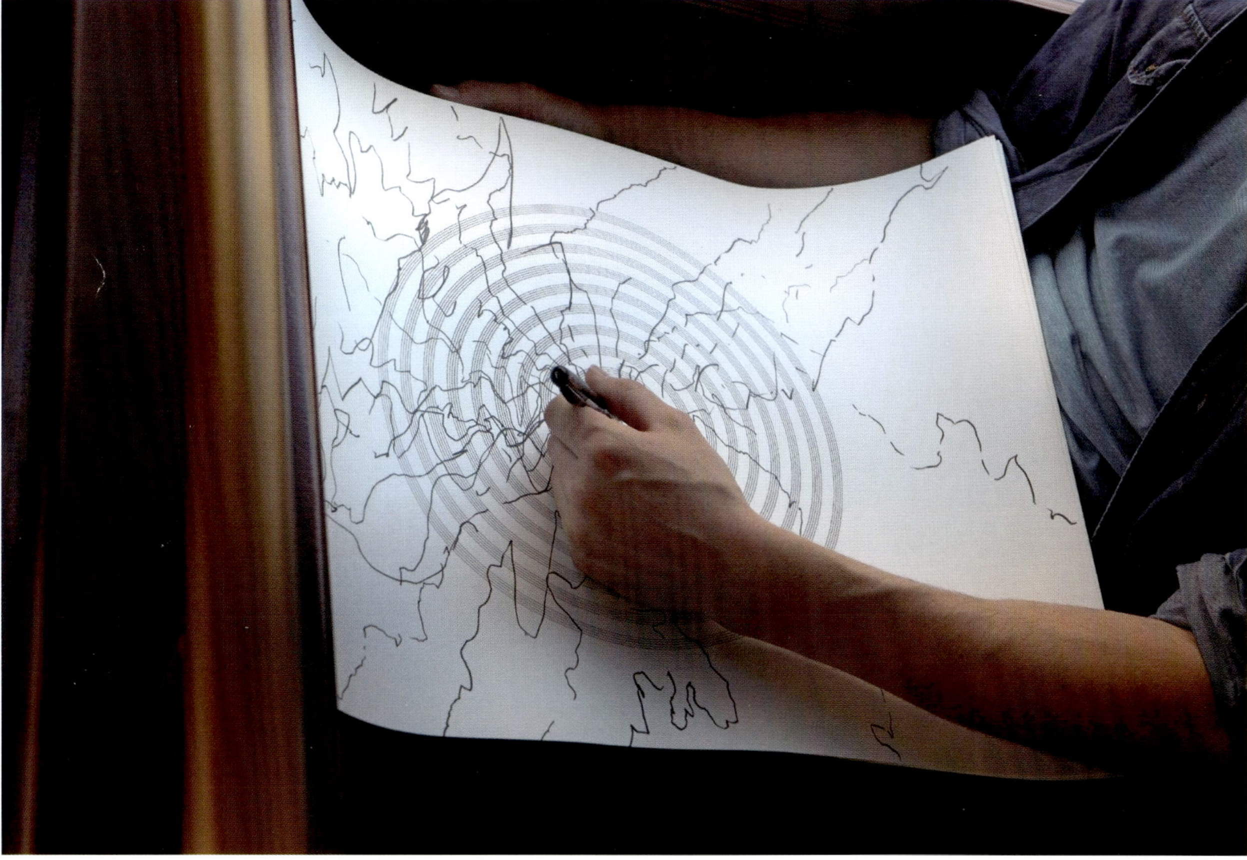

William Mackrell, *Gaps, glitches and speed bumps*, 2015, four days of performances on no 9 bus route in Central London with jazz, opera, classical and contemporary voice accompaniment, dimensions variable.

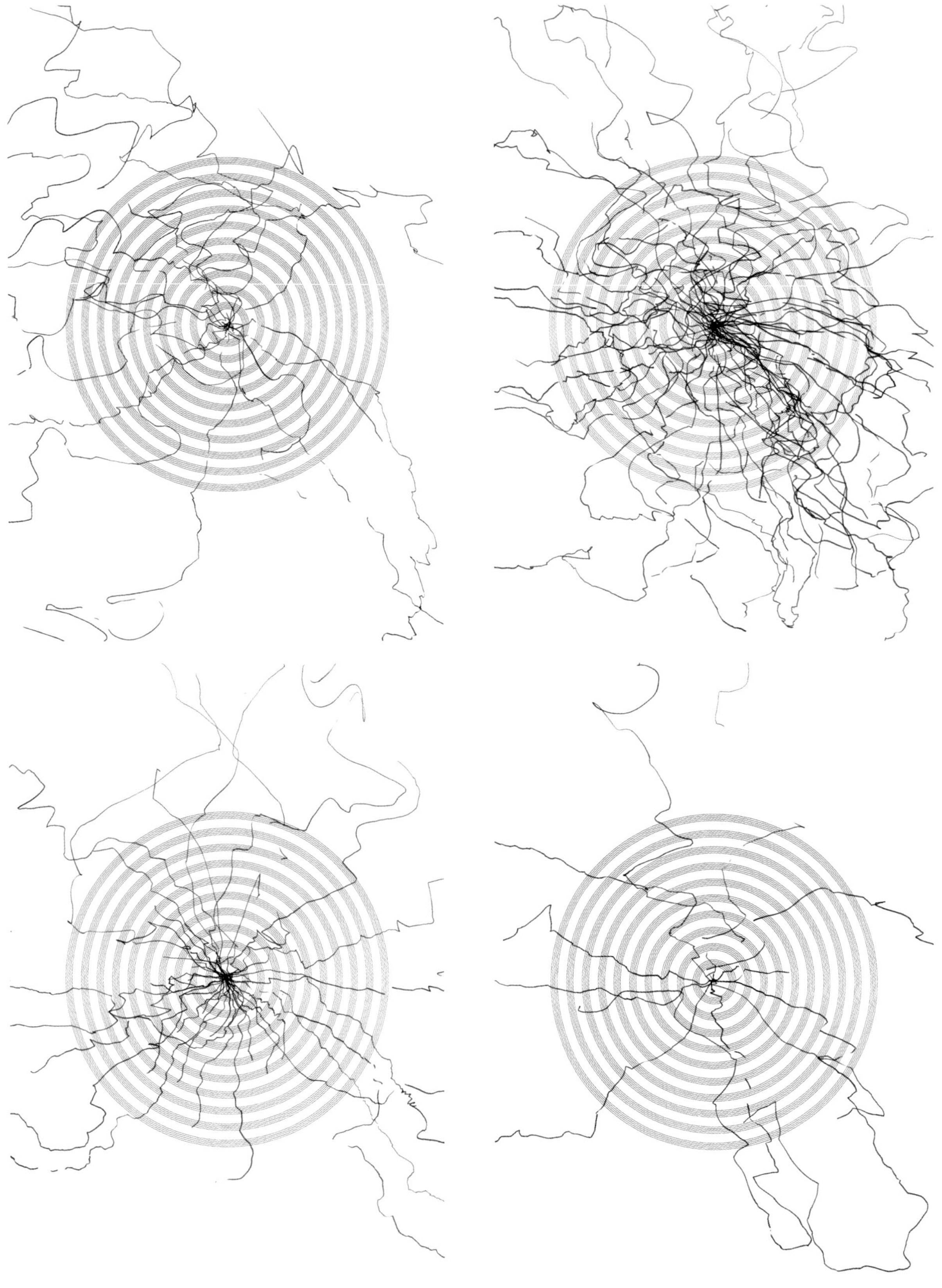

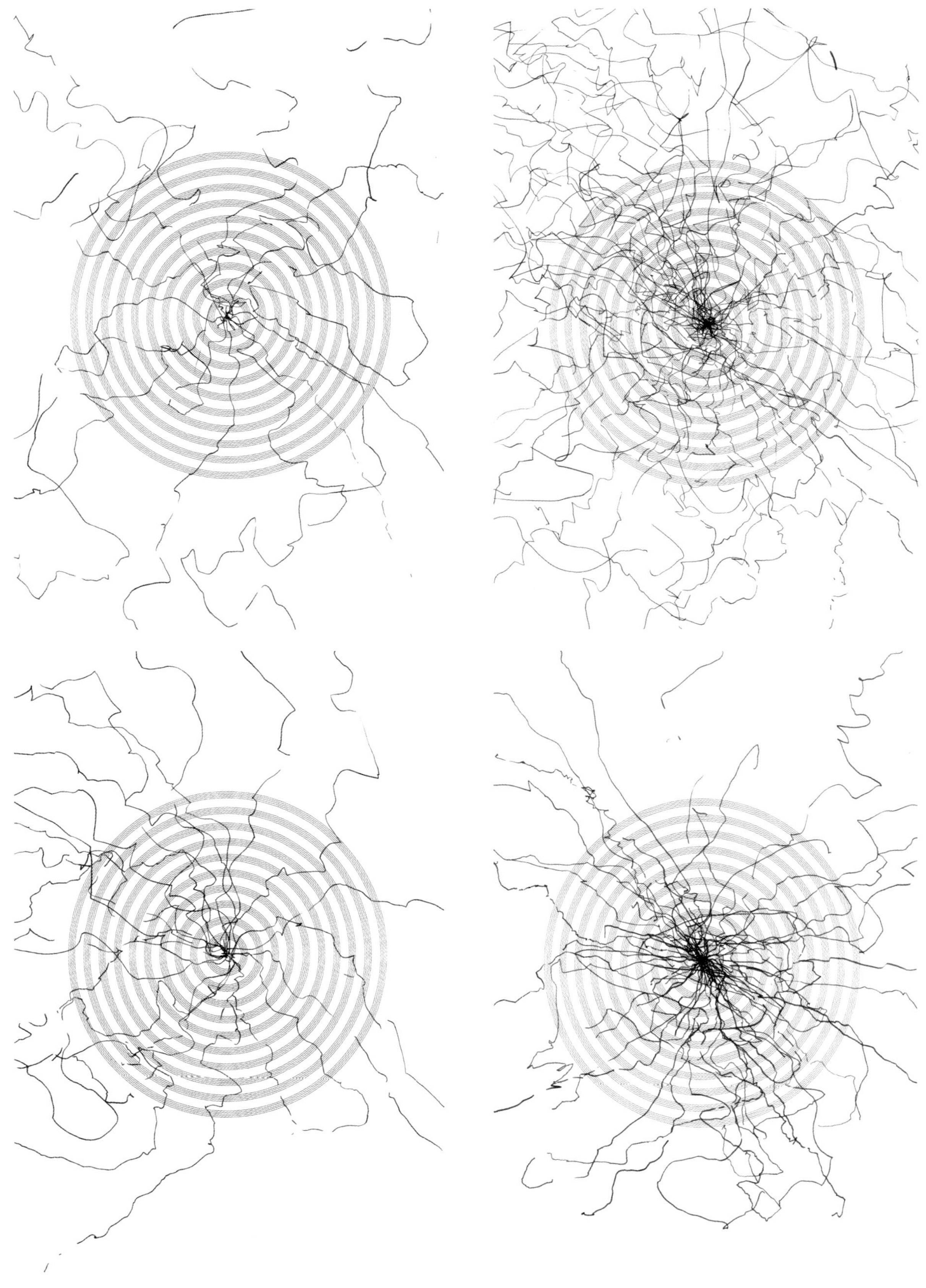

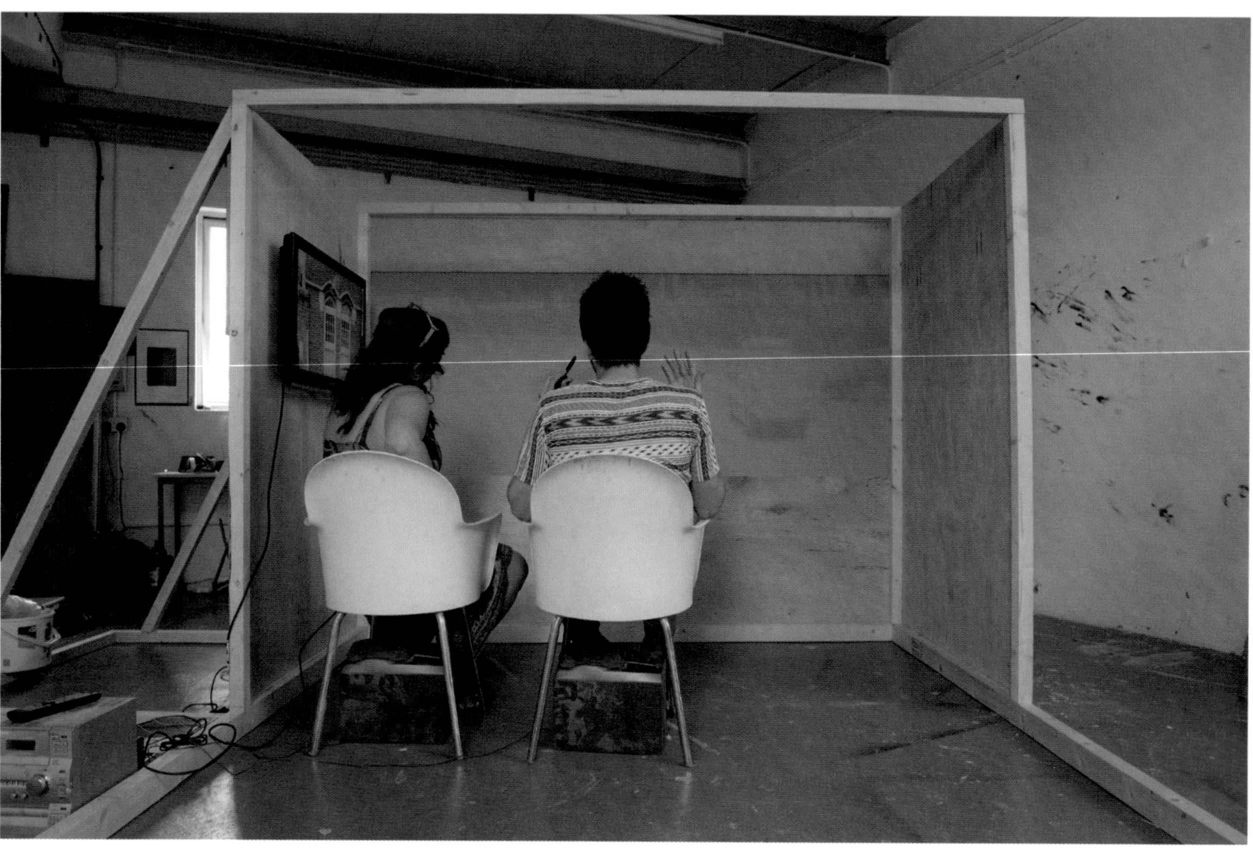

PP 74–75 William Mackrell, *Gaps, glitches and speed bumps*, 2015, hand-pulled screenprint with hand drawing in ink, 42 x 59.5 cm, edition of 30, each unique. Image courtesy the artist.

From left to right:

5 September: Route 52, Ladbroke Road, 4.33pm – Ladbroke Grove Station, 4.38pm, 5/30.

11 September: Route 9, Royal Albert Hall, 4.22pm – Aldwych, 4.50pm, 23/30.

5 September: Route 328, High Street Kensington, 4.20pm – Notting Hill Gate/ Pembridge Road, 4.28pm, 4/30.

5 September: Route 52, Ladbroke Grove Sainsbury's, 6.19pm – Willesden Bus Garage, 6.36pm (Bus driver shouts at me for missing final stop and ending up in the garage), 10/30.

12 September: Route 9, Hammersmith, 1.57pm – Road ahead blocked for march to support the refugees, turn around at Queens Gate and head back to Hammersmith, 1.41pm, 25/30.

12 September: Route 9, Hammersmith, 3.10pm – member of the public shouts "you guys need to see doctors" as we exit the bus at Holland Park Road, 3.17pm, 27/30.

5 September: Route 460, Willesden Bus Garage, 6.38pm – A friend from out of town coming to stay over calls me, I jump off at Melrose Avenue, 6.44pm, 11/30.

11 September: Route 9, Aldwych, 11.52am – Hammersmith Bus Station, 12.44pm, 20/30.

ABOVE William Mackrell rehearsing in his mocked up 'bus' at the studio during his residency.

Notes from the Studio

What made you decide to become a sculptor and when did your interest in performance develop?

Well, I think that the fluidity of working from a sculptural perspective has always appealed to me. Much of my work doesn't follow a particular medium and I see sculpture as loose enough to embrace my shifting process and the varying materials and methods I work with. It's interesting as, though sculpture is probably the closest category I would identify my work with, when I was at Chelsea College of Art for my BA, I was studying painting, although I would perhaps now recognise that, by the time I finished the degree, the work I was producing was more sculpture. I still have a strong interest in painting and along with drawing it has been a strong influence on my work from the start. The immediate act of a gesture, or a thought that mark-making evolves out of, is a key part of my practice now. For example, the series I recently performed at FOLD Gallery are very gestural: a wall drawing/sculptural intervention performance. Sculpture, for me, is taking the line of drawing and putting it into a three-dimensional and physical sphere where time and the unexpected all jostle and disrupt it.

With performance, I would say I fell into it quite accidently and only really began to recognise my work as performance in around 2009/2010. Around that time I made a work called *1000 Candles*, which was a response to a pocket torch I had in my studio which claimed to have 1,000 candlepower. I attempted to assemble 1,000 candles in my studio and then light them. This turned out to be very difficult. I couldn't reach, it got very hot, and then of course as soon as you got near the end, one would go out and you had to make the decision whether to stop or continue. When I made that piece, I had only ever thought about it as being a photograph, but when I got a video camera and started documenting, it really made me think about its physicality, the duration of the piece and the performative act inherent

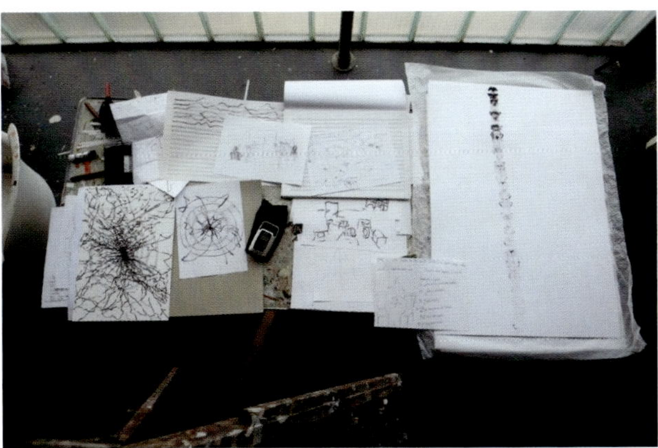

The artist's desk during his residency.

within it. So in a way I guess the performance aspect of my work was introduced through video, because it was video that helped me to see that *1000 Candles* was a live piece that didn't have to be contained within a frame. In fact, that's what I really like about performance: that it started freeing the work to be 'it is what it is' rather than trying to be 'art'.

But to confuse things further, I had actually been making performances long before then, but hadn't thought of them as anything more than a shot at finding a solution to a problem. In 2006, I was invited along with 30 other artists to a tiny island, Susak, in the Adriatic to see what might happen in a completely unfamiliar and isolated location. It was an idyllic place to be, but with all these artists it soon turned into an intense and claustrophobic atmosphere—a lot of people fell out. It became a like a Big Brother scenario, so I tried to escape for an afternoon by borrowing a table, umbrella and chairs from one of the two bars on the island and carried them into the sea in the hope of beginning a conversation offshore. Soon locals and people from the project joined with more chairs and then the guy working in the cafe waded out and asked if we'd like some drinks. That was probably the first performance to happen unintentionally, but in retrospect it holds a lot of value to me now for how I approach collective and participatory projects.

Who are the artists and theorists you most admire and which have had the greatest impact on your thinking and your work?

My tutor at Chelsea, Angela de la Cruz, was hugely influential in breaking down my work and helping me find my way to a language of working. Historic figures whom I hugely admire are Joseph Beuys—I am also quite curious about his shamanistic activities and his teaching and blackboard pieces—and, of course, Bas Jan Ader and filmmaker Andrei Tarkovsky. Their works delve deep into the poetic, political and absurdities of humanity. Also Paul McCarthy, particularly his really rough early works, which really bring out the madness of the studio and resonate so politically about their time and human folly.

Theorists I am interested in, and the two I have been looking at a lot recently as I find them particularly relevant to the ambulatory residency, are Henri Lefebvre and Paul Virilio. Lefebvre's *Rhythmanalysis* brings together the overlooked connectivity of rhythm, time and movement in the everyday, and has been in constant use over the last few months. And Virilio's book *The Aesthetics of Disappearance* unravels the delicate juncture between dreaming and being awake in the dizzying speeds of 24/7 culture and its relentless nature. For me both are a really interesting precursor to how we live now in an age of image saturation.

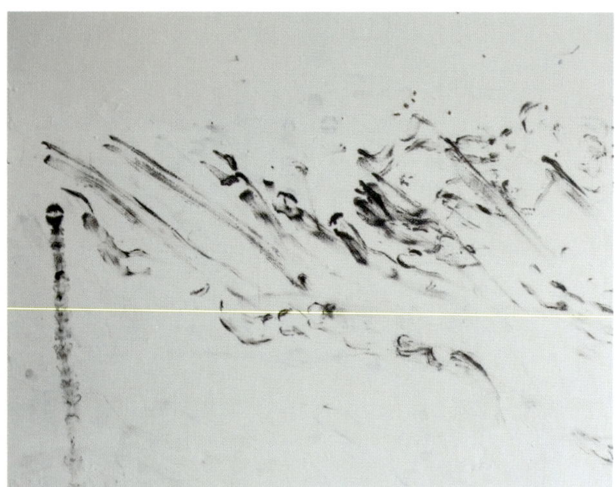

Preparatory lipstick wall drawings for the *In an instant* series of "studio feelings" performed during PerFORMa, FOLD Gallery, London, 2015.

Tell me about your interest in the site-specific and how it relates to performance as a genre?

It starts from the body being one's own site. *Gaps, glitches and speed bumps*, my intervention that will take place on a public London bus, explores the interrelation between the internal and external effect of the bus on the body. Looking at the way air moves through your lungs on the bus, how your diaphragm is effected by the reverberations and vibrations, and the way your body is thrown in an almost spherical direction by the bus in transit. I would say it's a hybrid of body and site, which makes this work site-specific because the viewer effectively becomes the site. It is also about the city and its rhythms as a site. The bus is not just a space on wheels; it feeds its way through the city with traffic and lights constantly disrupting and breaking its flow. The whole thing is about how time is always moving and, in a way, addresses the fact that the site-specific itself is more often than not a temporary experience.

I think that could almost be applied in any circumstance with art; even when you're hanging an artwork in a gallery you take into account small factors such as where the light is in the room.

I guess my interest in the site-specific started around the same time as my interest in performance developed, around 2010. I mean; the site-specific has really always just been there. I don't really know how to work without it, because I feel like it's so intrinsic to producing work. Whatever you are producing it is always in reaction to the time and space in which you are living. The site-specific is always there.

What is the importance of the audience experience to you and how do you hope your work will impact on those who witness your performances?

Considering your audience is necessary, as the live element of the work hinges on how you invite or position the audience within a live dialogue. Whether the work will be liked or not is something I cannot decide, but how they might reach the project, begin to enter into it, has to be thought about, and *Gaps, glitches and speed bumps* being the most precarious and unannounced live work I've attempted, I have to consider a range of responses I might receive from the public.

The key thing is really that the audience can step into the work quite quickly from a visual or sensory perspective. I am not looking to push a particular ideology or message onto the work, or onto the audience. It's about letting the audience come to the work and then letting them run with the idea. I like there to be elements you can grasp that are just about everyday experiences, how the work highlights their own space, their journeys, and the motions they go through within this familiar but transitional space.

Talk to me about your interest in incorporating sound into your work.

With sound, like time, it is the fragile and vulnerable qualities that attract me, its immediacy is an exciting prospect that leaves no trail of itself, but embodies the presence of memory by inhabiting a space for a moment. Like the smell of a club or music venue the morning after sound has this incredibly sensory power you can do so much with. In many ways I also find music more open, more democratic than 'art' in the fine art sense. So *Gaps, glitches and speed bumps* will attempt to work off music's relationship to line drawing.

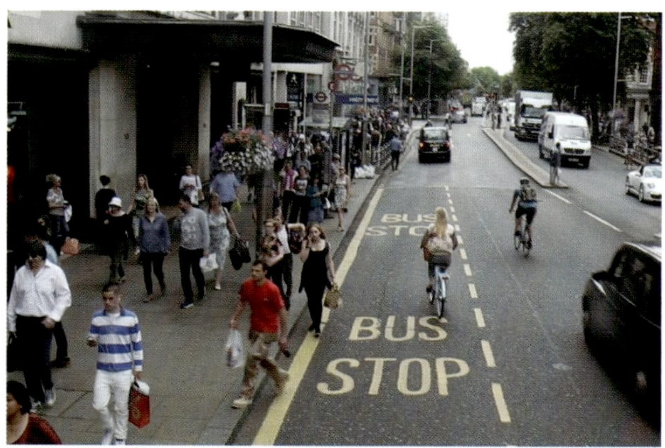

View from no 9 bus, High Street Kensington. Image courtesy the artist.

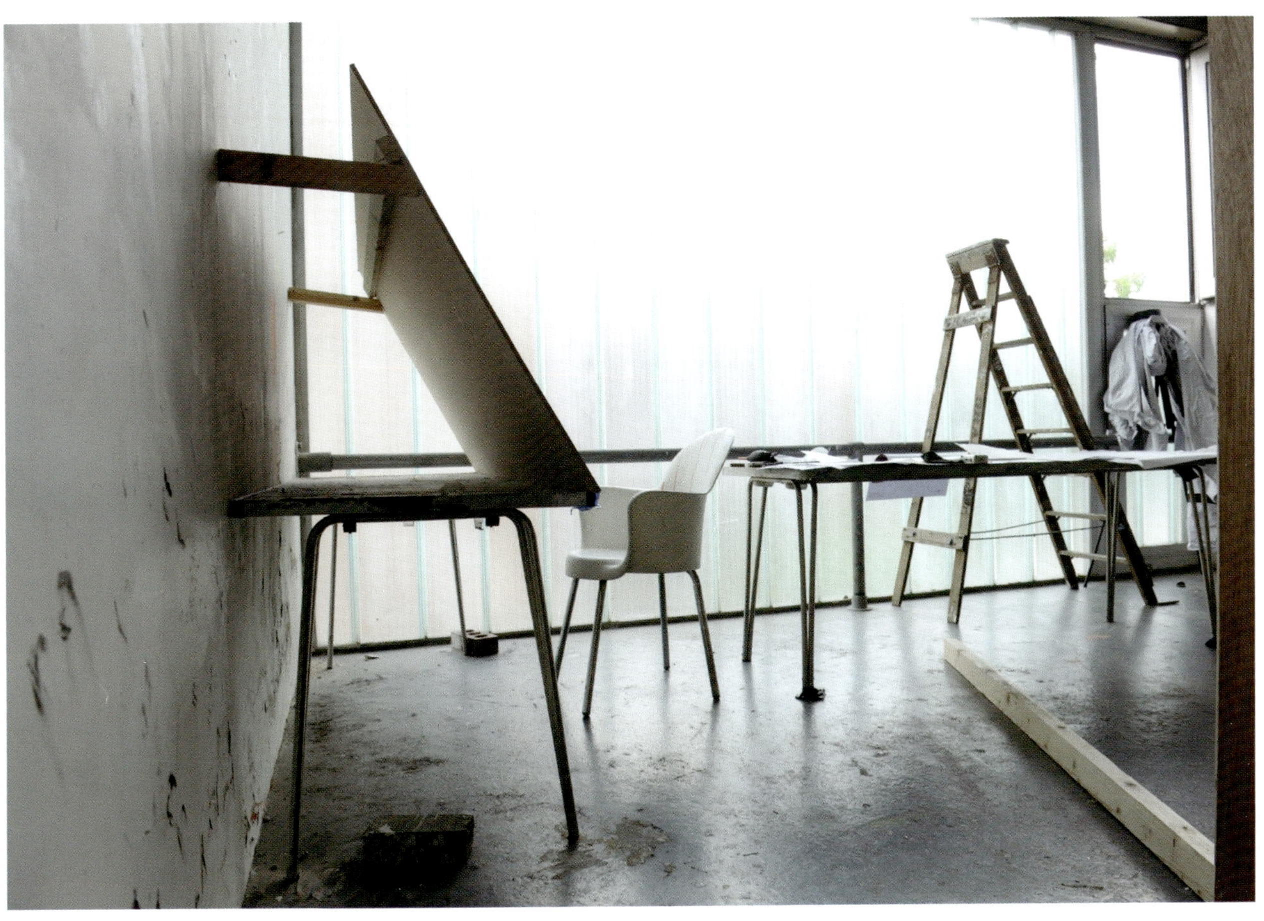

William Mackrell's studio during his residency.

William Mackrell's *Gaps, glitches and speed bumps,* 2015—Dave Beech

We understand space as the sphere of the possibility of the existence of multiplicity in the sense of contemporaneous plurality; as the sphere in which distinct trajectories coexist; as the sphere therefore of coexisting heterogeneity.

Doreen Massey

Performance is often described in terms of the body, spectatorship, duration, the spoken word, narrative. In art institutions, it is included among what has come to be known as time-based practices or live arts. Amelia Jones, for instance, notes that performance has been "privileged precisely through its ephemerality and immediacy". The current anxiety about the documentation and re-enactment of performance confirms the perception that performance is impermanent in a strong sense. Everybody knows that performances occur in spaces, but typically the performance is seen as something separate that is brought to the space and disappears from the space once it is over. In this way, performance has been theorised as primarily temporal rather than primarily spatial.

William Mackrell's work combines sculpture with performance (including print and photography too) in a way that not only adds a temporal dimension to the sculptural sphere of objects, but adds a spatial element to it as well. Not the kind of spatiality that animates installation art (a sort of extrapolation of the 'spaces' within paintings and sculptures), nor the bounded concept of space that attaches site-specific art to physical spaces. Mackrell's work traverses the spatial dynamics of geography. I am not thinking of the traditional conception of geography as the study of territory or the poststructural misconception of space as the "domestication of time", to use Ernesto Laclau's words. Mackrell's works respond to place and space through an embodied reflection.

Deux Chevaux, 2014, consists of a Citroën 2CV harnessed to two horses and driven, or ridden, through various specific places. Given its original purpose to supply motorised transport to farmers still using horses and carts in 1930s France, Mackrell's montaging of these two modes of transport into one functional vehicle is an historical conundrum. If conceptually it is a temporal folding of history upon itself, it has a strong geographical significance in its realisation. A great deal of Mackrell's time was taken up in negotiating with the local authorities to obtain written permission to take the horse-drawn car along specific routes at specific times.

His walking piece, *Going to the Gallery*, 2013, is a spatial study. Writing the words "going to the gallery" on a roll of paper as he makes his way on foot from the studio to the gallery, Mackrell links two places not only through his action but through his mantra. While still outside the studio he writes "going to the gallery", as if the two spaces were already, through his intention, bridged and bonded. As well as the movement of the artist from one place to another, a roll of paper, now absent from the studio is left in the gallery. This work thus transposes the experience of space into what might have once been called a piece of text art, which appears in the gallery as a little heap, not unlike Robert Morris' iconic piles of felt, of displaced material.

At least since the early eighteenth century, a man who walked from his studio to a gallery would be a bearer of spatial displacement. Daniel Defoe celebrated this in his panegyric to trade: "The cloth for the man's coat comes from Yorkshire;... the waistcoat... from Norwich. The breeches are... from Devizes, Wilts.... His yarn stockings are from Westmorland. His hat is a felt from

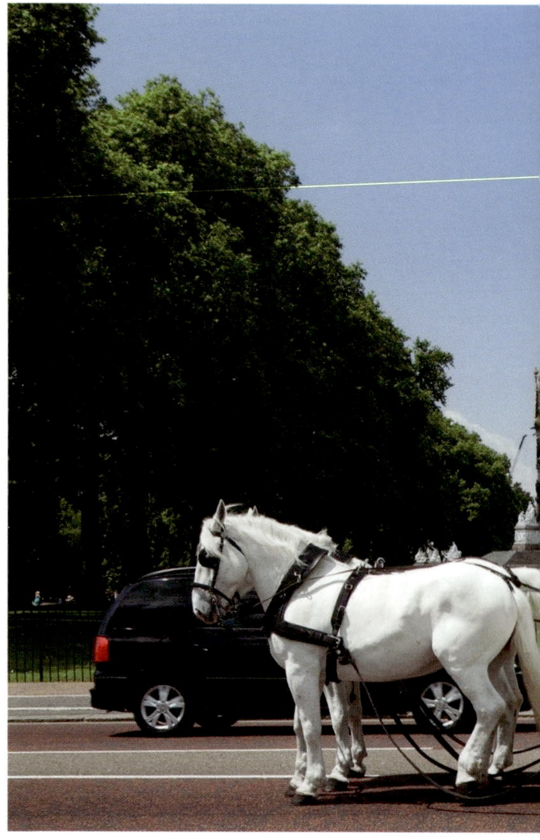

William Mackrell, *Deux Chevaux*, 2014, live performance, duration 5 hrs and 6 miles in which two horses towed the artist in the classic French "two horsepower" motorcar, the Citroën 2CV, through the streets of Kensington and Chelsea and Westminster via the Serpentine, Hyde Park, Natural History Museum and Royal Albert Hall. Image courtesy the artist.

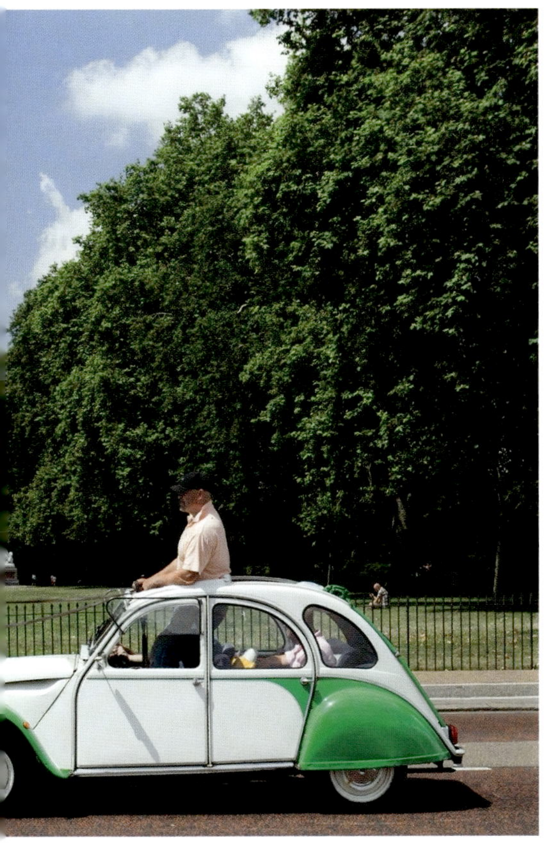

Leicester. His leather gloves come from Somerset, his shoes from Northampton." Today, David Harvey asks where your breakfast comes from (sugar, coffee, milk, cups, etc), saying that these products link you with millions of workers around the globe. He calls these "spatial linkages". Mackrell's works create spatial linkages that make visible the invisible threads that connect places together.

Gaps, glitches and speed bumps, commissioned by RBS for the Ambulatory category of Sculpture Shock in 2015, makes its way, eventually, to the gallery, but it takes place largely on public transport. Sat upstairs on the bus, Mackrell draws lines that are scattered by the swaying, stopping and swerving that jolts all the passengers. He draws on a print of sheet music in which the rows of lines have been bent into a circle. At the same time, four singers chart the journey with improvised sounds, stopping abruptly whenever the bus reaches a stop or a red light. Fellow travellers turn to listen and look, pointing and whispering, giggling and smiling.

"The real import of spatiality", critical geographer Doreen Massey says, is "the possibility of multiple narratives", or what she calls "coevalness". *Gaps, glitches and speed bumps* is Mackrell's most coeval work to date. The bus has a fixed route and is timetabled according to a semi-rigorous schedule, but the people who jump on and jump off have their own destinations and their own narratives. Buses are public, not in the Habermasian sense of places where opinions are exchanged and public opinion is formed collectively, but in the sense of a zone in which people come together temporarily and share space, like a park, a zoo or a shopping mall. Like the scenes portrayed by Manet, then, the bus is a conspicuous reminder of the city as a place of coeval existence. Mackrell's intervention in the bus, by adding just one or two new narratives to the scene, highlights the fact that there were multiple narratives here all along.

Mackrell did not hire a private bus to realise his drawings and improvised singing. It would have been reasonable to do so, but if he had, then the work would have remained spatial but would have been far less coeval. The route that the private bus took would have been determined solely by the artist and the fellow passengers would have been there to witness the work. By joining a public bus on its regular journey, carrying passengers to their individual destinations, Mackrell's work inserts itself into the space that others occupy for their own purposes, mid-stream so to speak. The work belongs in the same space, in the same intersection of journeys and narratives that any passenger would encounter walking down a busy street, catching a train or stepping onto the bus.

Taxi drivers famously enjoy the full benefits of coevalness, but taxi passengers do not. If we do not typically experience the coevalness of bus journeys in full, this is because our journeys are shaped by the polite avoidance of fellow passengers. In fact, coevalness is generally not something that we experience directly. It is a background feature that structures contemporary life. Like the spatial linkages that pins your breakfast to the world without you necessarily having any idea about what these linkages actually are, coevalness is structural not phenomenological. Mackrell makes coevalness phenomenological by assigning the movement and noise of passengers to the score of the work.

James Clifford roots the practice of travelling in the Greek term theoria: "Theory is a practice of travel and observation... a product of displacement. To theorize, one leaves home." Aesthetics is the result of a similar process, applied to objects and subjects alike. The modern institutions of art—including the public museum, the emergence of an art public and the publishing of art criticism—were unprecedented, but can be understood best as based on the modern experience of Greek and Roman artefacts displaced from their original contexts. Art and aesthetics are born when crafted objects left home, or, more precisely, were seised by foreigners. Art is in a perpetual state of leaving home. What *Gaps, glitches and speed bumps* demonstrates is that the displacement of the aesthetic from the museum does not return it to a pre-aesthetic function or utility, but percolates the aesthetic through small pockets of the everyday.

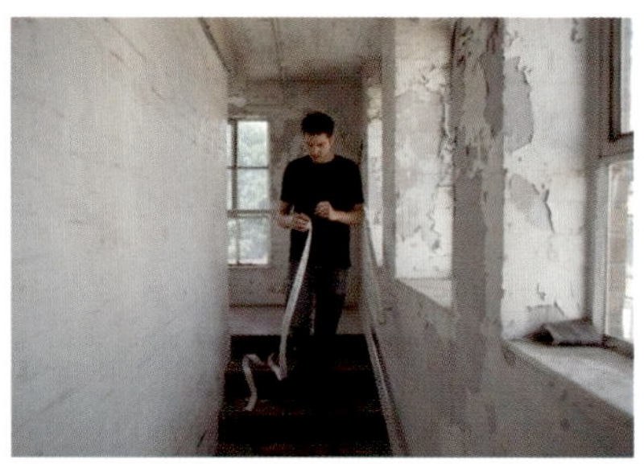
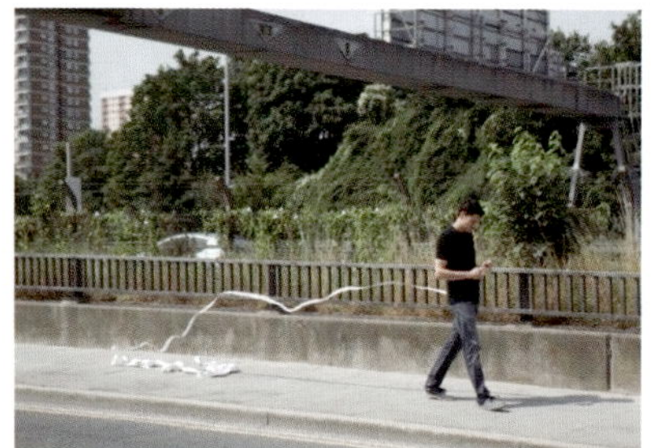
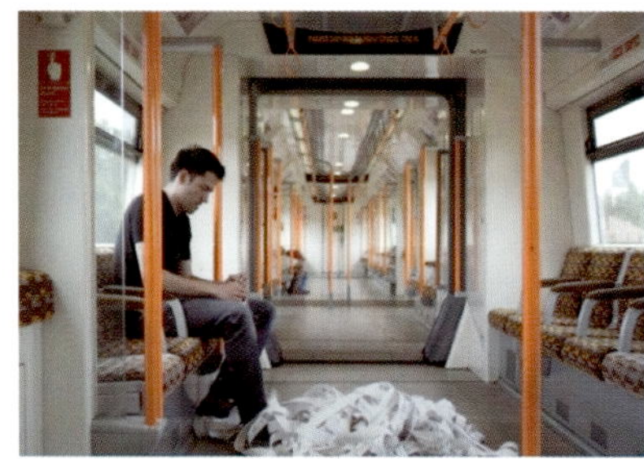
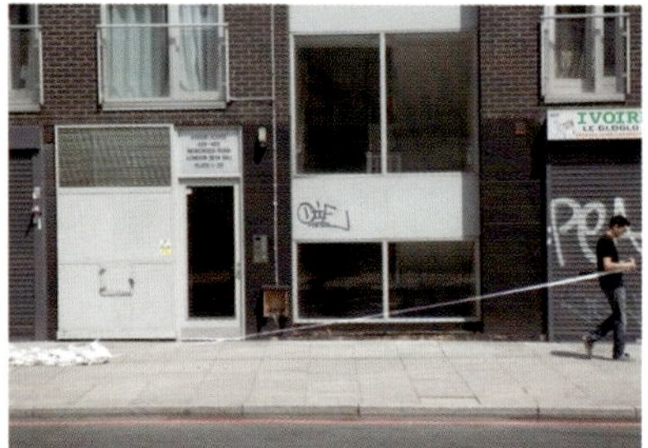
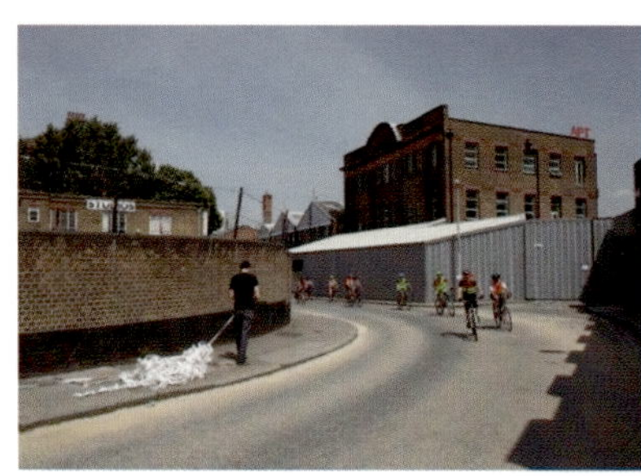
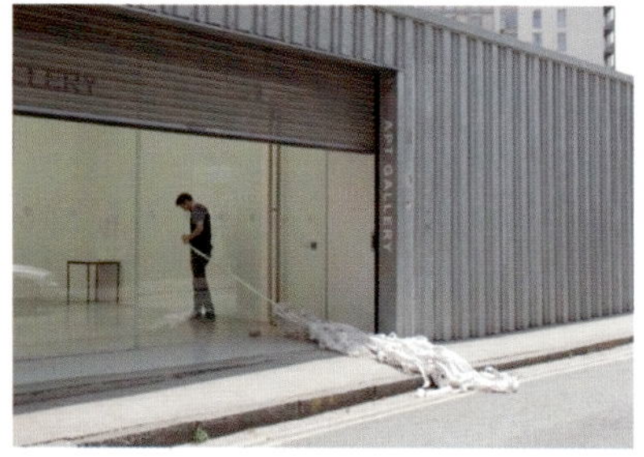

William Mackrell, *Going to the Gallery* (detail), 2013, live performance, repetitive writing in pen and ink on till roll from the artist's studio to the gallery, dimensions variable. Image courtesy the artist.

Site-Specificity and Recent Sculpture—Dave Beech

Modern sculpture used to occupy space with indifference. It was a matter of principle. Sculpture demonstrated its integrity by not being compromised by its site. Before modernity, by contrast, sculpture was more often than not commissioned for a particular purpose and place and was generally integrated into the architecture or other physical characteristics of the site. Modernism broke with tradition by breaking away from works being rooted in one particular place. This development has sometimes been interpreted as a consequence of art's new mobility as a commodity that passes from one owner to the next and from one collection to the next. However, the independence of artworks from their locations belongs to a much broader sequence of formal and technical emancipations of art from any trace of them being tokens of aristocratic magnificence. Art seemed freer when it was no longer encased in a particular physical space.

As high modernism congealed into a rigid dogma and subsequently lost its impetus to postmodernism in the 1960s and 1970s, the relationship between art and its sites shifted conscientiously from indifference to attentiveness. Issues around site became prominent for the first time with Land Art, epitomised by the work of Nancy Holt, and Robert Smithson's iconic earthworks such as *Spiral Jetty*, 1970, including his important theoretical distinction between site and non-site. One of the earliest published uses of the term "site-specificity" in art criticism came in Craig Owens' agenda-setting two-part article "The Allegorical Impulse" in *October* magazine in 1980 in which he describes Land Art as merging physically with its setting, like prehistoric monumentality. Following this, Rosalyn Deutsche made a critical distinction between assimilative and interruptive site-specificity.[1]

Site-specificity was stretched by being merged with what used to be called "environment art" or installation. While early installation art often filled the gallery and was experienced as an immersive whole, it was possible for it to be installed anywhere, even if it was held just once in a particular place. That is to say, the work did not address itself to the specificities of the site, but treated the space as an abstraction, as the frame for the work, as the empty background, or as having certain dimensions. What installation did, however, was to resituate the question of site indoors as a set of questions about buildings, places, occupancy and the social environment. Gordon Matta-Clark's key artworks included shooting at the windows of a building and removing sections of existing buildings. Rather than placing his sculpture within a building, he sculpted the site itself. Site-specificity now no longer belonged in remote encounters with monumental nature as it did with Land Art. The artist's engagement with site was expanded, not only to include urban spaces and buildings but also galleries and museums.

Site-specificity took on a new political hue when museums and galleries were subject to institutional critique.[2] Hans Haacke's exhibition at the Guggenheim Museum, which thematised the business dealings of the museum's trustees, was site-specific in a new way. Michael Asher removed the wall separating the gallery from the office space of Claire Copley Gallery in Los Angeles in 1974, making the site the form and content of the work. The work is not only specific to this site; the site provides the materials, theme and politics of the work. Miwon Kwon's poststructuralist rethinking of site-specificity as community specificity partly through an analysis of the work of Suzanne Lacy,[3] cross-fertilises site-specific sculpture with what used to be called community arts or socially-engaged art.[4] Sites are charged with social meanings by those who use them and the concept of site therefore is no longer restricted to physical or architectural qualities: the site is primarily a place occupied by social groups. Works by artists such as Pepón Osorio are site-specific not only by being exhibited in storefronts, department stores and private homes, but by working with local communities, their materials, their culture and their personal stories.

Insofar as the physical dimension of site-specificity has been downgraded, the historical bond between site-specificity and sculpture has been weakened. Sculpture, understood as an object experienced visually in three dimensions, had already lost ground to time-based mediums in the second half of the twentieth century, and appeared, therefore, to be anchored in modernism and had remained contemporary by interrogating site. Richard Wilson's site-specific deconstructions of buildings, such as *Turning the Place Over*, 2008, a slowly rotating 10-metre ovoid slice of a building's facade, imbues the physical properties of architecture with the qualities of dance or a video loop. Mike Nelson's constructions of interior spaces within galleries are less like performance and more like the theatrical setting for a performance. In both cases, however, contemporary sculpture takes on some of the qualities of time-based art. Adding time to sculpture separates it from the modernist sensibility that threatens to isolate it from contemporary concerns.

Site-specificity from the outset, even while it remained steadfastly physical, was conspicuously temporary. And sculpture had embraced temporality in the 1960s with the development of performance art. Before the term "performance" took hold, other terms such as "body art" appeared more accurate because this kind of art was an extrapolation of sculpture in which the body was the material to be sculpted. Gilbert and George's *Singing Sculpture*, 1969, and Bruce McLean's *Pose Works for Plinths*, 1971, are exemplary because they put performances in precisely those places set aside for sculptures. Performance injects the temporal into sculpture, and site-specificity grounds art practice in the networks and exchanges of place. When site-specificity merges with performance, therefore, two distinct traditions of contemporary sculpture are allied in a temporally and spatially dynamic practice.

Some recent sculpture has embraced performance and site-specificity without the burden of redefining what sculpture is or can be and without taking on the dreaded ontological question, "what is art?" Once it has been established that anything can be art and sculpture cannot delimit itself as a medium, the big questions lose their urgency and are replaced with countless micro concerns through form, technique, inter-subjectivity, meaning, agency, collaboration and dialogue. Participatory art, including relational aesthetics[5] and the social turn,[6] is always a kind of site-specific performance in which the distinction between the performer and the audience is called into question.

Amy Sharrocks, one of the Sculpture Shock artists in residence, uses performance within a participatory mode of address that has its roots in site-specificity and body art. She brings people together to participate in dialogical and physical acts that focus on the body as a simultaneously physical and emotional entity. For Sculpture Shock, Sharrocks led workshops in falling. Falling is more vulnerable than leaning, certainly in the way that Bruce McLean did it in 1971. Unlike the pose, the fall is not usually performed as a spectacle for others. If they are witnessed, you wish that they were not. Falling is almost always humiliating. If it were not so emotionally and formally charged, the idea of making art by falling might be considered to be scandalous. After all, anybody can fall. Infants fall before they can walk and consequently falling is infantilising. In Donald Davidson's terms, falling is an event not an act because it is not the result of an intention.[7] Falling is what you do when you lose control. *Season for Falling* confronts the shame of falling and dispels the *schadenfreude* of

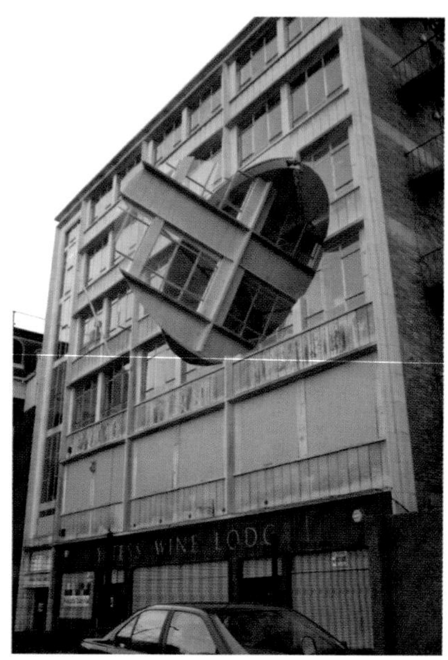

Richard Wilson, *Turning the Place Over*, 2008, Liverpool European Capital of Culture. Image courtesy the artist.

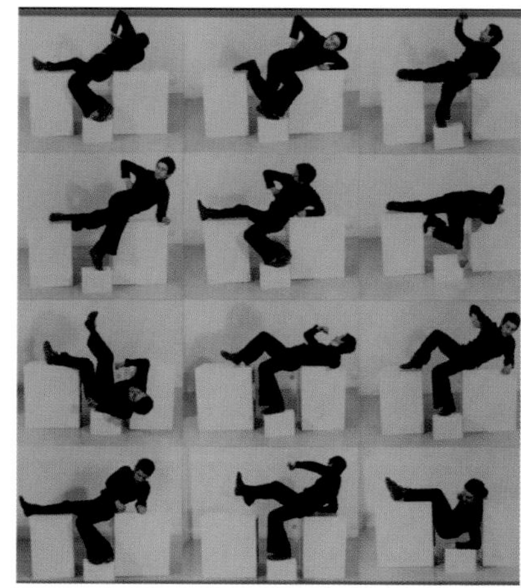

Bruce McLean, *Pose Work for Plinths 3*, 1971, 12 photographs, gelatin silver prints on paper on board, 75 x 68.2 cm. Photography © Tate, London 2016.

watching someone fall by constructing a community of care around meticulously choreographed collective acts of falling.

As well as connoting desire, tragedy and defeat (falling in love, the fallen woman, fallen heroes), falling pertains to one of the key conceptual concerns of modernist sculpture, namely gravity. Robert Morris' iconic piles of felt were the Minimalist answer to the traditional sculptural preoccupation with gravity. Rather than building materials up into sculpture, Morris simply let them fall to the ground as sculpture, forsaking the kind of mastery traditionally associated with sculpture for a different relationship to materials, dexterity, choice and authority. Falling, dripping, dropping and collapsing might be the negation of architecture, but they are legitimate processes for contemporary sculpture. Sharrocks' falling workshops are collective acts of pouring materials onto the floor. Bodies collapse not in pain or misfortune, but in deliberate acts of placement and arrangement. However, falling bodies cannot be considered in a purely aesthetic way. Falling is a bodily equivalent of bad taste: it occurs unintentionally and yet appears to show the world exactly who we are. This is why making sculpture from falling risks its own authority. By teaching us to think about falling differently, Sharrocks' *Season for Falling* asks us to be more humane to one another and simultaneously less dogmatic about sculpture.

Alexander Costello's Sculpture Shock work, ironically titled *Making Progress*, is a public performance in which the artist, wearing a white suit and attached in the place of a figurehead to the bow of a barge, points ahead while proceeding at 2 miles per hour along the canals between Tottenham and St John's Wood. It is classically site-specific insofar as it takes place on a specific route, and it classically puts the artist's body in a place set aside for sculpture. Despite these facts, the work has a more nuanced and critical relationship to the dual histories of site-specificity and performance. The specificity of site is sardonically abolished in Costello's leisurely cancellation of the future because, by eliminating the purpose from his journey, he annuls the difference between places. Movement, here, is absurd because nothing happens and nowhere counts as a destination. Nevertheless, *Making Progress* is also a reinstatement of site-specificity insofar as the work exists in a spatial sequence with no temporal qualities. By ridiculing time, this is a performance that moves at the speed of a monument. Temporal progress is sacrificed for spatial procession. Literally passing one place after another, in a non-hierarchical sequence, like a road movie or a Minimalist grid.

Making Progress is constructed around a narrative of the collapse of narrative which is also, simultaneously, an absurd gesture that confirms Berardi's theory of the death of the future.[8] Cruising the heritage waterways, Costello mocks the modernist belief in progress by subtracting historical time and its urgencies from the narrative of moving forwards. Costello epitomises the unrushed, gentle movement of leisure in a world of accelerated information and global traffic. His pointing finger is a "shifter", like the words "I", "here", "you" and "tomorrow", which says only "here", "here", "here", "here".[9] It subverts progress because it is indifferent about where it is going. *Making Progress* makes no progress not only because it gives the finger to the future but also because it doesn't point to anywhere specifically. Costello treats the implausibility of temporal progress as the absurd implausibility of getting closer to a destination, and also that it consists of a journey purposefully executed without the sense of an ending.[10] In this sense, Costello's task of endurance can also be interpreted as sculpture's revenge against time-based media. However, rather than succumbing to inertia, the pointing finger bears a trace of desire—of loss and drive—albeit in quotation marks.

Gaps, glitches and speed bumps is William Mackrell's conclusion to his Sculpture Shock residency. It takes an experiential and aesthetic interest in public transport that pays no attention to destinations, direction or any other mundane objectives. Instead, he uses the movements of the bus—stopping, starting, swaying and stuttering—in a technically precise act of deskilling: forcing his pen to move in directions not determined by the artist's hand or taste or skill or intention. Or, looked at from the other direction, so to speak, the bus uses Mackrell to draw a continual line across a page—a modified print of sheet music—in which time is turned into space. Time, which is usually apportioned in precise measures by musical notation, is cancelled or frozen in an infinite image of musical circularity on which spatial movement is inscribed. They look like wheels. Reading these scores is a form of tracing a journey as a bodily experience, which is to say an aesthetic experience of a journey uprooted from the linear narrative of origin and destination.

The four singers which augment Mackrell's public performance provide a kind of abstract running commentary on the movements of the bus that are guiding Mackrell's pen across the modified sheet music. Like a vinyl-record player, the pen resembles a stylus that converts movement into sound, with the singers acting as the speakers that amplify the shared experience of the bus moving along the street. Passengers experience the bodily jostling of the bus' more vividly as they hear the voices of these singers halt, soar, fizzle out and suddenly burst into song. Fellow travellers are turned into an embodied audience that is more than an aggregate of ears and musical taste, but is constituted of organs, flesh and bones that are carried by a form of mass transport. This work, therefore, merges site-specificity and performance with the techniques associated with guerrilla street theatre[11] or what Rebecca French and Andrew Mottershead call "micro interventions into everyday rituals".[12]

Mackrell's work plays on and against Gabriel Tarde's distinction between the crowd and the public. In his 1898 essay *"Le public et la foule"*, Tarde said the crowd is ancient whereas the public is only possible after the invention of the printing press. The crowd is a congregation of bodies in a place (Tarde specifies the pulpit, the lectern, the platform and the stage, but he might have also included the bus, the train and the aeroplane), whereas the public is linked by publications and is therefore spatially dispersed. Also, while it is possible to belong "simultaneously to several publics", one can belong only to "one crowd at a time".[13] Finally, while there is a limit to the size of crowds, "the public can be extended indefinitely".[14] Neither markets nor states produce a public. Consumers have cash, voters have votes, but members of a public have opinions, make judgements and hold values that they express by responding to and producing publications, including well-constructed arguments but also applause, heckles, chants and boos. Mackrell adds acts of publication—vocal performance and drawing—to the space of the crowd, which turns the crowd into a public, or treats the crowd as if it were or could become a public. Art always constructs its own social relations in the very act of constructing artworks. Mackrell's site-specificity is not a form of community-specificity, though, but a spatial act that transforms social relations with aesthetics.

1. Deutsche, Rosalyn, "Tilted Arc and the Uses of Public Space", *Design Book Review*, no 23, 1992, pp 22–27 and "Uneven Development: Public Art in New York City", *October* 47, 1988, pp 3–52.

2. Alberro, Alexander and Blake Stimson, *Institutional Critique: an Anthology of Artists Writings*, Cambridge, MA: MIT Press, 2009.

3. Kwon, Miwon, *One Place After Another: Site-Specific Art and Locational Identity*, Cambridge, MA: MIT Press, 2002.

4. Lacy, Suzanne, *Mapping the Terrain: New Genre Public Art*, Seattle: Bay Press, 1994.

5. Bourriaud, Nicolas, *Relational Aesthetics*, Dijon: Les Presses du Réel, 2002.

6. Bishop, Claire, "The Social Turn: Collaboration and Its Discontents", *Artforum*, February 2006, pp 178–183.

7. Davidson, Donald, *Essays on Actions and Events*, Oxford: Clarendon Press, 2001.

8. Berardi, Franco Bifo, *After the Future*, Arianna Bove, Melinda Cooper, Erik Empson, Enrico, Giuseppina Mecchia and Tiziana Terranova trans, Oakland, CA: AK Press, 2011.

9. A "shifter" is a technical term in the study of language. Shifters are those words, such as "here", "there", "now", "tomorrow", "you" and "me", whose meaning shifts according to who is using the word, when and where. See Jakobson, Roman, "Shifters and Verbal Categories", 1956, *On Language*, Linda R Waugh and Monique Monville-Burston eds, Cambridge, MA: Harvard University Press, 1990, pp 386–392; and Jespersen, Otto, *Language: Its Nature, Development and Origin*, London: Allen and Unwin, 1959 (1923).

10. The phrase "the sense of an ending" is emblematic of Frank Kermode's theory of narrative. See Kermode, Frank, *The Sense of an Ending: Studies in the Theory of Fiction*, Oxford: Oxford University Press, 1967.

11. Lesnick, Henry ed, *Guerilla Street Theatre*, New York: Avon Books, 1973.

12. Mottershead, French, "Micro Interventions Into Everyday Rituals", *Art Papers Magazine*, vol 30, issue 4, July/August 2006.

13. Tarde, Gabriel, *On Communication and Social Influence*, Chicago: University of Chicago Press, 1969, p 281.

14. Tarde, *On Communication and Social Influence*, p 281.

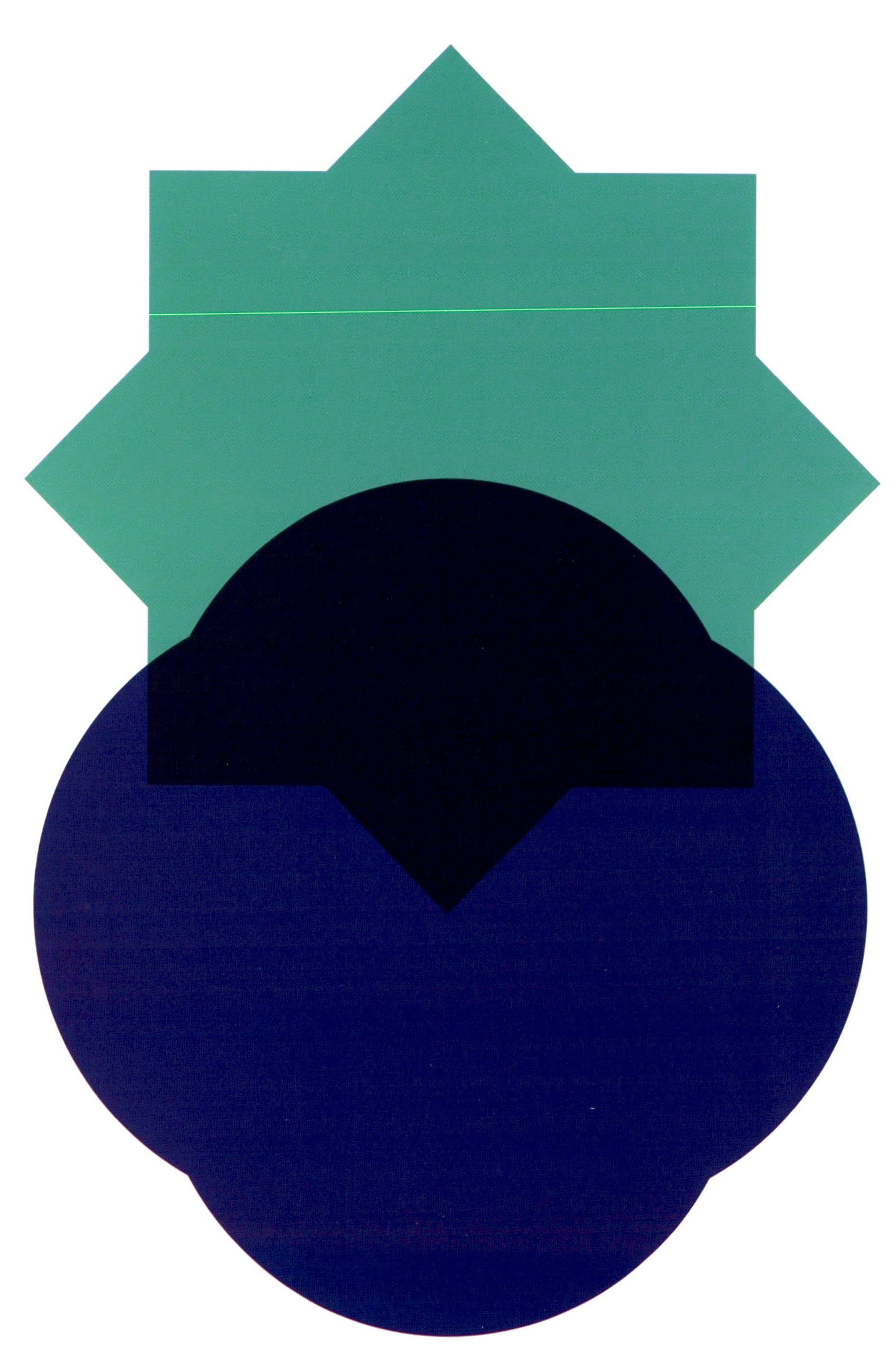

Historic

**Nika Neelova
Holy Trinity, Sloane Square, London**

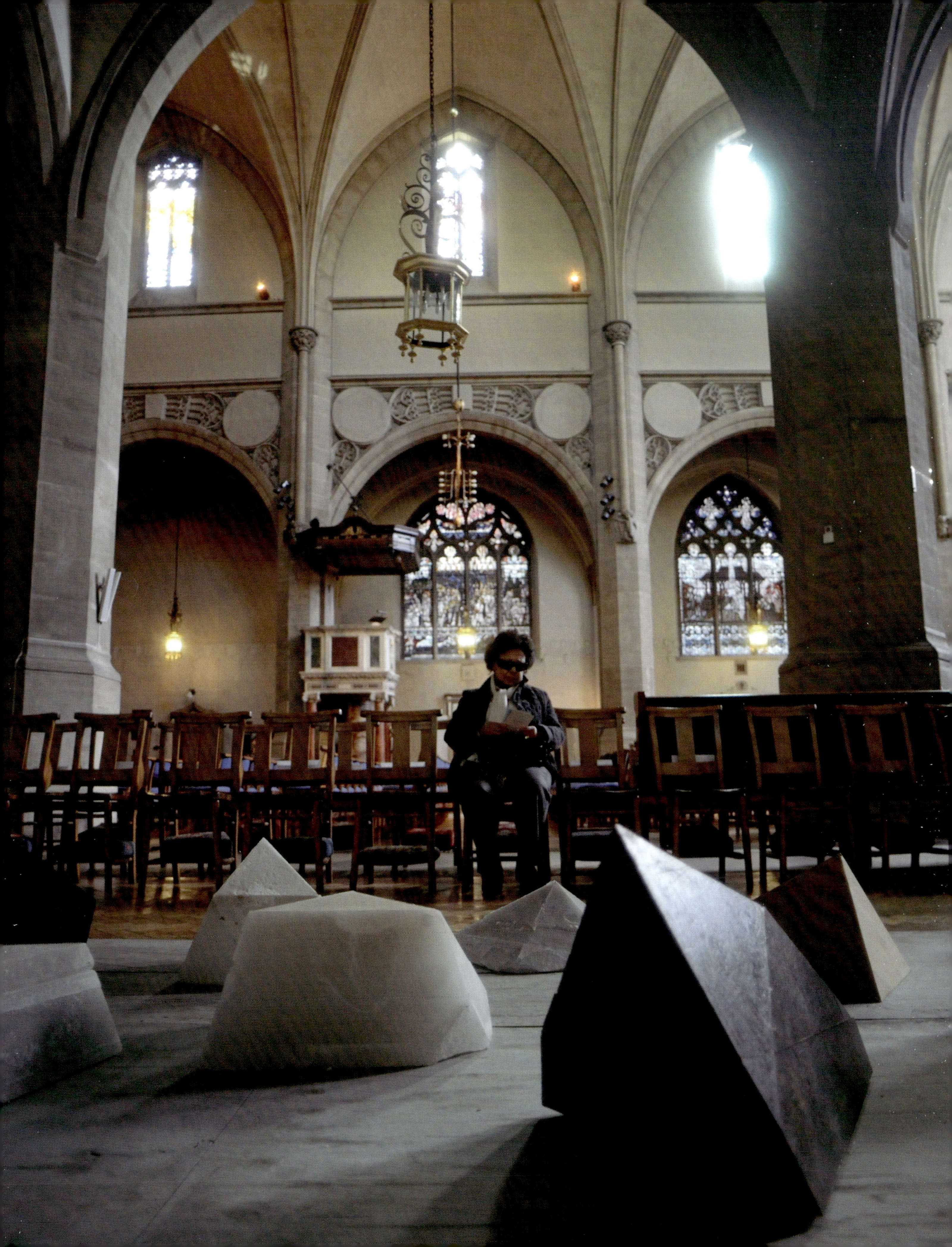

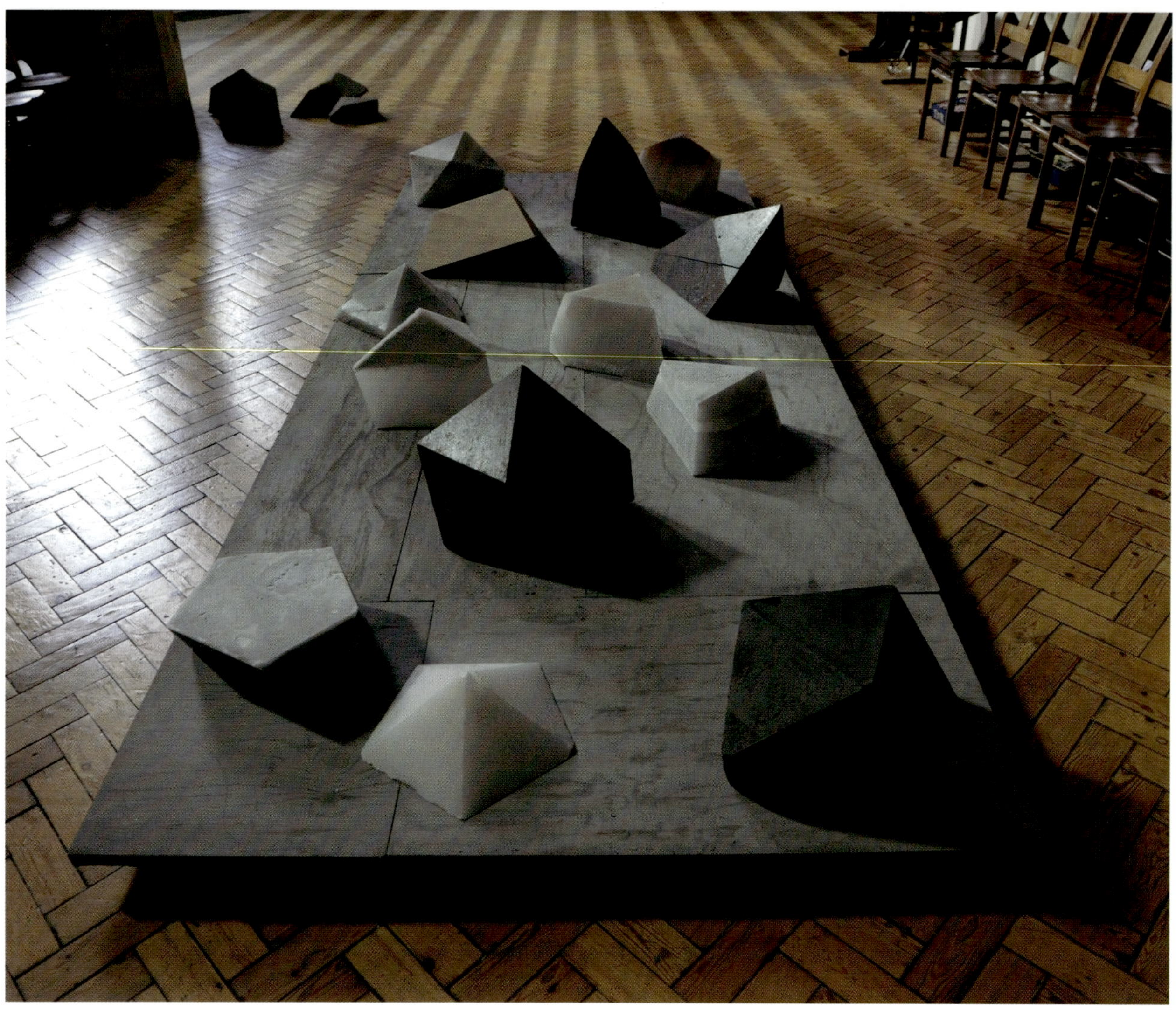

PREVIOUS PAGE, ABOVE AND OPPOSITE Nika Neelova, *North Taurids. Following the Meteor Shower*, 2013, cast concrete, cast wax and wooden table tops, 360 x 160 x 48 cm.

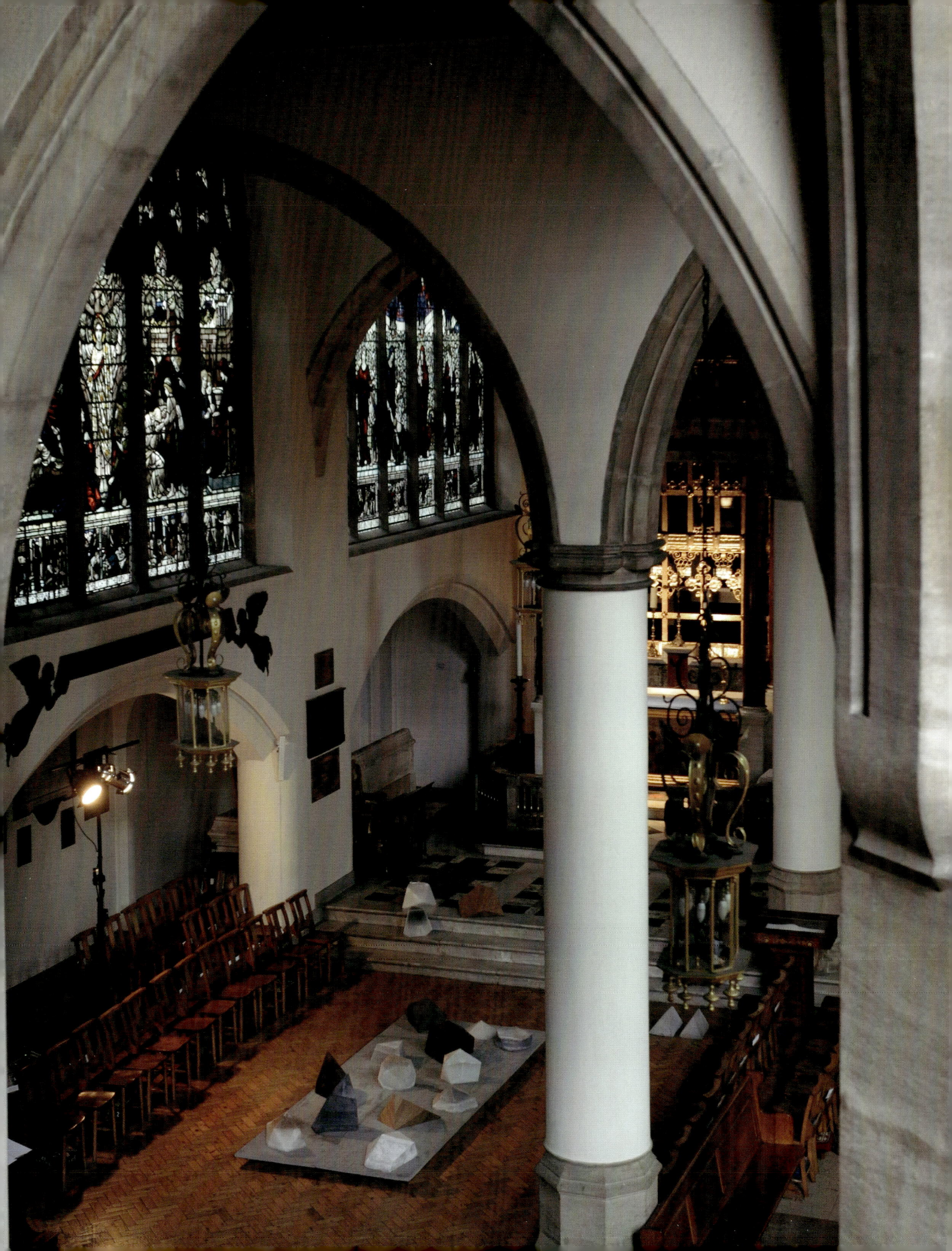

An Anonymous Philosopher's View

Spatial and temporal limitations define humanity. For centuries, art, science and religion have grappled with this existential dilemma. Trying to break free from these boundaries has been the impetus behind much of the creative processes that inhabit our societies.

Science seeks logic through geometrising the world. From Platonic sacred geometry to the tessellation of space with polyhedra of specific forms, science endeavours to explain space by revealing its underlying geometric nature. Therein lies a hope of reducing its immensity to a human scale.

Sculpture explores the act of creating new spaces from nothingness; by defining its own space where none existed before, this art of self-appropriation subordinates space to man.

Through her polyhedral creations, Nika Neelova is offering a certain alternative that lies at the confluence of both art and science. In Neelova's work, science and art combine in a dialogue that draws upon the strength of the other, further questioning our understanding of space.

Holy Trinity, Sloane Square, by the vastness of its architecture but also the silence that inhabits it, epitomises the spatial trauma of humanity and re-enforces the urge to find an answer. At the same time, in this very particular space, the act of questioning finds a different harmony and the struggle becomes contemplation.

Notes from the Studio—the Artist's View

Melencolia I of 1514 is an engraving by the German Renaissance artist Albrecht Dürer. It is an allegorical composition that has been the subject of numerous interpretations. It depicts Dürer's magic square and the truncated rhombohedron that became known as Dürer's solid. There have been various articles disputing the precise shape of this polyhedron. Although Dürer does not specify how his solid is constructed, it has been noted that it appears to consist of a distorted cube which is first stretched to give rhombic faces with angles, and then truncated on the top and bottom to yield bounding triangular faces whose vertices lie on the circumsphere of the azimuthal cube vertices.

Polyhedra have been part of the fabric of mathematics for 2,000 years. Anything which is bounded by flat surfaces and which has well defined corners has a polyhedral form. It has a significant presence in architecture as well as in nature, in the mineral, vegetable and animal kingdoms. They have been used widely in philosophical or scientific explanations of the world around us. As well as being part of the practical discipline of geometry, polyhedra have acquired symbolic value as artistic motifs appearing as an evolution of the Pythagorean-Platonic tradition, in studies of linear perspective, in ornament, and disguised in architecture and headwear. In nature, a striking example of polyhedral structures are crystals. Bounded by flat planes, their obvious geometric features contrast strongly with the more irregular qualities frequently found in natural forms. In the nineteenth century, the study of polyhedra and crystals led to the geometric analysis of symmetry.

In his analysis of cinematic moments, Gilles Deleuze describes the movement of temporality in a crystallised formation:

what constitutes the crystal-image is the most fundamental operation of time: since the past is constituted not after the present that it was but at the same time, time has to split itself in two at each moment as present and past.... Time splits in two dissymmetrical jets, one of which makes the present pass on, while the other preserves all the past. Time consists of this split and it is time that we see in the crystal... we see in the crystal the perpetual foundation of time.

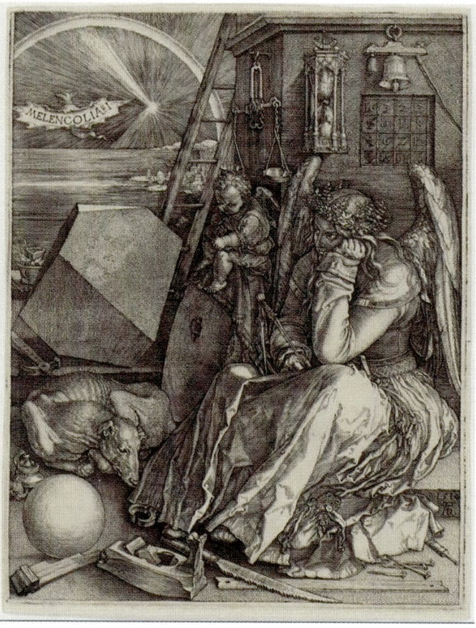

Albrecht Dürer, *Melencolia I*, 1514, engraving, 24 x 18.8 cm.

The Borgesian aesthetic contains numerous allusions to the spatialisation of time, its nonlinear and bifurcating nature. Borges regards the movements of time as flowing from the future into the past and thus as a ceaseless production of the past. In his short story "Tlön, Uqbar, Orbis Tertius", he imagines a civilisation that has developed a novel relationship to metaphysics: "For them the world is not a concurrence of objects in space, but a heterogenous

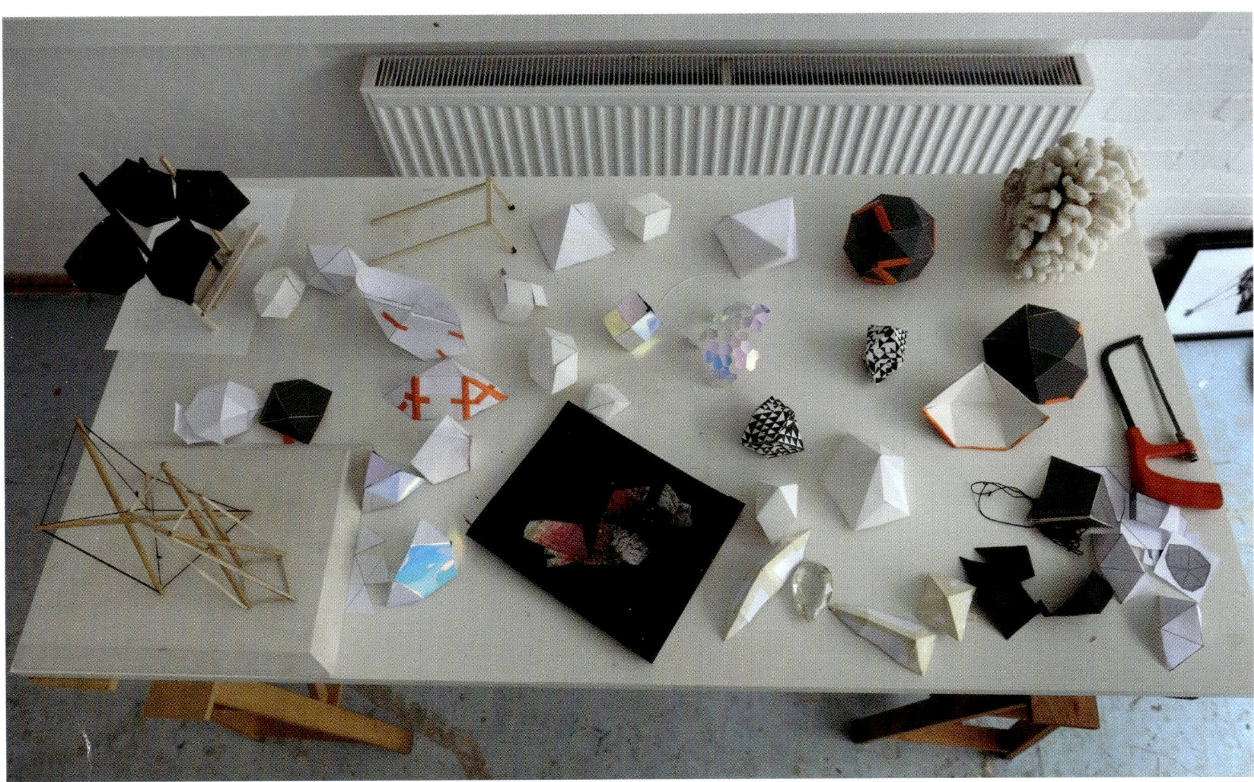

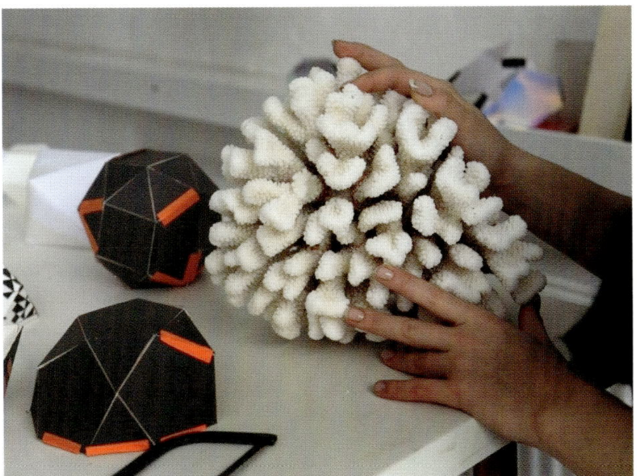

series of independent acts." In this civilisation producing, discovering and exhuming are one and the same, so the archaeologists of Tlön can just as easily invent the objects they exhibit as unearth them.

Similarly, the object-crystals displayed in the installation question their own origin, whether they have been created just now or in fact originated elsewhere a very long time ago, like unearthed pieces from an unfamiliar landscape or rock formation. The installation alludes to an excavation site, a descent into archaeological time toward eroded fragmented stones pointing to another system of beliefs. All the fragments are parts of each other and are completing each other, though the entity itself is never presented; a system of equations colliding with the forces of entropy and decay leading to the deconstruction of a devised system.

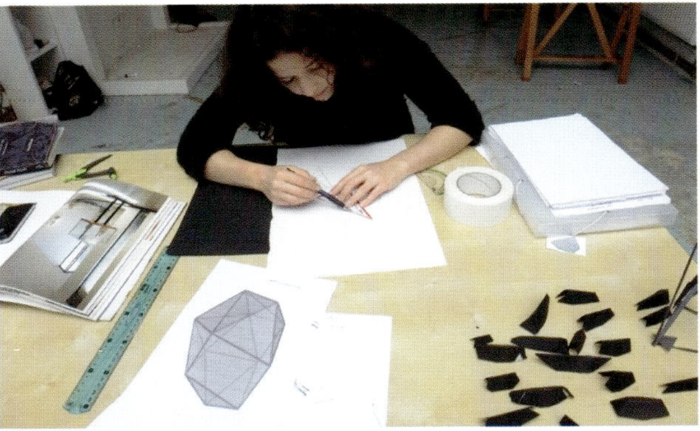

ABOVE AND LEFT Work in progress during Nika Neelova's residency.

Nika Neelova, Artistic, Sacred, Metaphysical Space: *North Taurids. Following the Meteor Shower, 2014*— Claire Mander

When faced with the challenging environment of the magnificence of Holy Trinity, Sloane Square, Neelova was filled with awe at the multitude of architectural detail, the overwhelming scale of the space and its sacred function. Described by former Poet Laureate, Sir John Betjeman, as the "Cathedral of the Arts and Crafts Movement", its architect, John Dando Sedding, believed that a church should be "wrought and painted over with everything that has life and beauty—in frank and fearless naturalism...", an aim which he achieved not least in the monumental stained-glass windows by Sir Edward Burne-Jones and William Morris.

Neelova had a challenge before her: how to create a work that responds and encapsulates a place so laden with artistic, sacred, metaphysical and spatial enormity. Her eye quickly moved from individual architectural elements and rested on the geometric patterns repeated throughout the church. Her research took this further and she quickly understood that all space can be explained through geometry, which strives to reduce space's immensity to a human scale, to the boundaries of human understanding. Everywhere there was evidence of the "sacred geometry", the belief that God created the universe according to a geometric plan, which is the foundation of much sacred art and architecture since ancient times. Plato reasoned that the entire universe could be understood through the interpretation of the five Platonic solids, which are polyhedral forms (namely solids in three dimensions with flat faces and straight edges), on which Neelova based her work. While this exploration took her into an increasingly abstract world of thought, she discovered the overwhelming presence of polyhedra in nature, in particular in the complex and compelling forms of crystals. Nature and mathematics became one.

Neelova then applied her research to the physical act of creation. She folded a wooden table top to form two hollow polyhedral vessels. These two wooden structures were used as casts into which she poured concrete, wax and marble dust to create fragments of the whole. Every one of the shapes could be fused together to recreate the two original polyhedra: all the fragments are part of each other, completing each other.

The origins and materials of the object-crystals in the installation are intentionally ambiguous. Resonant of the site of an archaeological dig, the fragments link the past to the present both in terms of material and systems of belief. She is presenting fragments of a cogent representation of the universe resulting in a quiet, contemplative work which does not battle with its environment, but becomes part of it.

OPPOSITE Nika Neelova, *Horizon Fold*, 2013, giclée print on paper, 42 x 59.5 cm, edition of 30, plus 6 artist's proofs. Image courtesy the artist.

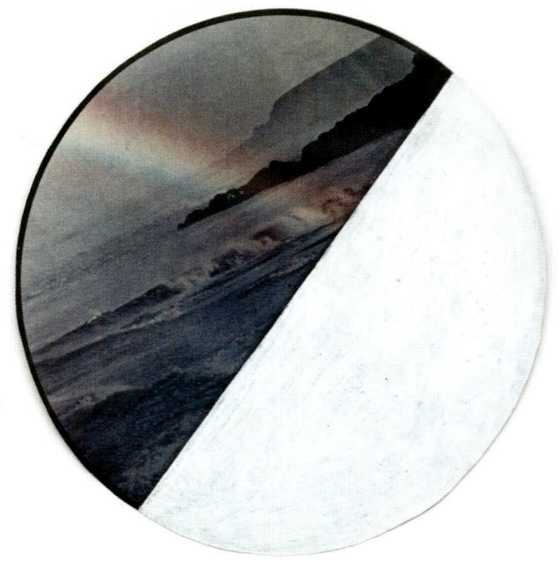

**Joanna Sands
The Asylum, Peckham, London**

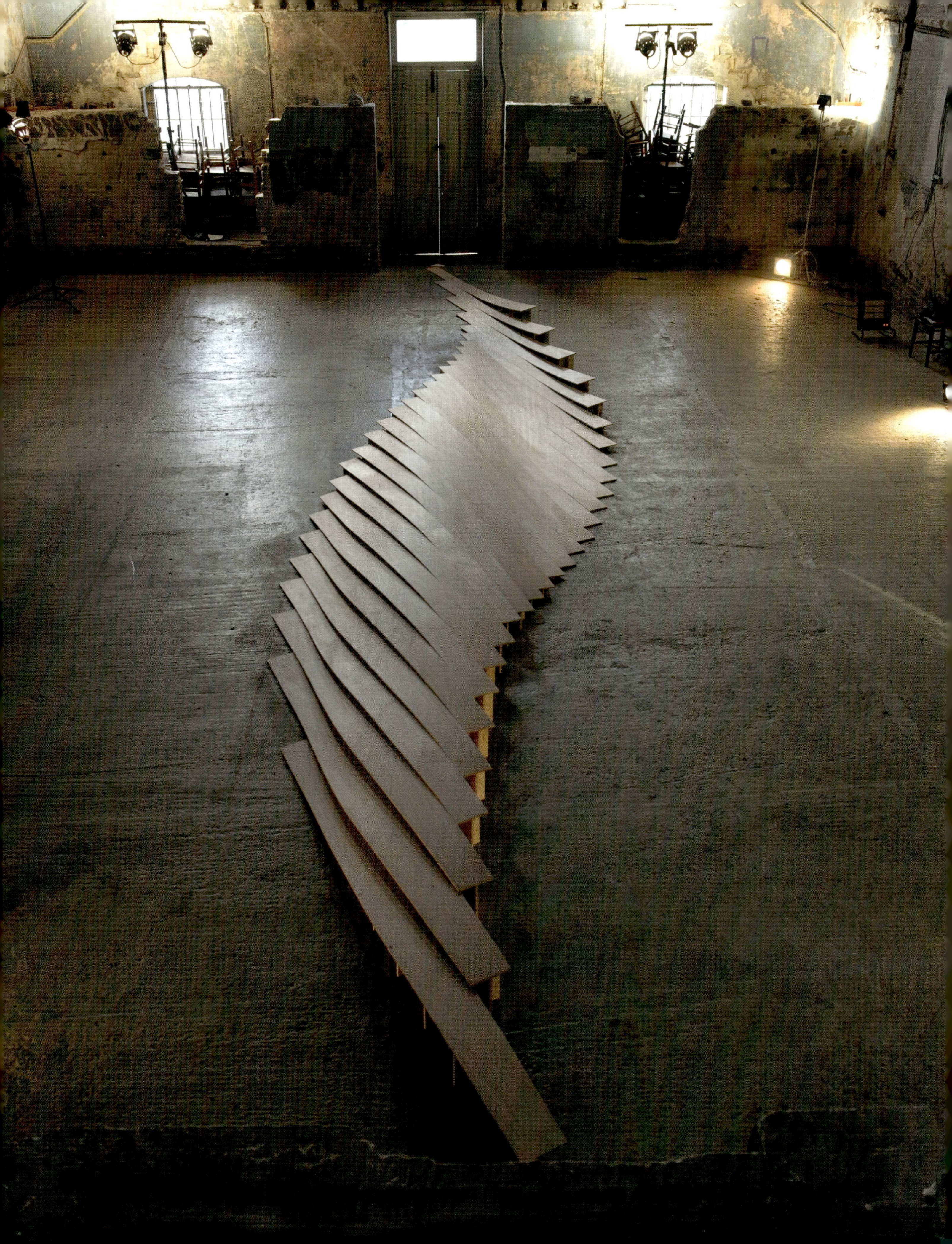

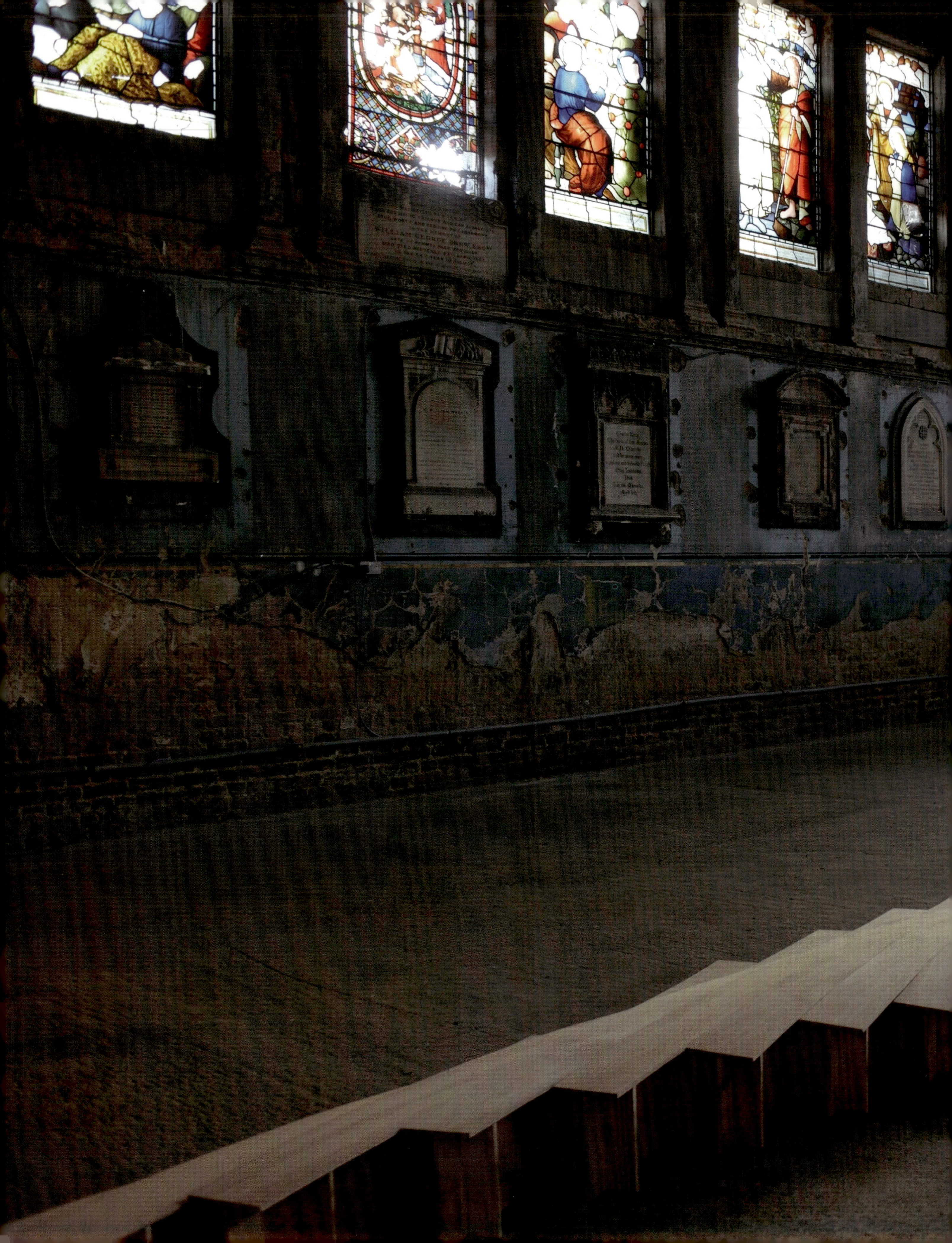

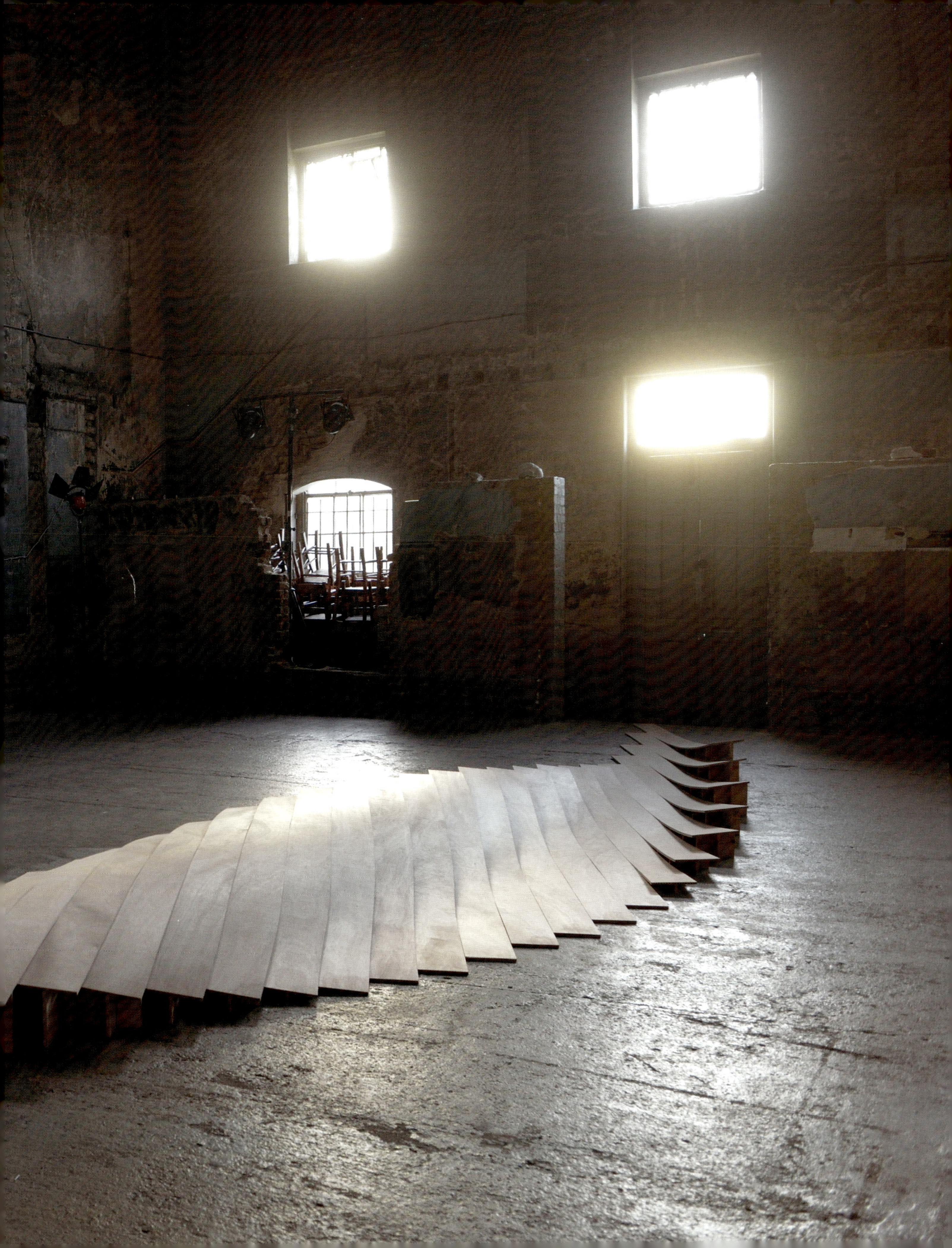

Notes from the Studio

Who are the artists, architects or designers you most admire and which have had the greatest impact on your thinking and your work?

Some of the biggest influences on my work when I was at college were Eva Hesse and her contemporaries, including Sol LeWitt, Robert Morris, Donald Judd, Carl Andre, Richard Serra and Robert Smithson. Out of those I have to say Carl Andre was probably the one I felt the most affinity towards in my work because his sculpture is a very physical response to material. His writing was also much easier to understand.

Another big influence was Gordon Matta Clark because of his physical relationship to pre-existing architectural space. I really admire the architect Peter Zumthor. His buildings are very beautiful and are as much about materials as their effect. His work has a very tactile quality and you can tell he has the knowledge of a maker.

You have said of your work that it often becomes an intervention into the space it inhabits and refers to the architectural characteristics of the surrounding environment. Can you elaborate on the importance of architecture to your work?

Well, the works relate to the surrounding architectural environment in many ways: scale, dimensions, the type of building, when it was built and who it was built for. All these factors allow that building to create a sense of place and I would like to think that the works become part of that.

As an artist who works site-specifically, the unpredictability of the site and its surroundings must have characterised many past projects, for example, when you initially worked in squats. How do you deal with this aspect of site-specific work?

Yes, it has, and I think you just have to roll with it. Lots of stuff happens that wouldn't happen in a gallery. You don't have any security, people don't know where you are or how to find you, and they can be reluctant to venture into these unknown spaces because they are difficult to access or scary. It's hard to publicise. Although having said that, at the time you don't think so much, if at all, about these aspects; you focus more on the opportunity it creates. You couldn't have created that particular work had you not been there in that place at that time; it gives the work a vitality the gallery space denies. You have the great advantage of freedom.

In his 1966 essay "Notes on Sculpture II", speaking of the reduced forms of the Minimalist aesthetic, Robert Morris stated, "The object itself has not become less important. It has merely become less self-important." When thinking of the impact you hope your work will have on the viewer, would you relate this to the key beliefs of Minimalist theory that focus on real space and unmediated experience or do you anticipate a more interpretive emotional response?

In general, what I hope to do with my work is to make something that relates to the space so that you are more aware of the environment you are in. It becomes an experience as it were. There is also usually a physical or formal narrative. To me that might be something very simple such as a curve which goes up and down across the room. Whether or not the work inspires a narrative in the viewer is really up to them. As Frank Stella said, "What you see is what you see".

In regards to the Minimalist aesthetic, I am not sure there is ever such a thing as unmediated experience; I don't believe you can take the self-expression out of art, but I do like the work of people who do. I like geometric

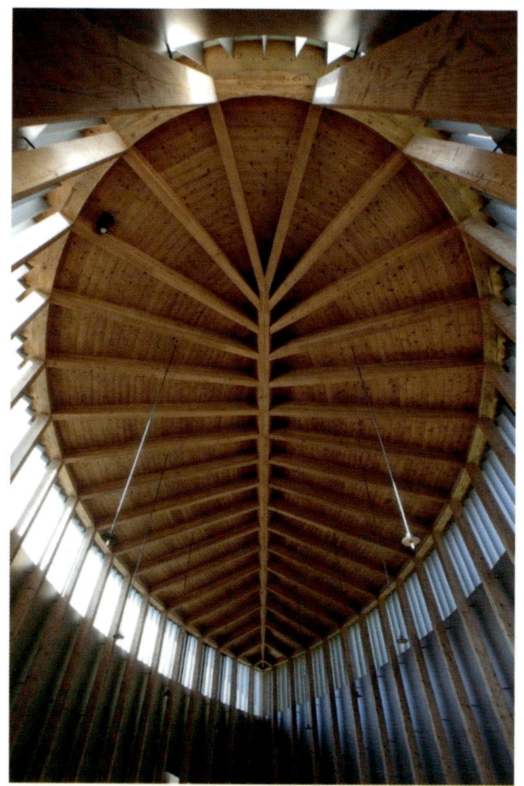

Peter Zumthor, St Benedict Chapel, Sumvitg, Switzerland, 1988. Image courtesy Felipe Camus.

PP 99–100 Joanna Sands, *Untitled (19 Princelet)*, 2014, plywood, 1300 x 240 x 30 cm.

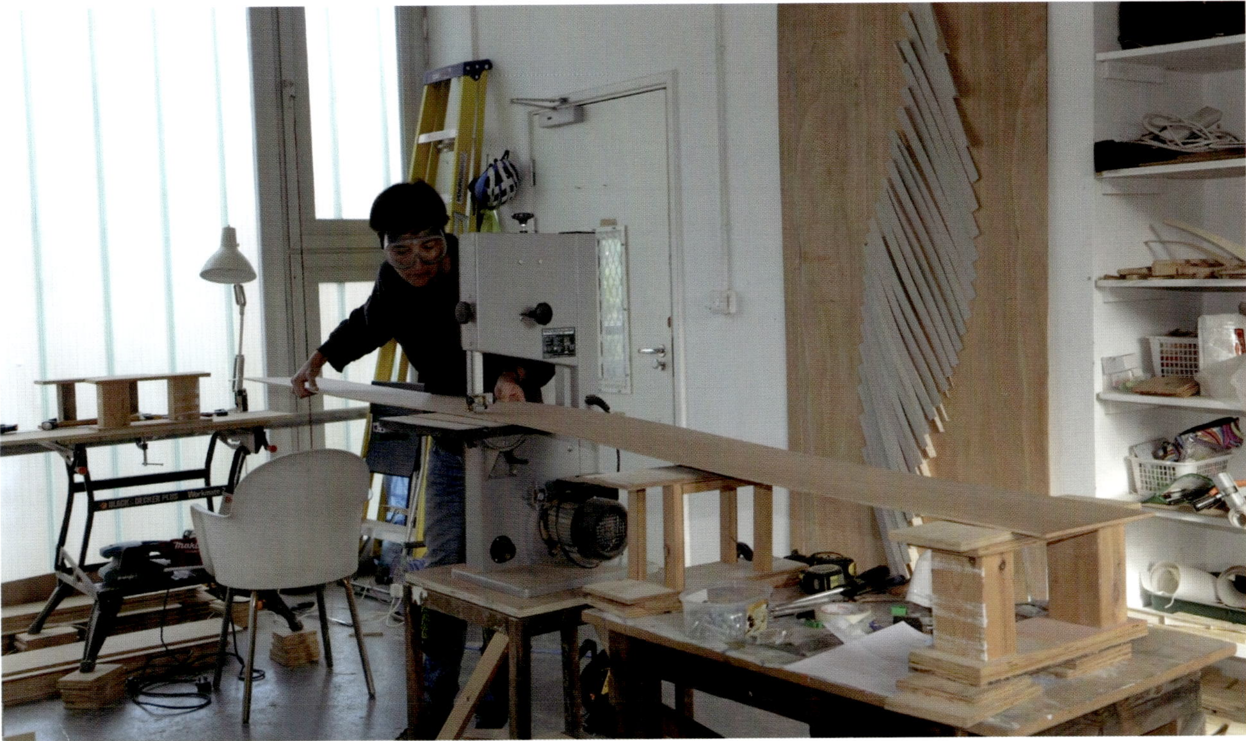

Joanna Sands during her residency.

forms, the use of repetition and simplicity, but I would say I am more of a materialist; I like the physical properties of the material I use, its weight, its patina, its texture and its presence.

You frequently use wood to create you work. Does the material you use inform/form your work or is it the nature of site-specific work that informs your choice of material? Have you always worked with wood? Are you committed to using wood as a medium?

No, I'm not. I like using found materials, recycled materials and building materials that come in standard sizes. My use of wood has probably come out of the fact that I have always had to move quite quickly in the space so all my tools have had to be easily movable and packable. Wood is a lightweight material, you can construct with it, and as a building material it's easily available. I also like using wood. I have nothing against using other materials, but at the moment it works for me and my practice. Obviously that may change in the future.

As part of your Sculpture Shock award you will be making a limited edition print. Is drawing part of your creative process and how will you approach the print?

Drawing is definitely an important part of my process. I tend to 'draw' first with models. In the back of my studio space there are hundreds of little models; sometimes at that point in the process it is easier to think through making. As I am used to thinking in three dimensions, it's easier just to get a piece of card and start that way. These models are not maquettes and I don't always make a maquette; it usually depends on the space and the potential cost of the materials.

Then drawing in the traditional sense comes after the three dimensional, at the point when I am trying to narrow down what I really want to achieve with the sculpture. I often draw when I want to record something because it's quicker than writing notes. I also use photography to document my work, but I find if I do a drawing I slow down and I observe more information and details than a photograph can convey. When I come across them later in sketch books, the drawings are often more meaningful than the photographs for this very reason. I also use drawing to plan my work and I was thinking of developing a version of one of these for the print.

What is the fate of your site-specific work after it is exhibited? How do you feel about the temporary nature of the work?

I sometimes recycle work and use the materials to make a new work and other times I just destroy it. It always exists in documentation, so traces of the work always remain.

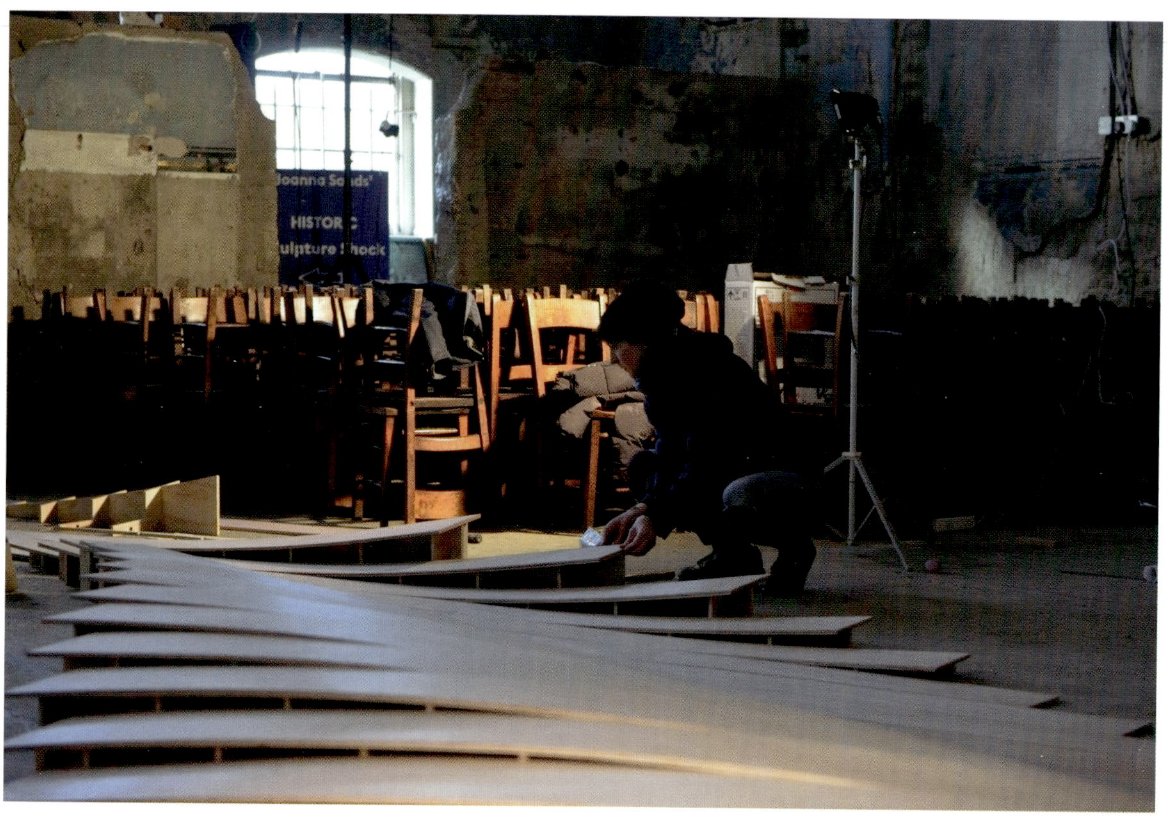

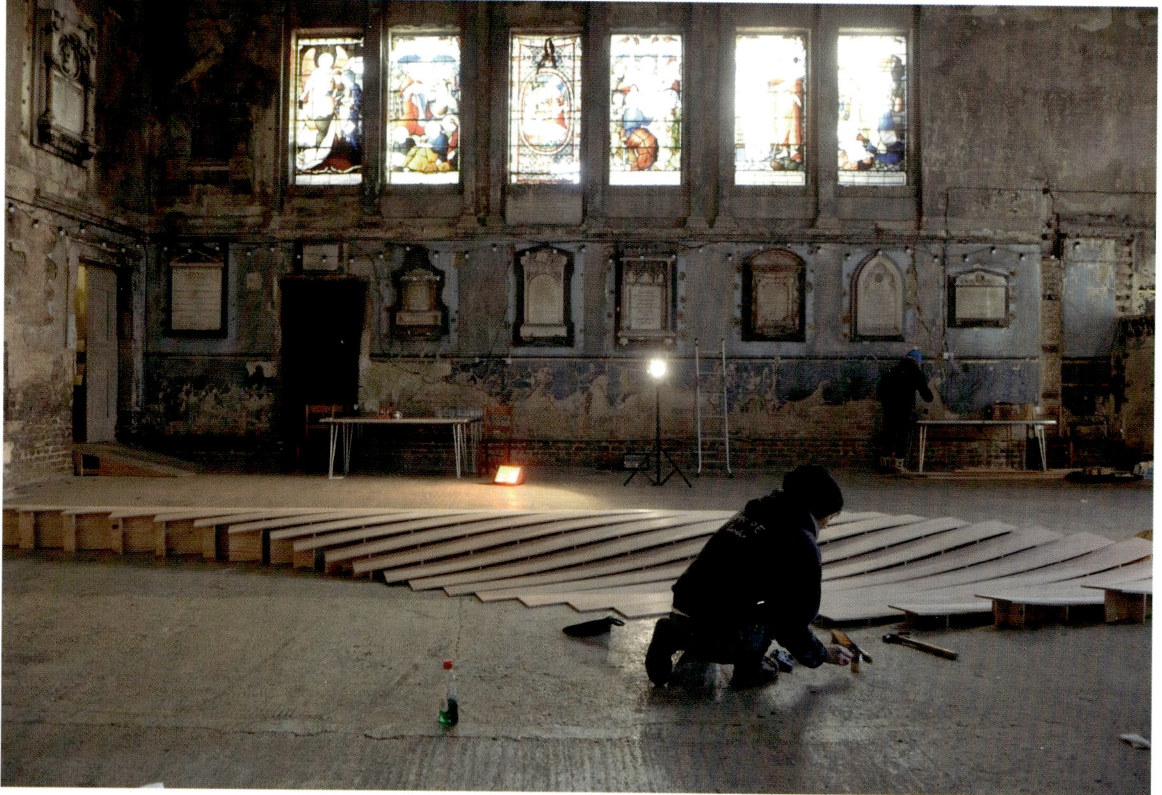

Joanna Sands installing her work at the Asylum.

Joanna Sands at the Asylum, 2014—Sarah Kent

Joanna Sands was chosen for the Historic category of Sculpture Shock, which involved creating an installation for the Museum of Immigration at 19 Princelet Street, a Huguenot house in Spitalfields that was home to successive waves of immigrants. Behind the house is a derelict synagogue and her plan was to link the two buildings with an undulating floor whose wavelike surface could evoke the insecurity and anxiety engendered by leaving one's home for a new country.

"I like working site specifically", she told me, "because the various difficulties and limitations become part of the piece; you have to contend with the unexpected." The unexpected came part way through the residency in the form of building work for Crossrail, which forced her to relocate to another abandoned religious building, the Asylum in Peckham. Sands took the move in her stride. "I saw the change from one site to another as just another element that I could use", she says. She modified the piece for the new venue and, inevitably, in this new context it takes on different connotations.

In Princelet Street her installation would have been a disruptive presence occupying the centre of the room, forcing viewers to the margins and thereby encouraging a sense of displacement. The Asylum chapel is much wider and more spacious, so rather than filling the room, the piece lies along the central axis between an entrance door and the altar. It feels less miraculous here; less like something (a broken wing, perhaps) that has fallen from the sky and more like a pathway, whose fluid curves invite one to approach the altar while, paradoxically, blocking the way.

The Asylum is a Georgian estate built by the Licensed Victuallers' Benevolent Institution to house retired publicans and 'decayed' members of the trade, those fallen on hard times. Located at the centre of this handsome complex, the chapel must have been rather fine, but in the Second World War, a German bomb destroyed the roof and much of the interior. Clinging to the walls, fragments of blue plaster offer glimpses of its former glory; while many of the stained-glass windows survive, the beauty of their luminous colours only serves to emphasise the dereliction of the rest of the building.

A corrugated iron roof prevents further decay, but it is still a melancholy place. Above the altar is a gaping hole crisscrossed by rusty metal struts that once supported a stained-glass window. Memorial plaques line the walls; one pays tribute to the chairman William Wallis, who secured the future of the Asylum by bequeathing it £630, a sum large enough to be worth recording for posterity. There's a maudlin beauty in this decay.

If the funerary monuments attest to the self-congratulatory ethos of the worthies they commemorate, Sands' unpolished boards bring to mind the 'decayed' colleagues who depended on their charity. A pompous display of wealth, on the one hand, a literal demonstration of fact or 'truth to materials', on the other.

The wood used for the installation may be ordinary ply bought from a builders' yard, but instead of the rough treatment meted out on a building site, it has been handled with a remarkable degree of subtlety and decorum. This humble material wreaks of impermanence and temporary solutions, but Sands' careful crafting invites respect. Her floor may seem unpretentious, yet close inspection reveals it to be surprisingly complex.

Made to bend in subtle, convex and concave curves by the rising and falling of the supporting structure, the lengths of ply overlap one another with understated elegance and reserve. The shape of each plank differs from that of its neighbour. Shining a light obliquely across the flanges, the artist mapped the shadow cast by each plank onto the one below, then added this shape to the plank so transforming straight boards into slow curves. She describes these additional segments as "the ghost or memory of a shadow. It encourages you to read the shape as a story unfolding in time, with a momentum that builds up and dissipates."

The dual identity of the installation—as a temporary structure soon to be dismantled and a carefully crafted sculpture—is like an embodiment of the paradox that makes this estate and its chapel such a fascinating place. There's a certain irony in the fact that while the almshouses still provide modest homes for the less well-off, the building that proudly honoured the founders of the estate is now derelict; the lavish decoration that celebrated the wealth and generosity of the donors has been all but destroyed.

A German bomb stripped the chapel of its flamboyant decorations leaving only the basic structure intact, sans pomposity. And I am inclined to see these melancholy remains as a three-dimensional vanitas, a salutary reminder of the brevity of life and the transience of worldly goods.

OPPOSITE Joanna Sands, *Asylum 2014*, 2014, giclée print on Southbank Smooth, 42 x 59.4 cm, edition of 30, plus 3 artist's proofs. Image courtesy the artist.

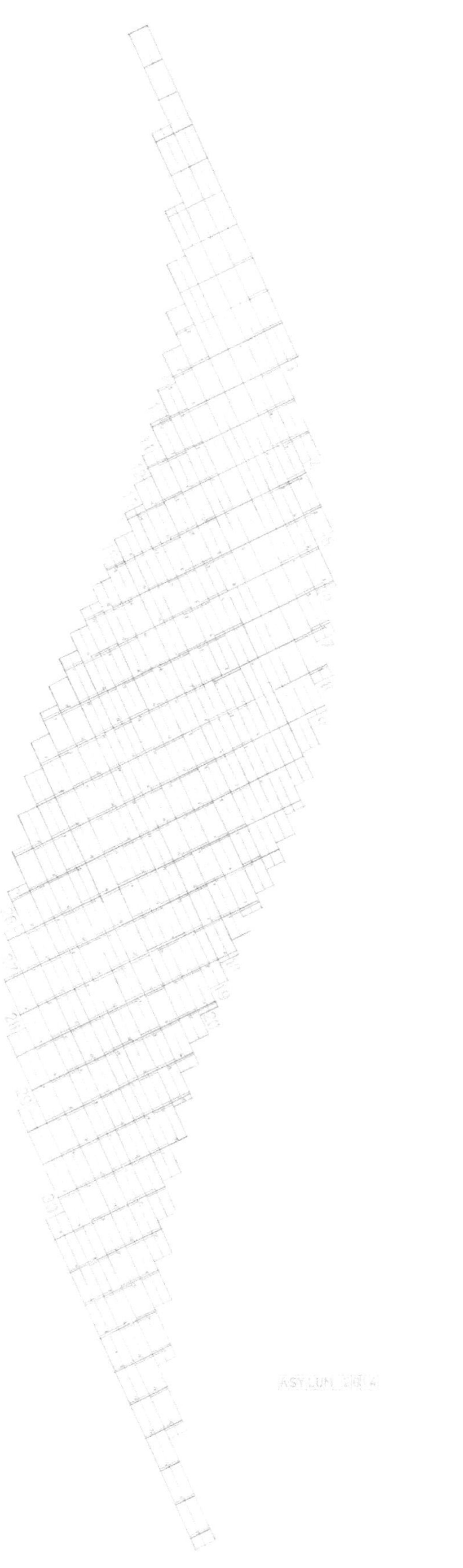

Hanna Haaslahti
The Ionic Temple, Chiswick House and Gardens, London

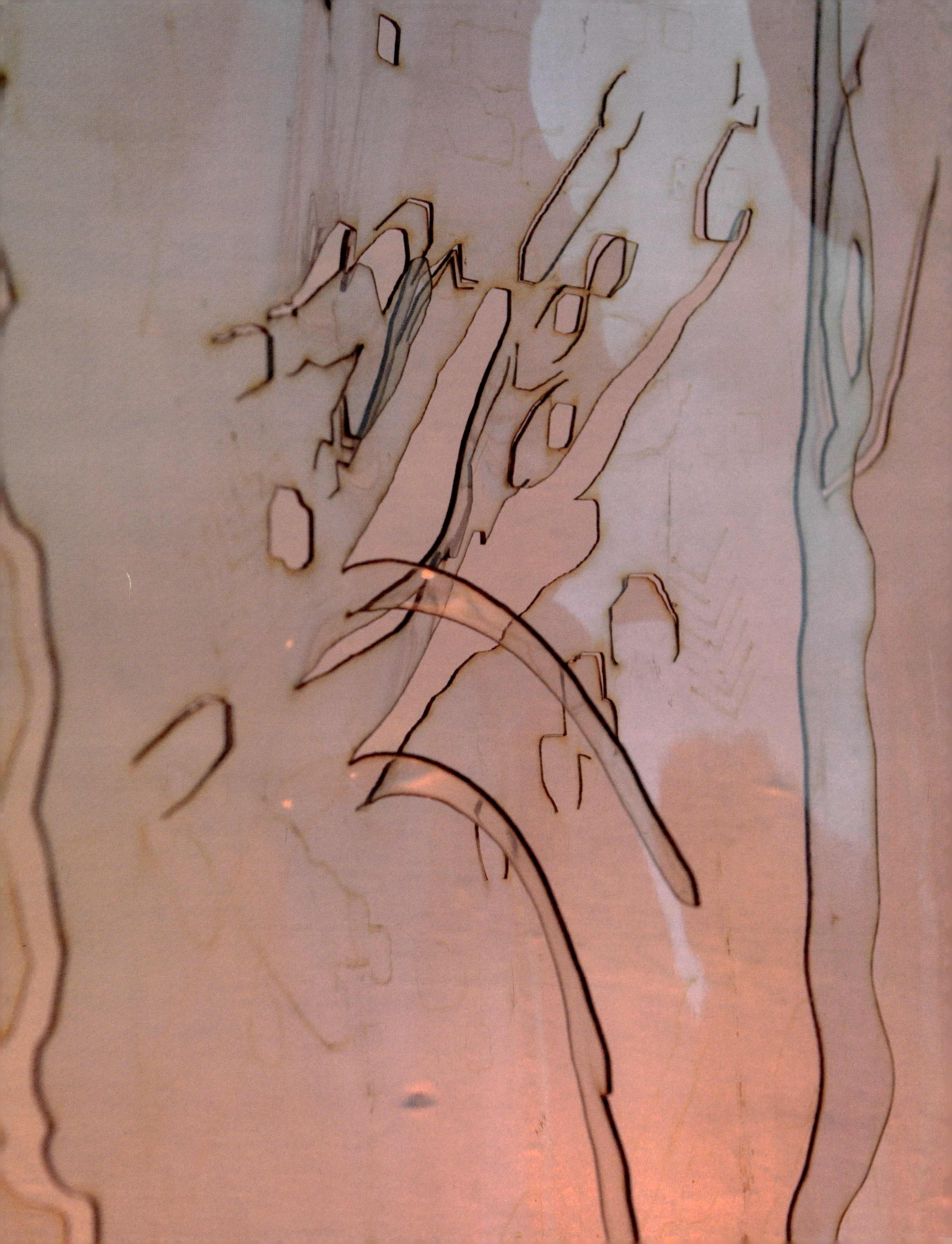

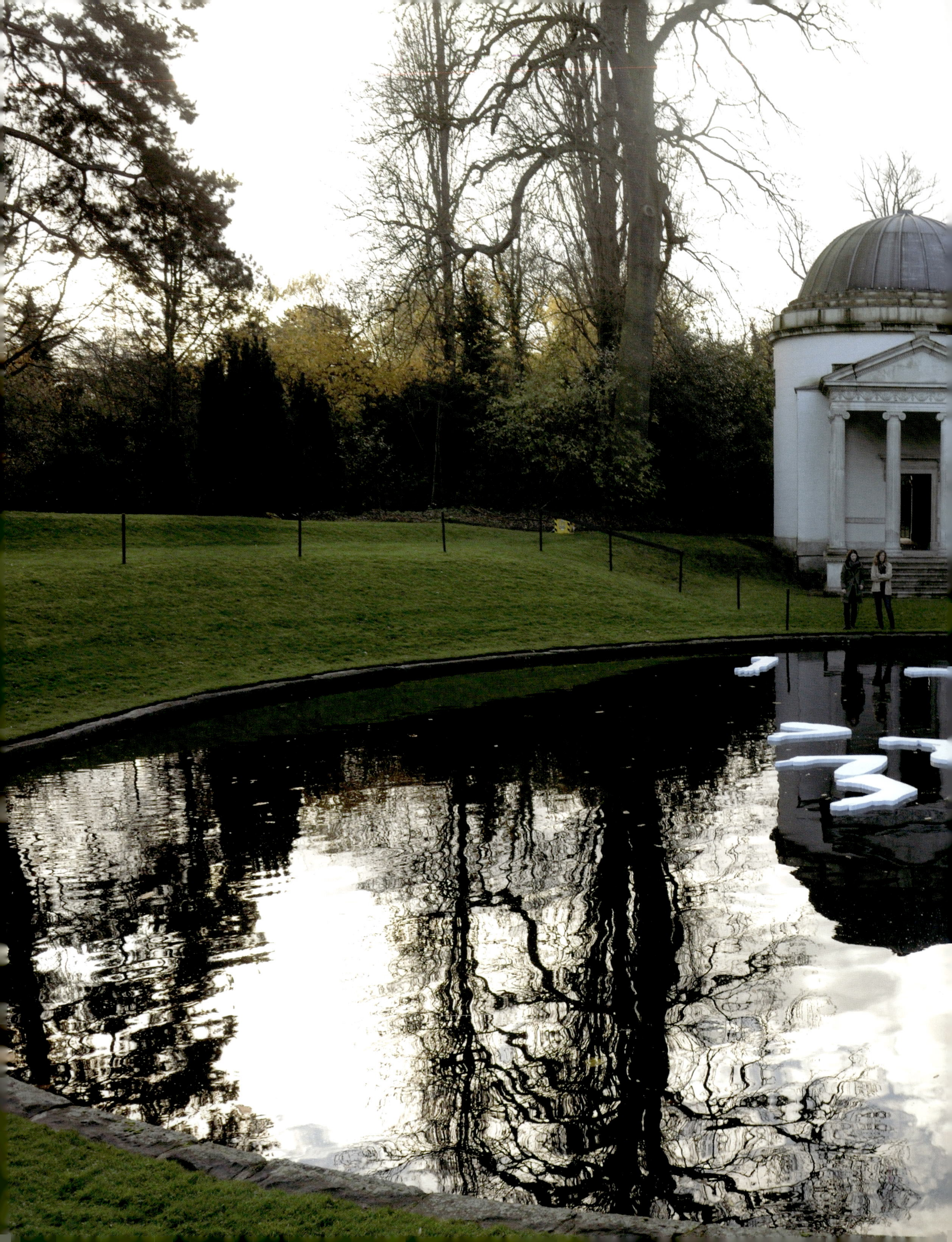

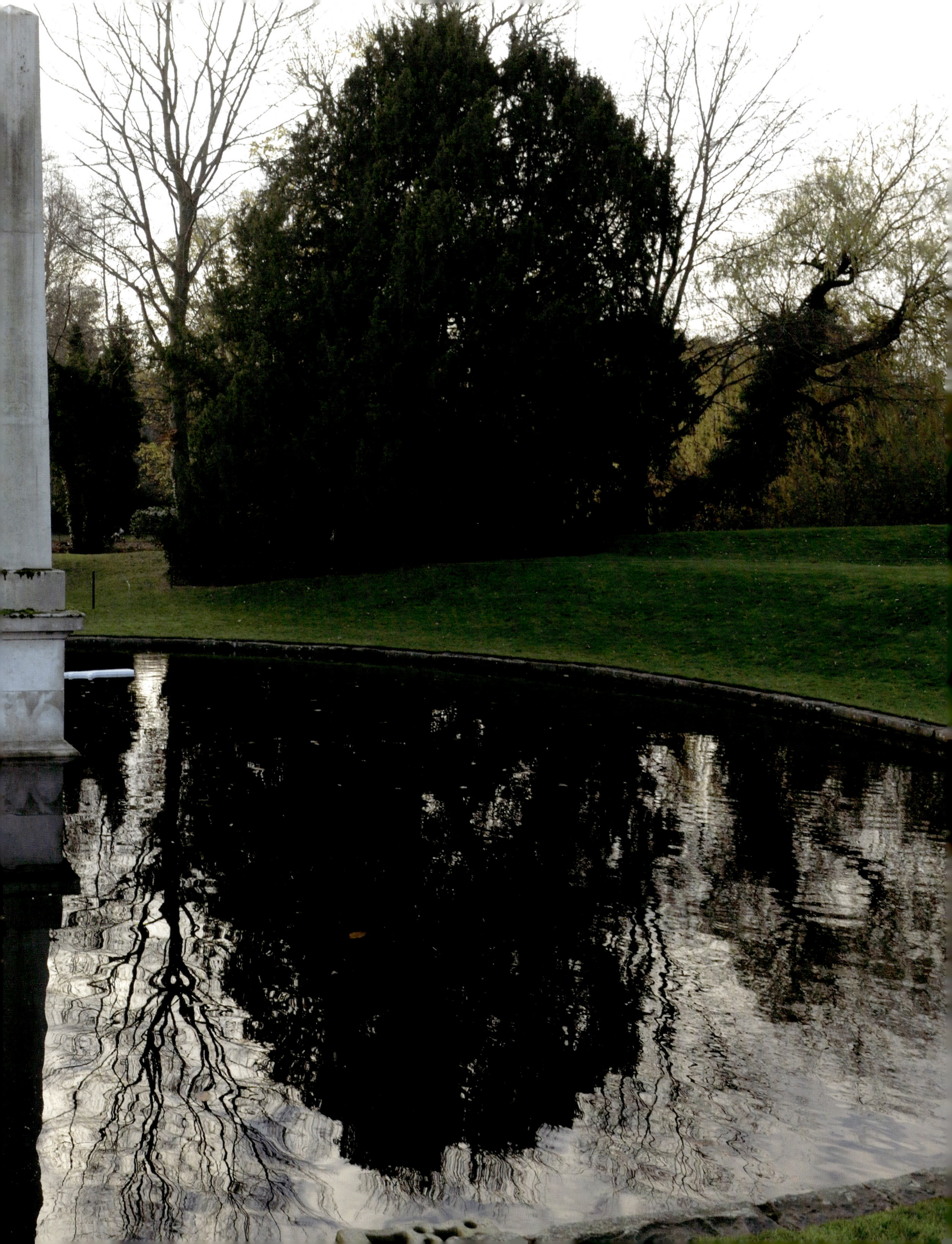

Notes from the Studio

Who are the artists, thinkers, theorists from any field of endeavour that you most admire and which have had the greatest impact on your thinking and your work?

Many people influence my work and thinking as research is an important part of my working process. At the moment, Timothy Morton, an English philosopher who writes about object-oriented ontology (OOO) is of particular interest. The idea that objects comprise both surface and essence— the surface/appearance being easily comprehensible while the essence can never be seen or known—is somehow magical and endlessly sought after.

Discovering gestalt psychology was a revelation for me. It explains how the brain processes our perceptions of the world by filling in missing gaps and creating whole forms, before our cognitive mind has had a chance to intervene. I am also fascinated by studies around the psychology of the group and phenomena surrounding 'herd mentality'. Malevich is an artist whose work and manifestos are, for me, an iconic turning point in thought and image. The utopian architectural constructions of Haus-Rucker-Co made in the 1970s, at a time of increased fear of environmental issues, interest me in the way they incorporate plastics into pneumatic air structures. They wanted to provide creative solutions to environmental and social issues. Today we do not have room for utopias; we are the generation that has to clean up the trash from the past and move on. I also admire Bjørk for her energy and her imagination.

You have created work which responds to historically important places in the past, for example, *Sincere Lies*, 2013, at Sinebrychoff Art Museum of Old European Masters in Helsinki. What aspects of the historic appeal to you?

Certain ideas are associated with certain historical periods; there has always been a manipulation or control of what we know, what is passed down, what is revered and what is not discussed and in this sense history is a perceptual formula. I am interested in the 'back streets of history', not the official line. Our age, the digital age, is characterised by a flow (or flood) of information stated quickly and simply, which does not describe a true or fair view of the complexity of an event. I am interested in presenting the possibilities of alternative narratives, not necessarily based on research or re-presenting facts; new information does

P 109 Hanna Haaslahti, *Ionic Temple* (detail), 2015, polystyrene, PVC, interactive light projection, smoke machine, dimensions variable.

PP 110–111 Hanna Haaslahti, *Mirror Lake*, 2015, exterior showing limbs floating on blackened Mirror Lake.

not help. After all, information is not communication. I am talking about different ways of perceiving the world. The images you see every day in the media make you blind and powerless, but sometimes you catch a glimpse of something revealing. Take the image of the new Chief Executive of BMW who dramatically fainted at the conference, an image that went viral. The pose is almost religious, the fall so out of place; it revealed human fragility so carefully hidden inside the machineries of power.

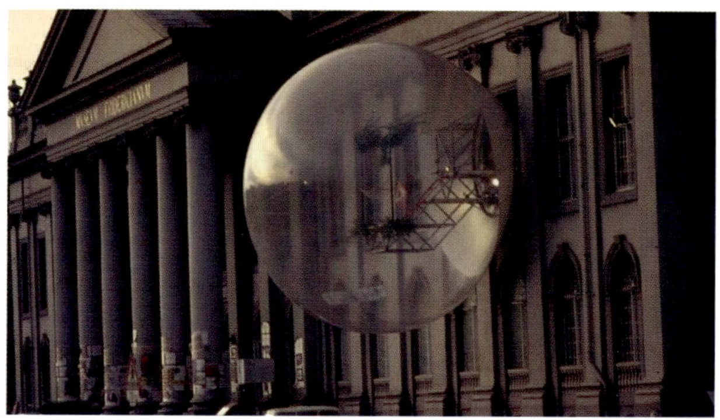

Haus-Rucker-Co, *Oase no 7*, Fridericaianum, documenta 5, Kassel, 1972. Photograph copyright Hein Engelskirchen, © Haus-Rucker-Co Archive.

Tell me about the importance of digital technology and the possibilities it opens up in the visual world?

Digital technology introduced instability as the unexpected side effect of high-tech society. Objects are no longer solid and enduring; buildings are made to last a decade rather than millennia; events seemingly take place here, on the other side of the world and on various platforms simultaneously, as do images of ourselves. An instantaneous, ephemeral, speeded up digital world; we are not sure how to understand this new dimension of immateriality. Concepts of physical presence and absence have dissolved. Now we are present all the time in different ways in different media; images of ourselves are on social media, sent back and forth, selfies everywhere. Our paranoia about surveillance cameras seems to have disappeared and now we suffer from FOMO; we throw ourselves into the proliferation of images and now we live with our own digital images constantly. Next year I am embarking on an art+science research project in Aalto University, Helsinki, called Life as an Image, to explore new technologies around image-making and three-dimensional sensing and their social reverberations. The relationship between human perception and computer vision—how computers see the world—is fascinating. Three-dimensional sensing technology adds another element to the RGB of image creation—the

D of Depth, also called point cloud—which dispenses with traditional perspectival systems of vision. Three-dimensional sensing moves around the object and builds up an image from all angles. Liberating image-making from the chains of perspective is exciting and contains many possibilities.

I am positive about digital technology; we cannot turn back the clock and it is here to stay, so there is no point being negative about it or yearning for analogue technology. But we can and should try to take control of it. We are in a honeymoon period of intense love with our social screens, creating a generation of young iPhone zombies as we say in Finland, but I am hopeful that technology might lead ultimately to a new understanding of time, presence and materiality.

How did you approach your Sculpture Shock residency and making the work?

Not in front of a computer screen! Chiswick House and English Heritage have been very supportive and I have spent many days at the Temple, in the archives and in the grounds. The history of the Ionic Temple is fascinating and multilayered. As with all historical research, as many things are hidden as are revealed. Just as the obelisk that stands in front of it, the Temple itself is a monument and monuments are selective in their statements about past deeds.

Certain aspects of the Temple caught my imagination: the empty niches in the interior, the armless sculptures in the grounds and the idea of building a bridge between the past and present—of invigorating a space which is not open to the public.

The two empty niches in the Temple once contained copies of classical sculptures that are now in the main house. Replicas of these stand in the gardens outside the Temple area. They have lost their arms and hands—their gestures—and without them the sculptures have lost their means of communication. I wanted to study gestures of classical sculpture to link past and present by incorporating them into the installation. The concept of "heroic nudity" invented during Archaic period resonates strongly with contemporary anxieties surrounding beauty and the toning of muscles. These same gestures reappear again and again in sculpture over the millennia and now they float in their contemporary incarnation on the surface of the Mirror Lake. Certain visual effects just keep repeating themselves throughout history.

Much of the apparent richness of the interiors of Chiswick House is due to its carefully gilded surfaces. This interested me as I primarily work with light, which creates a similar type of surface effect. Gilding, though, is a way of making materials look more desirable and expensive, creating this rift between the surface and the essence. I decided to invert this treatment and re-cover the solid materials of the Temple with a contemporary non-precious, artificial-looking material. So much of the contemporary world is made up of cheap fake things mimicking old precious things, like cheap vinyl oak-looking floors or fake marble tiles, which I wanted to make the viewer think about. I wanted to create an installation that highlights the disjunction between the solidity of this grand building and the instability of the contemporary world.

How do you hope your Sculpture Shock intervention for the Ionic Temple at Chiswick House will be read by its audience and what impact do you hope it will have?

The audience is the key link between the building and my work and between past and present. The interactive light work will ensure that visitors are in the spotlight, if only for a moment. They will be the fulcrum of the work; actually generating and moving the light. The audience is not passive; they will not just stand and watch. Their function is to challenge the border between installation, viewer and site. I hope their perceptions will be altered and they will be animated by the space as much as they animate it themselves.

How has Sculpture Shock assisted you in the development of your practice and what are your artistic ambitions?

This programme really opened a new perspective in my artistic practice. I had labelled myself as a media artist and now I have a broader sense of what I do. Why do we have to have these divisions anyway? As an artist I want to be able to always do whatever is necessary.

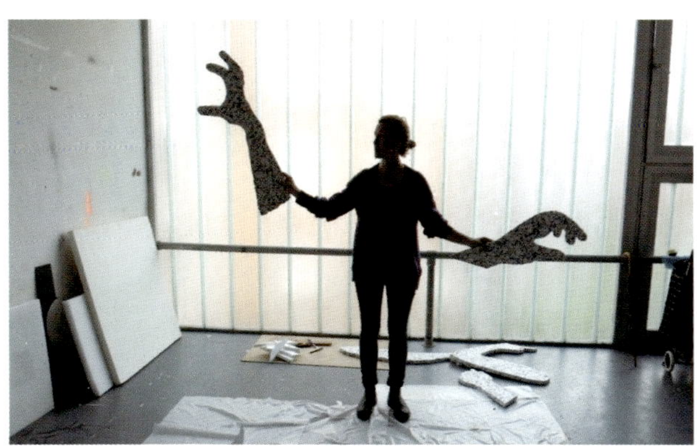

Hanna Haaslahti experimenting with gestures in the studio.

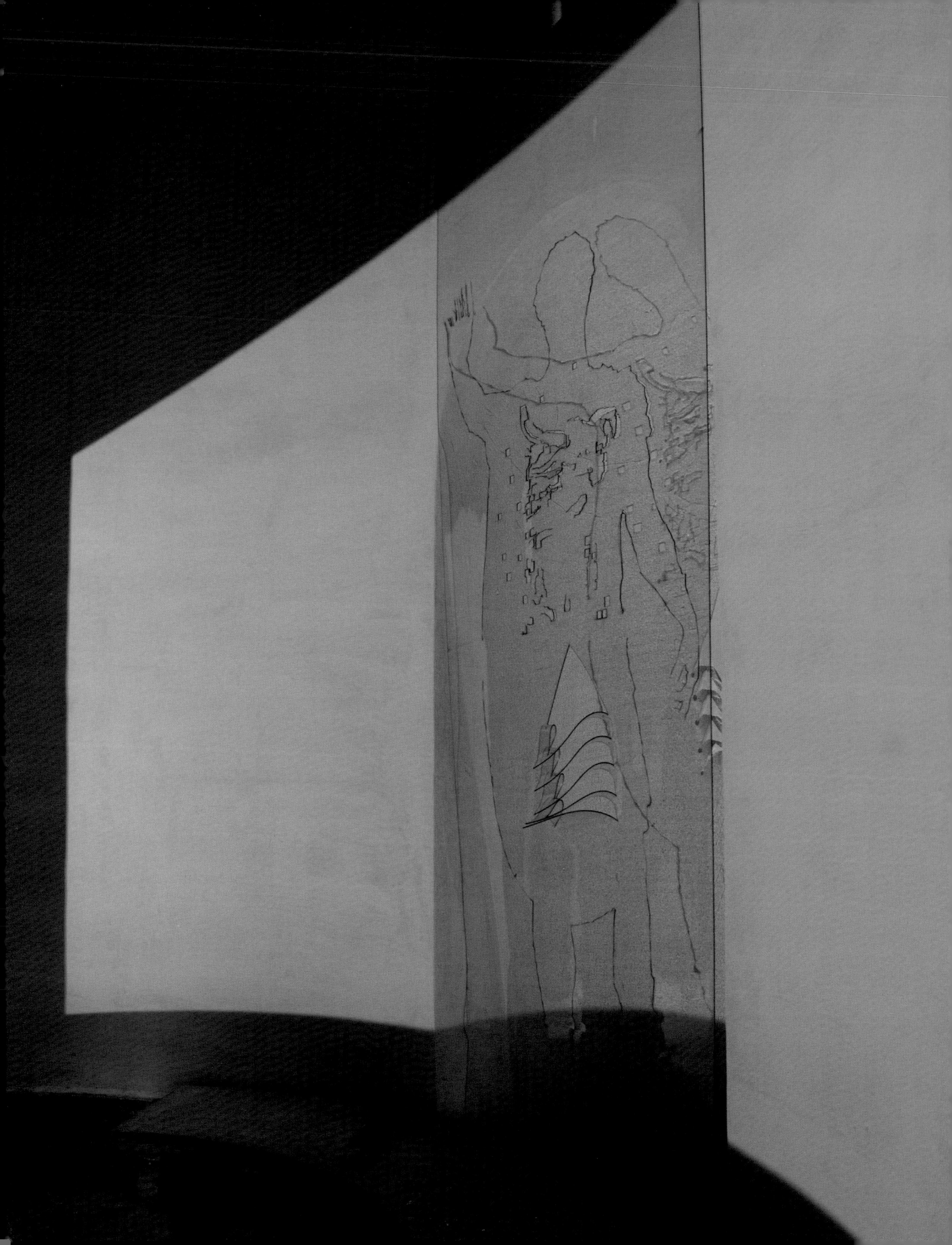

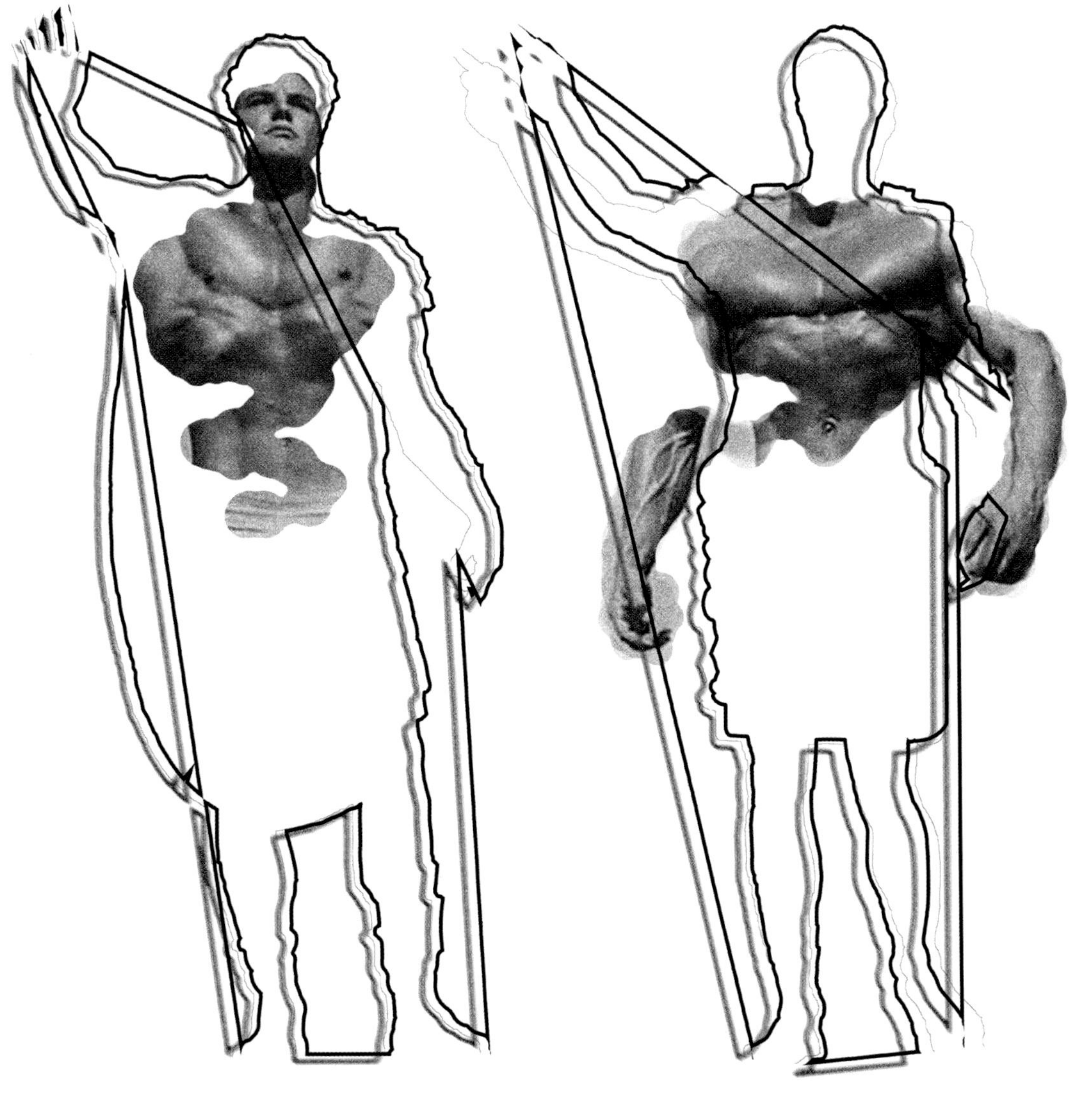

OPPOSITE Hanna Haaslahti, *Ionic Temple* (detail), 2015, niche within the interior, laser-cut PVC.

ABOVE Hanna Haaslahti, *Cosmetic Space*, 2015, hand-pulled screen print, 42 x 59.4 cm, edition of 30, plus 3 artist's proofs. Image courtesy the artist.

Sculpture Shock: Historic—Richard Cork

Today, the whole notion of making a site-specific work in a historic building is regarded as an extraordinary challenge. Most artists are displayed in galleries or museums, which continue to proliferate across the world. The usual exhibition spaces for contemporary art are white and minimal, allowing our attention to be focused entirely on the work rather than its surroundings. So the willingness of these three Sculpture Shock participants to make temporary interventions in historic contexts seems courageous indeed. Nika Neelova, Joanna Sands and Hanna Haaslahti all felt immensely stimulated by the opportunities they were given to install their three-dimensional art in locations as diverse as a church, an asylum and a temple. Moreover, they proved that the outcome of such experiments can invigorate viewers and prompt us all to enlarge our ideas about the unexpected possibilities which might well become available to artists in the future.

Working in historic buildings also links up with the ambitious and memorable projects undertaken by masters of the past; anyone exploring Renaissance art in Italy quickly realises that it was installed in a whole variety of settings. These historic places emphasise the uniqueness of artworks not simply by enhancing them, but also by showing how many images seem to spring from their particular locations. In most galleries nowadays, art appears to exist in a curatorial- or dealer-manipulated context, cut off from nourishing connections with the life that initially brought it into being. In Renaissance Italy, by contrast, the place and the image housed inside were often parts of an indissoluble whole. We cannot possibly remain oblivious of the connections between them. Walking into the Milanese refectory where *The Last Supper* is housed, we appreciate how well the damaged fresco was attuned to the dimensions of the immense wall at Leonardo da Vinci's disposal. The architecture within his painting appears to be an uncannily plausible extension of the room surrounding it, while the monks eating and drinking there must have provided an appropriate context for the rather more exalted biblical meal depicted on the wall above them.

Renaissance artists refused to be overwhelmed by the buildings they enhanced and Nika Neelova summoned a similar amount of courage to tackle the opportunity provided by Sculpture Shock in Holy Trinity, Sloane Square, an outstanding Chelsea church hailed by Sir John Betjeman, who worshipped there regularly, as the "Cathedral of the Arts and Crafts Movement". Both its architects, John Dando Sedding and Henry Wilson, wanted Holy Trinity to be embellished with the finest artworks they could commission, so they persuaded William Morris and Sir Edward Burne-Jones to design stained-glass windows. But Neelova, who was born in Russia before studying in The Hague and London, approached this historic interior with an independent vision, far removed from the figurative carving of the Crucifixion above the main altar at Holy Trinity.

Her work is uncompromising in its use of abstraction. At the same time, however, Neelova was subtle enough to make something discreet rather than dominant and exclamatory; her sculpture could not be seen from a distance by people entering Holy Trinity, so nobody was able to accuse her of violation. Instead, she took her cue from Plato's theory that the universe should be seen through an interpretation of the five Platonic solids, polyhedral forms which enabled her to explore a more geometric approach in sculpture. The main part of her installation, called *North Taurids. Following the Meteor Shower*, consisted of elemental pieces made of cast concrete and cast wax. Inspired in particular by the formation of crystals, they also evoked pyramidal forms found above all in Egypt.

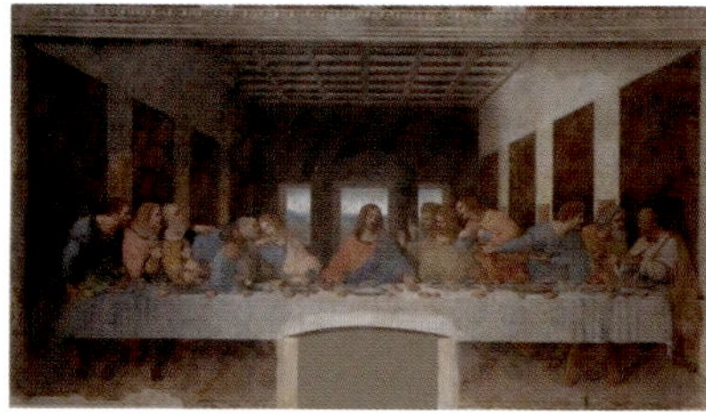

Leonardo da Vinci, *The Last Supper*, 1495–1498, Santa Maria delle Grazie, Milan, tempera on gesso, pitch and mastic, 460 x 880 cm.

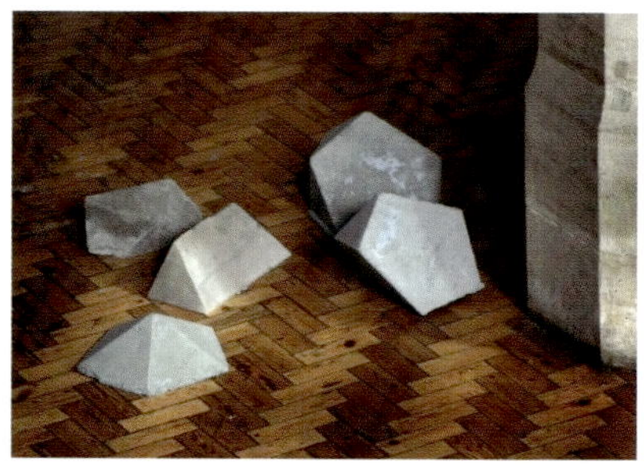

Nika Neelova, *North Taurids. Following the Meteor Shower* (detail), 2013.

Restrained in colour, ranging from white through warm wood to mottled grey and deep black, they suggested an elemental and primordial world, far older than the Arts and Crafts images produced by artists for Holy Trinity's interior when it was built. The more I looked at Neelova's forms, the more calm and architectural they seemed. At first glance, they had looked like the fragmented results of a cataclysm; in tune with the aftermath of the meteor shower mentioned in the work's title. After a while, however, I realised that they seemed surprisingly ordered. And expectant, too, as if waiting for humans and animals to invade their privacy. While I was there, nobody in the church wandered among them: everyone either stopped and gazed, or sat down on the chairs ranged at the side for a longer look at *North Taurids*.

Nothing like this had ever been seen in Holy Trinity before, and so Neelova's bold intervention could in this respect be regarded as a 'shock'. All the same, people in the church were quietly contemplating its significance rather than reeling backwards with anger or dismay. They appeared to be responding in a meditative mood, and their reaction clearly delighted the artist herself. She explained that "I wanted to do something quiet and contemplative, which is quite new in my work. I aimed at getting rid of the aggressive spectacular: it hits the viewer too much. I wanted the geometry of nature, [to be] placed in a kind of excavation site where archaeological research is conducted. It lets my forms spread into the space and engage with the architecture." Neelova's *North Taurids* could hardly be more different in style from the bronze angels flying in Holy Trinity, or the Virgin and Child who seemed to be staring down sadly at her work. Yet she succeeded in making me look at the church's familiar art in a new and refreshing way, discovering primal shapes even within the most detailed and highly decorative religious images on display there.

In dramatic contrast with the Holy Trinity project, Joanna Sands was offered derelict buildings for her Sculpture Shock intervention. At first, she received an invitation to make a work for the Museum of Immigration and Diversity at 19 Princelet Street, formerly a Huguenot house in the East End of London. Immigrants once lived there, and regarded it as their home. But Sands was also fascinated by the abandoned synagogue behind the house. In her eyes, this melancholy structure revealed a great deal about the anxiety felt by successive waves of people who found themselves struggling to create new lives in a foreign country. So she set to work on an undulating floor made of birch plywood, which would link the house and the synagogue by stressing their occupants' sense of insecurity.

Suddenly, however, Sands herself was obliged to experience a change of venue which might have unsettled her in a negative way. The Crossrail enterprise, invading and disrupting so many areas of London today, made it impossible for her to proceed at Princelet Street. Sands retained her composure and succeeded in adapting her plans without undue alarm to the alternative location in Peckham, which would prove just as stimulating as its predecessor. And besides, her willingness to be involved with Sculpture Shock in the first place meant that she was an artist energised by the advent of an unexpected challenge.

The Asylum became the most elaborate almshouse complex built in nineteenth-century London. Covering no less than 6 acres, it was intended by the Licensed Victuallers' Benevolent Institution to house and look after so-called 'decayed' members of the trade, as well as pub landlords in their retirement years. Its ambition was summed up by the grandeur of the chapel in the middle of the site, containing stained-glass windows which heightened the significance of the funerary monuments erected inside to honour the worthies. But during the Second World War a Nazi bomb wrecked its roof and severely damaged a great deal of the interior. Sands was confronted here by a melancholy space, far larger and more dilapidated than its predecessor in Princelet Street.

Rather than forcing herself to produce an alternative installation, she adapted the wooden floor piece and gave it a radically different meaning in the Asylum Chapel. No longer filling most of a modest-sized room with its presence, this undulating work now stretched across the centre of an ample interior where visitors had far more space to walk on either side of it. Yet its significance was not lessened. On the contrary: proceeding from an entrance door towards the altar, it managed to heighten the meaning of the Asylum Chapel as a place offering spiritual consolation while at the same time reminding us of the Second World War's destructive impact.

Moreover, the fact that the wood looked like recycled building material emphasised our awareness of the amount of damage inflicted by the German bomb. These raised floorboards accentuated the building's plight, not to mention the suffering experienced by the 'decayed' victuallers who needed help to cope with their own ordeals in old age. Although Sands was influenced as a young artist by the simplicity and geometric repetition of the Minimalist aesthetic, it became in the Asylum Chapel a means of enabling her to express an almost ghostly feeling, filled with insights into the sadness of a derelict Asylum Chapel now covered by a corrugated iron roof.

No such patch-up material was ever applied to the neo-Palladian Ionic Temple erected so proudly in its own self-contained garden at Chiswick House. Located very near the Thames in West London, the House and Temple were designed by their original owner Lord Burlington. Working with William Kent, he aimed to create an eighteenth-century English residence which would pay homage to the classical tradition. Lord Burlington succeeded in achieving his goal, and a recent £12.1 million restoration has returned both garden and buildings to their former geometrical precision. No wonder Hanna Haaslahti was fascinated by Sculpture Shock's ability to offer her an installation there. She is a Finnish media artist, far removed from creating sculpture in the traditional sense. Having studied photography, set design, and arts and technology in various countries before entering the Medialab at Helsinki's University of the Arts, she became well-acquainted with the ever-expanding possibilities inherent in digital technology. But that does not mean she felt uninterested in exploring the history of the Ionic Temple. Far from it: Haaslahti immersed herself in the multilayered meanings of this extraordinary location, and counted herself lucky that a building normally closed to the public became a place she could investigate and transform with an audacious intervention.

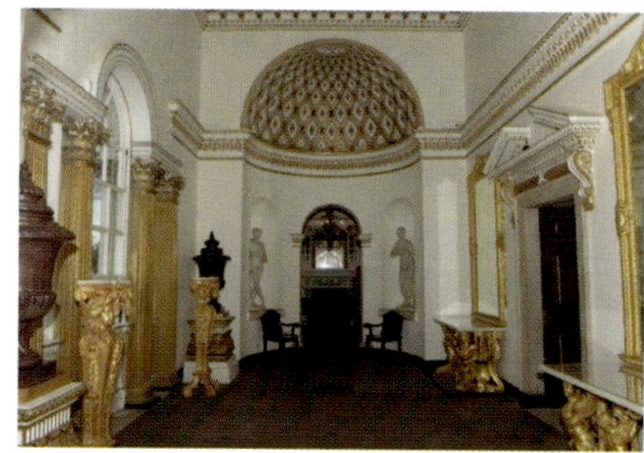

Lord Burlington and William Kent, Chiswick House, completed 1729 (interior). Courtesy of English Heritage.

Especially intrigued by the niches inside the Temple, Haaslahti discovered that copies of classical sculpture were formerly installed there. Although they are now in the main house, replicas stand in the gardens where she pondered the loss of their arms and hands. These naked figures, who once personified muscular and fully formed prowess, now look deprived of their anatomical grandeur. More akin to victims than heroes, they chime with our acute contemporary awareness of human vulnerability. Haaslahti decided to recreate them floating like helpless fragments on the surface of the pond outside the Temple, where they gestured in different directions as though determined to bewilder visitors entering this once-serene locale. An obelisk, part of the original self-contained garden designed for the Temple, still stands proud and erect near the water's edge. But

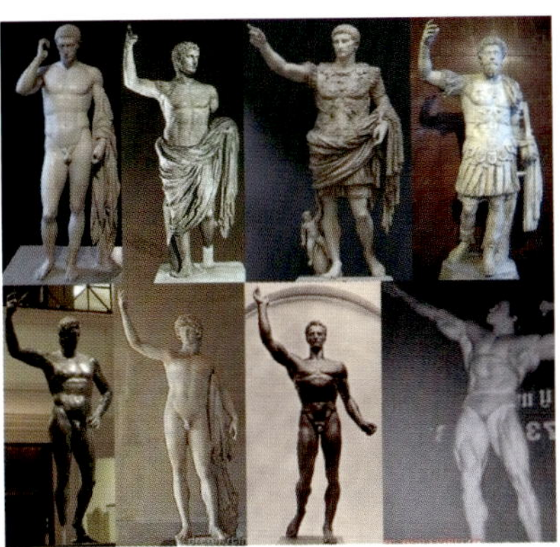

Hanna Haaslahti's work in progress during the Sculpture Shock residency: "muscle architecture from classics to more recent mutations".

Haaslahti's white fragments contradicted the obelisk's single-minded vertical stillness, pointing everywhere as if to make us feel disorientated or even lost.

Moving into the Temple itself did not provide visitors with any reassurance. Haaslahti used her knowledge of digital technology to subtly undermine the harmonious certainty that once reigned throughout this classical interior. Because the prominent niches in the Temple's walls are empty now, she could not resist making visitors an integral part of the installation conceived for the building's interior. Moving through this space, we found ourselves becoming triggers for the action of light. It constantly changed everything, so that the grand solidity and permanence originally celebrated by Lord Burlington grew elusive. The instability so often dominating our perception of present-day existence was evident wherever we looked. Haaslahti transformed the Temple, not least by giving its interior a PVC covering that was frankly artificial. Because this material was non-precious, it implicitly challenged the gilded surfaces lending the rooms within Chiswick House their air of desirable richness. Haaslahti presented a radical vision which made us question everything we encountered in the Temple, replacing the calm order of the classical style with a ceaselessly unsettling alternative.

Taken together, all three of these projects in the Sculpture Shock enterprise prove that the 'historic' dimension can turn out to be immensely rewarding. Whether the context is well preserved, like Holy Trinity in Chelsea, or as derelict as the Asylum Chapel in Peckham, artists can find plentiful inspiration for the work they install there. The sense of adventure generated by these experiments is compelling indeed, and it suggests that a whole stimulating new world of alternative locations lies waiting to be discovered and transformed in the future by everyone who thrives on the challenge of risk-taking innovation.

End Matter

Alexander Costello MRBS is a sculptor, video and live artist. He has an MFA from the Slade School of Art and a BA Hons (Class I) in Fine Art from Middlesex University. His work continues to be exhibited both nationally and internationally and he lives, works and teaches in London.

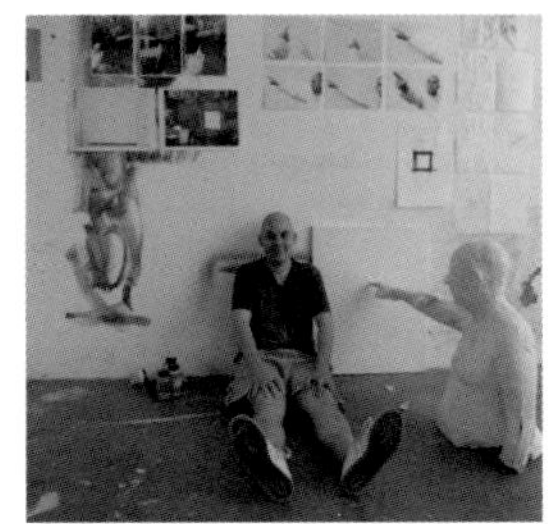

Lynn Dennison MRBS graduated from the Slade School of Art in 1987 and obtained a distinction in her MA at Central St Martins in 2013. She has exhibited widely in London, Beijing and Tokyo including Waterfall, De La Warr Pavilion, Bexhill on Sea, 2014, and Lookout Tower, Aldeburgh, Suffolk, 2013–2014. She lives and works in London.

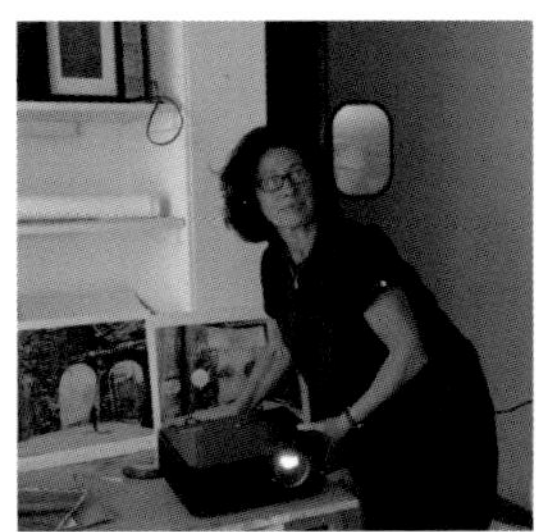

Hanna Haaslahti has a background in photography and set design and completed her MFA in media studies at the Medialab at the University of Arts and Design Helsinki in 2001. She has exhibited extensively across Europe, has undertaken residencies in Brussels, Paris and St Petersburg and has received many awards including the prestigious AVEK-award. She lives and works in Helsinki, Finland.

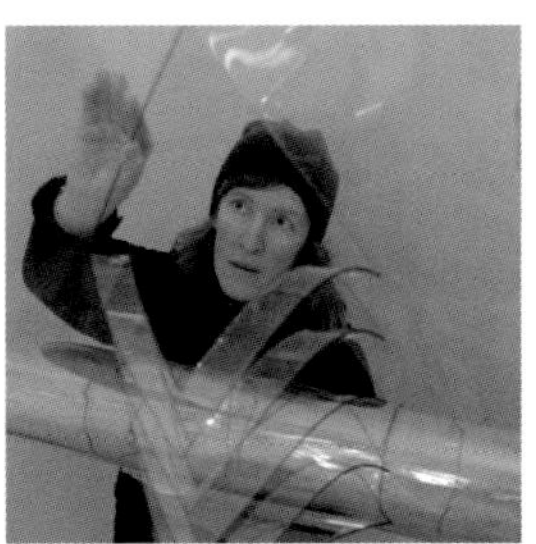

Patrick Lowry MRBS obtained a DipAD from West Surrey College of Art and Design in 1971 and an MA from Falmouth University in 2003, where he is now visiting lecturer. He has exhibited widely in the United Kingdom, France and the Netherlands including American Dream, Exchange Gallery, Penzance, 2013; Crushing the Tate, BIKINI Espace d'art Contemporain, Lyon, 2012; and Escalator, New County Hall, Truro, Cornwall, 2007. Lowry is also a director of Back Lane West an artist-led project space. He lives and works in Falmouth, Cornwall.

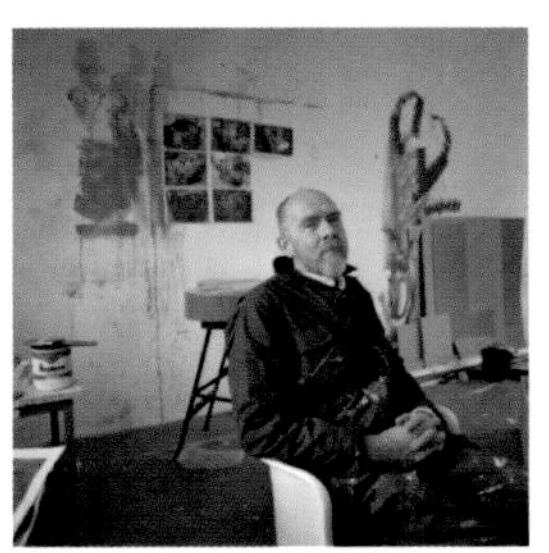

William Mackrell MRBS graduated from Chelsea College of Art and Design in 2005 and obtained an MFA from Goldsmiths in 2016. He has exhibited nationally and internationally, including Dundee Contemporary Arts and Two Rooms Gallery, Auckland. He was shortlisted for the Jerwood Drawing Prize in 2015 and selected as artist in residence at Krinzinger Projekte, Vienna in 2013. He lives and works in London.

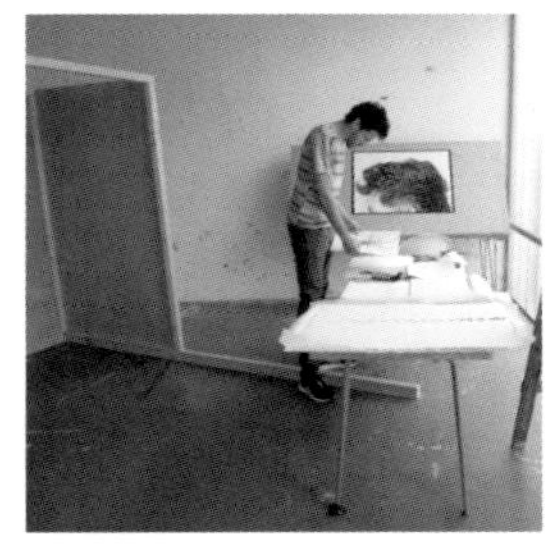

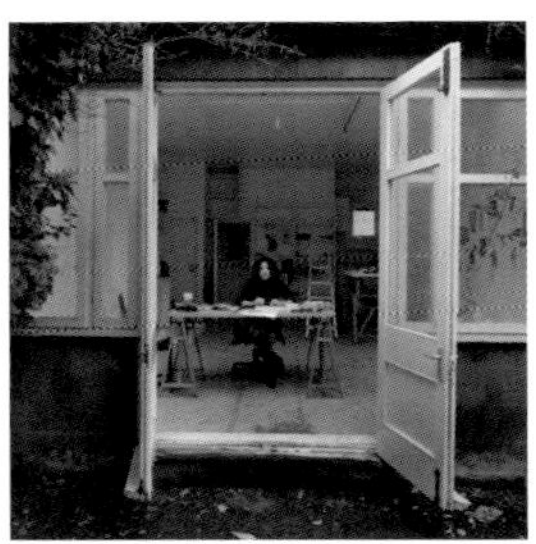

Nika Neelova was born in Moscow, Russia, studied at the Royal Art Academy in The Hague and received her MFA from the Slade School of Art in London. She received the Kenneth Armitage Young Sculptor Prize, the Land Security Prize Award, the Royal British Society of Sculptors Bursary Award and was the winner of the Saatchi New Sensations Award. Neelova's work has been exhibited in the United Kingdom and internationally. She is represented by Vigo Gallery and lives and works in London.

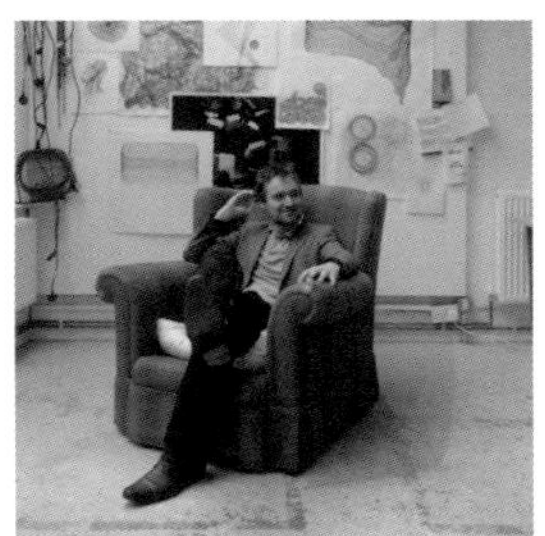

David Ogle MRBS obtained a BA Hons (Class I) in Fine Art History and Practice in 2009, an MA (Distinction) in Contemporary Arts Research in 2012 from Lancaster University and is currently undertaking an AHRC funded doctoral research project at the University of Liverpool/FACT. Recent exhibitions include Loomings, Bury Art Museum, 2016; In Another Light, Croft Castle (The National Trust), 2014; Regenerate 14, Berlin/Copenhagen, 2014; and the Catlin Art Prize, London, 2013. Ogle is represented by Mark Devereux Projects and Kinetica Museum, London and lives and works in Liverpool.

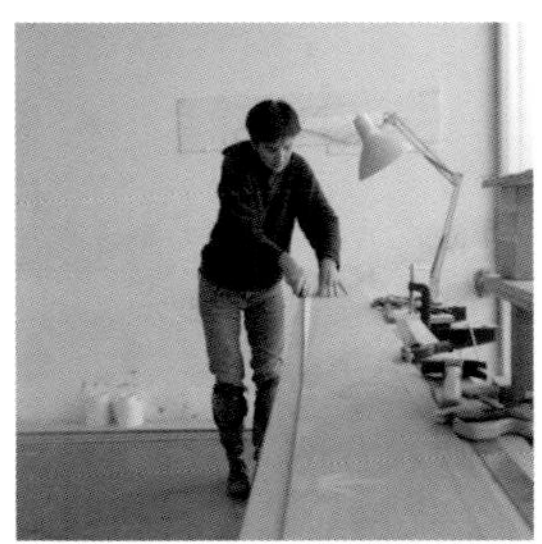

Joanna Sands MRBS graduated from Maidstone College of Art in 1986 and took her MA at Chelsea School of Art in 1987. In 1989 she received a DAAD scholarship to study in Berlin. She is the recipient of a Pollock-Krasner Foundation grant and The Woo Foundation Award. Sands has exhibited widely both in the UK and Germany and lives and works in London.

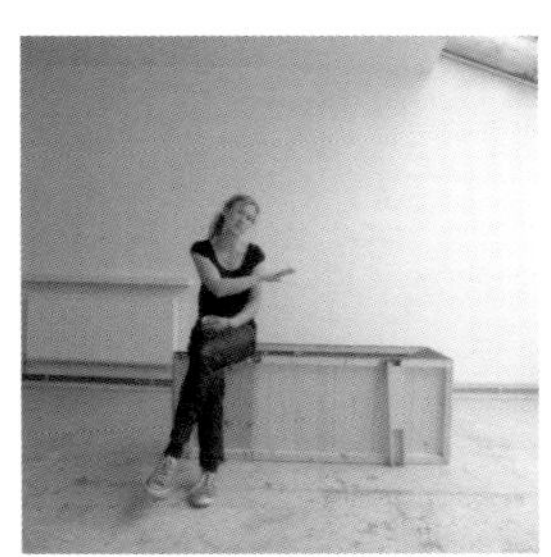

Amy Sharrocks obtained a BA in Fine Art from Camberwell College of Art and was shortlisted for the Arts Foundation Fellowship Award in 2015. Her award-winning *Museum of Water*, which toured the UK and Europe from 2013 to 2016, is nominated for European Museum of the Year 2016. She has published essays on falling in live art in *Performance Research*, no 18 and *The Live Art Almanac* 4 and publications on her works *SWIM* and *Museum of Water*. *Swim the Thames*, a mass swim across London's famous river, is her next project. She lives and works in London.

Dave Beech is a writer, curator and artist in the collective Freee. He studied painting at Leicester Polytechnic and then Cultural Theory at the Royal College of Art, where he researched the historical development of the concept of philistinism from Romanticism to postmodernism. He has written widely on the politics of art, as well as the legacy of the Avant-Garde and Conceptualism. He has also contributed to debates on participation and art's publics, in books such as *In Search of Art's New Publics*, 2010, and *Curating and the Educational Turn*, 2010, as well as being a founding editor of the journal *Art and the Public Sphere*. As an artist he has exhibited at the Istanbul Biennial, 2013, and the Liverpool Biennial, 2010. He also curated the exhibition We Are Grammar at the Pratt Institute, New York, 2011 (co-curator Paul O'Neill).

Clare Burnett PRBS has worked on site-specific sculptures and installations for a number of years, each work a direct response to the history and visual language of its location. Using a pared-down, abstract language, she explores how colour and material change with context, and how they can be used to draw attention to what surrounds them. Previous projects include installations of works in West Norwood and Brompton Cemeteries, in Le Corbusier's Unité d'Habitation and Leighton House. She is President of the Royal British Society of Sculptors.

Richard Cork is an award-winning art critic, historian, broadcaster and curator. In 1969 he became Art Critic of the *Evening Standard*, and then Chief Art Critic of *The Times*, Slade Professor of Fine Art at Cambridge and Henry Moore Senior Fellow at the Courtauld. He has curated major exhibitions at Tate, the Hayward Gallery, the Royal Academy and the Barbican Art Gallery. He broadcasts regularly on the BBC, and was appointed an Honorary Fellow of the Royal Academy in 2011. Cork's many books include a ground-breaking study of Vorticism, awarded the John Llewellyn Rhys Prize in 1977; *Art Beyond the Gallery*, winner of the Banister Fletcher Award in 1986; a major monograph on David Bomberg in 1987; *A Bitter Truth: Avant-Garde Art and the Great War*, winner of the Art Fund Award in 1995; *The Healing Presence of Art*, 2012; and *Face to Face: Interviews with Artists*, published by Tate in 2015.

Sarah Kent was visual arts editor of *Time Out* magazine for 30 years and Director of Exhibitions at the ICA, staging over 50 exhibitions. She was a jury member of the Turner Prize, John Kobal Photographic Portrait Award, New Contemporaries, the Royal British Society of Sculptors' Bursary Award and the Arts Foundation Award for Arts Journalism amongst others and has written catalogues for the Hayward Gallery, ICA, Saatchi Gallery, White Cube and Haunch of Venison and books such as *Shark-Infested Waters: The Saatchi Collection of British Art in the 90's*, 2003. She studied painting at the Slade School and was an artist and lecturer until 1977.

Ezra Konvitz is the co-founder of ArtStack, the social platform for art. ArtStack is a new way to discover and share art with friends, professionals and an international community of art lovers, and is enabling emerging and established artists, curators and thought leaders to reach a global audience. Ezra previously led on strategy at the Serpentine Gallery, London, and focused on media and technology clients as a strategy consultant at Bain & Company. He holds an MA from the Courtauld Institute of Art, and an MPhil and a BA from the University of Cambridge.

Claire Mander is Deputy Director and Curator of the Royal British Society of Sculptors, which she joined in 2011. She has curated many exhibitions and site-specific interventions including SKULPTUR: Contemporary Sculpture from Denmark, Finland, Iceland, Norway and Sweden, showcasing the work of 17 artists across three sites in London; Boyle Family Contemporary Archaeology: The World Series, Gotland Site 1968/2015; and the Napoleon Garden commission for female sculptors. She is a qualified litigation solicitor and holds an MA (Distinction) from the Courtauld Institute of Art, MA Honours in French and History of Art from Edinburgh University.

Terry New PPRBS was the Head of Fine Art and Head of Sculpture at the Royal Academy from 1986 to 2011. He is a practising sculptor and has had solo exhibitions at the Serpentine Gallery, Plymouth Museum and Art Gallery, Martini Arte Internazionale, Turin, Italy, as well as having work in public and private collections including the Art Gallery of Western Australia and the Sharjah Art Museum and Merck, Sharp & Dohme, UK. He is a Fellow and Past President of RBS.

Cornelia Parker OBE RA formalises things beyond our control in her work, allowing the viewer to witness the transformation of the most ordinary objects into something compelling and extraordinary. Nominated for the Turner Prize in 1997, Parker is known for her installations and interventions, including *Cold Dark Matter: An Exploded View* in 1991 at Tate Modern and *The Maybe*, a collaboration with Tilda Swinton at the Serpentine Gallery in 1995. In 2010, she was awarded an OBE and elected to the Royal Academy. She has works in collections including the Tate Collection, MoMA New York and The Metropolitan Museum of Art, New York for which she obtained The Roof Garden Commission for Transitional Object (PsychoBarn) in 2016.

Richard Wilson RA is one of Britain's most renowned sculptors, often singled out for his concentration on site-specific projects, his name synonymous with the idea of installation art in Britain. He has exhibited widely nationally and internationally for over 40 years and has made major museum exhibitions and public works in Japan, US, Brazil, Mexico, Russia, Australia, Iraq, China, Hong Kong and throughout Europe. Wilson represented Britain in the Sydney, São Paulo and Venice biennials and the Yokohama Triennale. He was nominated twice for the Turner Prize and was awarded the prestigious DAAD residency in Berlin in 1992–1993. In 2006 Wilson was elected a member of the Royal Academy.

Nina Wisnia trained as a dancer at the Balett Akademien in Stockholm and then as a visual artist in London and holds a BA from Central Saint Martins College of Art and Design and an MA from the Royal College of Art. She has written and illustrated four books published by Editions du Rouergue in France and Sweden, for which she was awarded the Opal Book Prize and Bologna Book Fair Award. Formerly a graphic designer in the Arnell Group in New York and London, she currently pursues her own artistic practice which focuses on drawing, collage and the body and is involved in various contemporary art projects.

Bibliography

Bishop, Claire, *Installation Art: A Critical History*, New York: Routledge, 2005

Bishop, Claire, *Artificial Hells: Participatory Art and the Politics of Spectatorship*, London: Verso, 2012

Bourriaud, Nicolas, "Relational Aesthetics", *Documents sur l'Art*, Simon Pleasance and Fronza Woods with the participation of Mathieu Copeland trans, Paris: Les Presses du Réel, 2002

Crimp, Douglas, "Redefining Site Specificity", *On the Museum's Ruins*, Cambridge, MA: MIT Press, 1993

de Oliveira, Nicola, Nicola Oxley and Michael Petry, *Installation Art*, London: Thames and Hudson, 1994

Doherty, Claire, *Public Art (Now): Out of Time, Out of Place*, London: Ar/ Books Publishing Ltd, in association with Situations, Public Art Agency Sweden, 2015

Doherty, Claire ed, *Contemporary Art: From Studio to Situation*, London: Black Dog Publishing, 2004

Kaye, Nick, *Site-Specific Art: Performance, Place, and Documentation*, London: Routledge, 2000

Krauss, Rosalind, "Sculpture in the Expanded Field", *The Originality of the Avant-Garde and Other Modernist Myths*, Boston, MA: MIT Press, 1985

Kwon, Miwon, *One Place after Another: Site-Specific Art and Locational Identity*, Cambridge, MA: MIT Press, 2004

Lippard, Lucy R, "Art Outdoors, In and Out of the Public Domain", *Studio International*, March–April 1977

Lippard, Lucy R, *The Lure of the Local: Senses of Place in a Multicentered Society*, New York: The New Press, 1997

Meyer, James, "The functional site; or, the transformation of site-specificity", *Space, Site, Intervention: Situating Installation Art*, Erika Suderburg ed, Minneapolis, MN: University of Minneapolis University Press, 2000

Selz, Peter and Kristine Stiles eds, "Installations, Environments, and Sites", *Theories and Documents of Contemporary Art: A Sourcebook of Artists' Writings*, Berkeley, CA: University of California Press, 1996

Rugg, Judith, *Exploring Site-Specific Art: Issues of Space and Internationalism*, London: I B Tauris & Co Ltd, 2010

For more information and contemporaneous comment about the Sculpture Shock project please visit sculptureshock.rbs.org.uk

Thanks are first and foremost due to the Sculpture Shock artists who all worked with great gusto during their residencies to create their surprising site-specific interventions, always undaunted and always flexible. Thanks also to the large community of sculptors who supported the award.

A project of this scale and ambition involves many individuals and I am deeply grateful to all the staff of the Royal British Society of Sculptors, including Anne Rawcliffe-King for welcoming me into the RBS and supporting the development of the project; Susannah Kingwill for her meticulous application and enthusiasm as well as Michelle Butler who gave invaluable project management assistance; Julie Beech and Cynthia Scoville who ran the lively education programme as well as Helen Bayer, Monica Cornforth, Aïcha Mehrez, Alannah Pirrit and Verity Whiter for their support; Matt Moser-Clark for installing at all hours; Leo Loebenberg for lending his voice and compositional flair to his collaboration with Lynn Dennison; and the many essential volunteers including Elodie Fillon, Ana Isabel Bento, Cristina Centelles Villanueva, Davide Restifo, Lucia Stamati, Octavia Young and the 14-strong team of volunteers for William Mackrell's *Gaps, glitches and speed bumps*.

A huge thank you to the members of the jury who gave their time dispensed their judgment so brilliantly: Dave Beech, Clare Burnett PRBS, Richard Cork, Sarah Kent, Ezra Konwitz, Terry New PPRBS, Cornelia Parker OBE RA, Richard Wilson RA and Nina Wisnia.

For the encouragement and open-mindedness of organisations, many of which made their first foray into contemporary art, including Holy Trinity, Sloane Square and particularly The Revd Rob Gillion and The Revd Graham Rainford; Robert Hulse and Katie Edwards of The Brunel Museum; Man Somerlinck and his floating Fordham Gallery; Tristan Appleby of Network Rail; Roger Burton at The Horse Hospital; and the team at Chiswick House and Gardens Trust, including Clare O'Brien, Diane Schaefer, Geraldine King, Sophie Larner, Becki Bryan, William Rallison, Peter Beagley and Esmé Whittaker of English Heritage.

For the generosity in giving advice and providing contacts during the long project development stage including David Shreeve, Environmental Adviser to the Archbishops' Council of the Church of England; Charlotte Fergusson, Westminster City Council; and to John Hampson, Arts and Culture, Royal Borough of Kensington and Chelsea for its initial grant and for providing the studio space in Chelsea formerly occupied by Dame Elisabeth Frink for the first year and for allowing live art to briefly inhabit its streets.

Sculpture Shock would not have been possible without the immense and sustained support, both financial and intellectual, of Samuel and Nina Wisnia through their CoLAB Programme.

Claire Mander, Deputy Director and Curator of
the Royal British Society of Sculptors

The Royal British Society of Sculptors is an independent artist-led organisation and is the oldest and largest organisation dedicated to sculpture in the UK. It is committed to engaging, inspiring and informing all about contemporary three-dimensional art through its exciting and varied programme of awards, residencies, exhibitions and its educational programme. Established in 1905, it is a membership society of 600 plus professional sculptors and are a registered charity with its HQ at 108 Old Brompton Road, London.

Sculpture Shock and this publication was made possible with the generous support of Nina and Samuel J Wisnia through their CoLAB programme.

Sculpture Shock: Site-specific interventions in Subterranean, Ambulatory and Historic contexts

Subterranean:
David Ogle, The Vaults, Arch 233, Leake Street, London, SE1 7NN, 18–21 April 2013
Patrick Lowry, The Horse Hospital, Colonnade, Bloomsbury, London, WC1N 1JD, 15–19 May 2014
Lynn Dennison, The Brunel Museum Rotherhithe Shaft, Railway Avenue, Rotherhithe, London, SE16 4LF, 14–17 May 2015

Ambulatory:
Amy Sharrocks, World's End Place SW10 0DR, Outside 1–5a Thistle Grove, SW10 9RR, various locations on Old Brompton Road SW7 3RA, 13–23 July 2013
Alexander Costello, waterways from Camden Lock to Tottenham Hale, 4–7 September 2014
William Mackrell, No 9 Bus Route, from 10–13 September 2015

Historic:
Nika Neelova, Holy Trinity Sloane Square, Sloane Street, London, SW1X 9BZ, 15–18 November 2013
Joanna Sands, The Asylum, Caroline Garden's Chapel, London, SE15 2SQ 9–11 December 2014
Hanna Haaslahti, The Ionic Temple, Chiswick House Gardens London, W4 2RP, 3–6 December 2015

Curated by Claire Mander

Black Dog Publishing Limited
10a Acton Street, London, WC1X 9NG
United Kingdom

t: +44 (0)20 7713 5097
e: info@blackdogonline.com
www.blackdogonline.com

Designed by Rita Pereira at Black Dog Publishing Limited
Edited by Claire Mander, Royal British Society of Sculptors

All photographs are by Anne-Kathrin Purkiss unless otherwise stated.

All opinions expressed within this publication are those of the authors and not necessarily of the publisher.

British Library in Cataloguing Data
A CIP record for this book is available from the British Library

ISBN 978 1 911164 18 0

Black Dog Publishing Limited, London, UK, is an environmentally responsible company. *Sculpture Shock: Site-specific interventions in Subterranean, Ambulatory and Historic contexts* is printed on sustainably sourced paper.

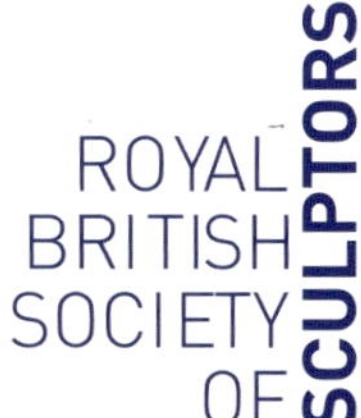

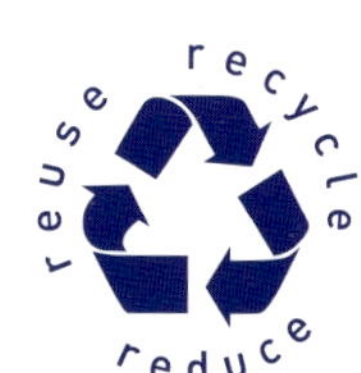